GENDER, RIGHTS AND SECURITY

GENDER, RIGHTS AND SECURITY

SIDDHARTHA SARKAR
Department of Commerce
Dinhata College
Dinhata, Cooch Behar
West Benga, India

SERIALS PUBLICATIONS
NEW DELHI

First Published–2010

ISBN: 978-81-8387-331-4

Published by

SERIALS PUBLICATIONS
4830/24, Prahlad Street, Ansari Road
Darya Ganj, New Delhi-110002 (India)
Phone : 23245225 Fax : 91-11-23272135
E-mail: serials@satyam.net.in

CONTENTS

PROLOGUE

Promoting human security requires measures to protect people from disruptions to nations and households. It also requires addressing the many sources of risk that affect poor people including children–lack of food and adequate water, ill health, unemployment, and other environmental risks.

The article 'why do people want children?' examines how similar the fertility theory of' 'crisis in the population question' is to neoclassical economic theory of fertility. It is similar in conferring time cost of children and in the discussion of the quantity-quality tradeoff.

The coverage of information economy in terms of women's accessibility and opportunities for economic empowerment in developing countries has been explored in 'technology,. economic opportunities and women empowerment'.

The paper 'women in watershed development' advocates that the homogeneous and focused women groups need to be formed and supported if they are to expand viable income generating activities depending upon the skills they already possess and the training imparted in such activities which should be conducive to watershed development.

In an effort to 'gender, vulnerability and informality', it has been recognized that in general the informalisation of work has had a negative impact on women workers and has meant low wages, job insecurity, isolation and lack of opportunities to organize. The informal economy is a part of survival and household strategies for the poor; nevertheless its contribution to well being remains inadequately understood and largely unnoticed by policy makers.

Some explicit questions have been raised in the study of 'farmer committing suicide' to be familiar with the circumstances under which the farmers have been committing suicide and to what extent these could be attributed to agriculture-related indebtedness.

Report on 'land rights of women in achieving sustainable livelihoods' stipulates that with a view to bringing together the diverse perspectives, proficiency and knowledge of global institutions, governments, technical agencies, and civil society stakeholders, the existing information available on rural women and land resources can be used to generate a comprehensive outlook of rural women's access to, control of, use of, land and related resources like water, extension services, credit etc.

In 'cooking with biofuel and women health' it has been estimated that indoor air pollution from burning of biofuel causes a substantial exposure to the health of rural women and children. The basic focus of the study is on the risks to health arising from exposure of women and children to smoke in the kitchen and by and large consequences of this for the health of rural poor women who are somehow engaged in informal activities.

Jamila Ahmed Chowdhury advocates that like many other developing countries Bangladesh is also facing numerous problems in ensuring access to justice through its formal judiciary. The available traditional adjudicative system performed at the local level by local elites is also inundated with corruption and pro-male biasness. So one alternative method of dispute resolution getting increased recognition now-a-days is NGO mediation conducted by local leaders under the supervision of some practicing NGOs which try to establish quick and just settlement of the disputes arises in their respective locality.

The government of Botswana, through the Department of Culture and Youth has made attempts to solve the problem of youth unemployment and integrate them into the general economy by economically empowering them. This has been done through many programmes including out-of-school youth grant whose aim is to enable unemployed youth to create self-employment.

Public opinion is one of the instruments through which people can express their concern over the security issues and may influence their governments on such sensitive issues. The article 'women and the nuclear issue' states that if there were a nuclear war or leakage in a nuclear plant or nuclear accidents, woman would be more vulnerable victim than man as a mother, as a wife and as the one who takes enormous responsibility of the family.

Tabitha W. Kiriti-Nganga explains that women in Kenya form over 50 percent of the population and over 60 percent of the voting population. They have been relegated to the position of second-class citizen by cultural and institutional impediments that assign certain roles and assignments to them. This socialization has led to poor enrolment of women in learning institutions, low employment levels, over-representation in agriculture and the informal sector and an increase in gender violence.

Lewis B. Dzimbiri's paper discusses trade union-government relations with examples from east and southern Africa and offers an economic and political explanation for the dismal relationship between governments and organized workers. It further questions the applicability of some internationally evolved 'best practices' to the late developing societies of Africa and how such an imposition can create an environment in which there is a discrepancy between the legal framework for human rights and the actual practice on the ground.

N. Narayana in his paper states that gender inequalities that leave women in a subordinated position to men prevail despite the commitment of governments all over the world to achieve gender equality.

Siddhartha Sarkar

List of Contributors

Siv Sofia Gustafsson: Professor of Economics, University of Amsterdam and Fellow at Tinbergen Institute, The Netherlands.

N. Narayana: Professor of Economics, University of Botswana, Botswana.

Falendra K. Sudan: Reader, Department of Economics, University of Jammu, Jammu and Kashmir, India.

Siddhartha Sarkar: Faculty, Department of Commerce, Dinhata College, Dinhata, Cooch Behar, West Bengal, India.

G. Sreedhar: Professor, Department of Rural Development, SK University, Anantapur, Andhra Pradesh, India.

K. Dasaratharamaiah: Associate Professor, Department of Economics, SK University, Anantapur, Andhra Pradesh, India.

Rosalud de la Rosa: Chair, Women Organizing for Change in Agriculture and Natural Resource Management, Italy.

Alexandra Aquino-Fike: Gender & Rural Development Consultant, USA.

Jamila Ahmed Chowdhury: Lecturer, School of Law, Bangladesh Open University, Bangladesh.

Donatilla K. Kaino and Martin P. Ntongana: Faculty, Department of Economics, University of Botswana, Botswana.

Adluri Subramanyam Raju: Associate Professor in Political Science, Centre for SAARC Studies, Visakhapatnam, Andhra Pradesh, India.

Tabitha W. Kiriti-Nganga: Senior Lecturer, School of Economics, University of Nairobi, Nairobi, Kenya.

Lewis B. Dzimbiri: Senior Lecturer, Department of Political and Administrative Studies, University of Botswana, Botswana.

1

WHY DO PEOPLE WANT CHILDREN?

SIV SOFIA GUSTAFSSON

INTRODUCTION

Age specific fertility statistics has been collected in Sweden since 1751. During the first 150 years the total fertility rate never decreased below four children per woman and it never reached 5 children per woman. At the time when Alva and Gunnar Myrdal wrote 'Crisis in the Population Question' (1934, Fourth Edition 1935) the total fertility rate showed a rapidly decreasing negative trend for the first time in history and in the 30 years since 1900 had decreased to only 1.77 children per woman in 1931-1935. This was around 30 per cent fewer birth than the fertility rate required for the Swedish population to replace itself according to their computations (Myrdal and Myrdal 1935). It is no wonder that people were worried about the rapid fertility decrease. Would the negative trend come to a stop? The Myrdals (1935) projected that it would not unless by public policies, the underlying reasons for people to refrain from becoming parents were changed. This paper is about how the Myrdals theorized about determinants of the number of children that a rational calculating couple with free access to contraceptives would have and how their theories compare to modem economic theory of fertility. There are often references to the Myrdals in policy analysis but in economic theory analysis (Hotz, Klerman and Willis 1997) such references are lacking. One purpose of this paper is to point out this caveat. Recently the Swedish fertility rate has fluctuated but with the exception of 1990 remained below replacement.

However such fluctuations of fertility rates are not specific to Sweden, but has been observed in all European countries. In Spain and Italy fertility rates are now as low as 1.1-1.2 children per woman and if such a low fertility rate would persist it means that the population will be halved in one generation. Fluctuations in the size of different birth cohorts is not without problems, also if the average over a longer period is close to the replacement rate. In Sweden today there are 30 per cent more children who are born in 1990, than there are children who are born in 1995, and those who were born in 1982 belong to a cohort of the same smaller size, as these 1995 cohort. Such fluctuations cause problems in the planning of school buildings, the planning of teacher resources, the planning and recruitment of teaching staff on different school levels. Further, when the ageing population will be of a bigger size than the supporting economically active population, there will be problems in the pension systems and the recruitment of personnel for the care of the old (Cutler, Poterba, Sheiner and Summers 1990; MacKellar 2000). Further the size of different cohorts can affect the standard of living not only by its distribution between the young and the old, but there can also be a negative effect on the total size of the cake to share if less resource is put into productivity enhancing investments in human and physical capital. However, the Myrdals were perturbing not about fluctuations but about a consistently negative trend. The issue brought up by Alva and Gunnar Myrdal 1934 on whether family policies can assist couples to afford the number of children they desire is just as important today as it was then.

ECONOMIC THEORIES ON FERTILITY

Academic economic research about the family is a lively field closely connected to the Nobel Prize winner for economics of

1992 – Gary Becker from University of Chicago (Becker 1981; Ermisch 2003; Gustafsson 2001). The Myrdals asked the question as 'why did fertility fall from four children per woman to 1.77 in Sweden in only 30 years from 1900 to 1930?' They did not ask why fertility increased rapidly in the 1940s, and why there is a cyclical pattern with some years of much childbirth and other years with little childbirth. The Myrdals did not return to the population issue in this sense, not even to claim, that the social policies, which were gradually introduced as a result of their arguments in the 1930s were causing the fertility increase in the 1940s. Other researchers asked these questions. The most famous one of these is Richard Easterlin (1980). He claims, that the cyclical pattern of fertility in the United States with many births in the 1950s and few births in the 1960s followed again by many births in the 1970s, and again few births in the 1980s, was caused by what he called 'the relative income hypothesis'. Each small generation has an easy way in the labour market because of few competitors and each large generation experiences the opposite. Therefore large generations have fewer children and more women work in the market. Small generations have many children and few women work in the market. Therefore they could afford to live on husband's income and delegate to the wife to be at home and have many children and so the 1950 cohort became large. Rivaling this hypothesis is the opportunity cost of time hypothesis, that claims, that the value of women's market time has increased relative to their home making time, so that we can expect increasing trends in women's market work and women would not adjust their inputs in market work only to supplement the incomes of heir husbands (Gustafsson 1992 compares the Easterlin and the neoclassical view). The 'opportunity cost of time' view has also been called the Columbia-Chicago School because of contributions by Jacob Mincer (1962) from Columbia University and from Gary Becker (1965) from Chicago University. The opposing school was the Pennsylvania school because Easterlin was active there.

An interesting analysis of the opportunity cost of time hypothesis is Schulz (1985). He studies the fertility transition in Sweden 1860-1910. Sweden of the 1860s was a basically rural country. Most people were employed in agriculture and much of it was producing subsistence for own needs. However, Sweden was also a grain exporting country for example to the wealthy Amsterdam. But quicker ships totally changed the picture when grains could be exported from the vast farmlands of the United States and the Russian steps. The small farmlands in Sweden were no longer competitive and the price of grain decreased dramatically. This caused a decrease in the relative price of grain to butter and diary products, which were other Swedish exports.

Schultz (1985) claims that the relative butter to rye ratio can be used as an indicator of the female to male price of time, because in pre-industrial agriculture milk, butter, cheese were women's work, while working on the fields were men's work. The more expensive female time now induced a substitution away from having many children to care about and in favour of more lucrative diary production.

The Easterlin relative income hypothesis can be seen as a special case of the general neo- classical theory. Only when the income effect is more important than the substitution effect the Easterlin hypothesis will be true. This is the case if people put more emphasis on how many children they can afford for a given income, than on how much more money a wife could cam on the market rather than her value as a housewife. The neoclassical theory or the opportunity cost of time view is more similar to the Myrdals view in emphasizing time and money costs of children as determinants of fertility. However, modem neoclassical economies describe the theory in an algebraic condenses way and specifying which factors are of importance for determining those costs are only hinted at. For Alva Myrdal on the other hand in 'Crisis in the Population Question' (1934) and in 'Nation and Family' (1941) making visible the social and economic situation of families with children is the main focus.

BENEFITS AND COSTS OF HAVING CHILDREN

The decision for a prospective parent or a prospective parent couple is to compare costs and benefits of having a child. Then the couple will have a child if benefits of having a child are larger than costs, or equivalently net benefits are positive i.e., larger than zero. Which are the benefits of having children? In traditional agricultural societies children are put to productive work in the family business at an early age, and if there is no public old age pension children are also the only source of support for old people. In such a society it is economically beneficial to have children, and this is one reason, assuming rationality and knowledge about contraceptives, that have kept rural families over the world bigger than urban families. However, with urbanization and increased schooling also in rural areas and the introduction of public pensions the financial motives for having children have decreased or disappeared. Both the Myrdals (1944) and Becker (1981) discuss this change in benefits. What remains as benefits is the joy of having children. But having children is costly and the costs are higher the higher the quality of life you wish for your child. Because parents finance child related expenses out of a given budget there is enough for either a big number of children of low quality or a smaller number of children of higher quality. The social situation in Sweden in the 1930s analyzed and described so convincingly by the Myrdals (1935) the quality of life of each child needed to be increased. The Myrdals propose a large amount of quality improvements. Becker (1981) proposes, that the wish of the parents to increase the quality of each child, have lead them to demand fewer children of better quality, when incomes have increased. In the overpopulated, high fertility developing countries of the world it is necessary to increase the quality of life of each child and as a result the number of births will decrease. This thinking fits very well with the sociological theory of Caldwell (1980) proposing that the introduction of mass education would determine the fertility transition in a country i.e. the time when fertility rates become close to the replacement rate of about two children per woman. The means to reach this result is education and empowerment of women (World Bank 2001) as well as men. Extending education and empowerment only to the male population does not produce this result and there is therefore no contradiction between policies for economic growth and policies for gender equality. Policies for gender equality can not wait until economic development has been achieved, because women's empowerment is a prerequisite for economic growth, in that educated mothers produce healthy, well educated children ready to invest in their human capital and develop the economy of their country.

The costs of children are of two aggregate categories namely, time costs and money costs. The time costs or opportunity costs of time arise because time spent in childbearing and childcare cannot simultaneously be spent in market work unless there is market non-parental childcare. In addition to time costs there are also money costs like a bigger house, food, clothes, toys, music lessons, schooling expenditures etc. One important difference between the work of Alva Myrdal and that of most modern mainstream economists, who theorize on population, is that Alva Myrdal worked out her proposals in political details. She took part in polities, chaired government committees, wrote newspaper articles, and gave many public presentations to promote her ideas. Typical of a modern economist is what the answer Gary Becker gave at the European Society for Population Economics Meetings in 1990 in Istanbul, to a Turkish economist asking: what can Turkey do to decrease fertility? I think Becker must have said, that contraceptives must be made available, and that all children must go to school but what I remember him saying was: 'Turkey should do the opposition of Sweden i.e. increase costs of children, rather than the Swedish policy of decreasing costs of children'. Of course Becker does not want to impoverish more of Turkey's children. But a less thoughtful use of his advice could have that effect. An increase of the opportunity cost of time by stimulating women's market work would however make children more expensive and could lead to less poverty. Therefore it is important to be more specific in policy advice. Which policies to increase costs of children would simultaneously result in lower fertility and better quality of life for the children. Obviously the introduction of mass education would be such a policy.

MAINSTREAM ECONOMICS OF FERTILITY

Recent reviews of the economics of fertility include Cigno (1991), Hotz, Klerman and Willis (1997) and Ermisch (2003). The origins of the economics of fertility by Hotz *et al.* (1997) as consisting of two important contributions namely the first, the quality-quantity model of fertility, acknowledges that parents not only demand numbers of children but also children with certain qualities. The second contribution was to acknowledge the importance of parental time, especially mothers' time in the rearing development of children.

Much of this early literature in collected Gary Becker's own contributions is synthesized in Becker (1981). Becker (1981) proposes that parents value both the number of children (N) and the quality of life of each child (Q) in addition to their own consumption (C). This assumption produces a utility function of the form:

$$U = U\ (N, Q, Z)$$
$$S.T.Y = \Pi_2\ z + \Pi_c\ NQ \qquad (1)$$

By this assumption Becker is able to explain the puzzle, that children are likely to be normal goods with poor substitutes, and yet we have witnessed in Europe a hundred years of fertility decreases as income increases over time, rather than a positive correlation between income and fertility, which Malthus (1798) predicted. Becker (1981) suggests, that parents simply invest more money in each child, than have more children when their incomes increase.

Parents derive utility from the number of children (N), the quality of each child (Q) and adult standard of living (Z). Assuming that each child gets the same amount of resources invested in him or her by their parents; children can only come in quality-adjusted packages NQ, rather than having N and Q as separate adjustments in the utility function. Family full income (y) must then be used to pay for adult standard of living ($\Pi_z Z$) and the cost of children ($\Pi_c NQ$).

Both NQ and Z are produced in the household by inputs of tie and goods and services bought on the market.

Becker (1965) argues that it is not the market goods like vegetables, meat, olive oil that enter our production function but a much more limited number of commodities like a pleasant meal, a nice home, affection and company that we produce combining market goods and services with our own time. That means that child quality Q is produced.

$$Q = f\left(\frac{x_c}{N}, \frac{t_{mc}}{N}, \frac{t_{fc}}{N}\right) \tag{2}$$

where X_c are market goods and services bought for the child like clothes, food, school fees, child care center fees, toys, music lessons etc. Child quality also needs mother's time tmc and father's time tfe.

Adult standard y living is produced in a similar way

$$z = g(x_z, t_{mz}, t_{fz}) \tag{3}$$

where X_z are adult goods and services. It can be difficult to distinguish between X_c and X_z but it is easy to agree that time use patterns of adults, who do not have children will include more of eating out, going to concerts, exercising sports like skiing and sailing, traveling long distance and the like where children can not so easily be brought along.

Changes in costs of children using this framework can then be written following Ermisch (2003):

$$N_c = \frac{P_c X_c}{\Pi_c NQ}(pc) + \frac{Wmtmc}{\Pi_c NQ}(wm) + \frac{wftfc}{\Pi_c NQ}(wf) \tag{4}$$

where Π_c is the shadow price of children. The three right hand terms express the costs of the three factors of production X_c, t_{mc} and t_{fc} that enter the production of child well being Q according Q according the expression (2). T

The cost of the three factors of production costs is made up of their prices times their shares in the budget of the parents.

The right hand side of (4) reads: the price of market goods and services (Pc) times its budget share ($PcXc/\Pi_c NQ$) plus the price of mother's time (W_m) times its budget share and the price of father's time (W_f) times its budget share. Of course X_c is a composite of many different goods and services and its price Pc is a weighted average of all these different prices. The price of mother's time (W_m) and father's time (W_f) are generally taken to be their market wages or in case of any of the parents do not perform market work it will be their potential market wage, which they would have earned had they had a job. If the mother cares fulltime for her children and the father has a fulltime, the mother's time expenditure is a large share of the costs of children (Π_c) while the father's time cost is small and his market earnings instead come into paying for the market goods and services used in the child well being production.

It is often interesting to know what happens to the cost of children if there are changes in the prices, which determine the cost of children. By taking the logarithms we get an expression for percentage changes:

$$d\ln\Pi_c = \frac{P_c X_c}{\Pi_c NQ} d\ln(pc) + \frac{W_m tmc}{\Pi_c NQ} d\ln(W_m) + \frac{W_f t_{fc}}{\Pi_c NQ} d\ln(W_f) \qquad (5)$$

Decreases in p_c result for example if the government subsidizes children by child benefits, child tax credits, tax financed schools or elementary, secondary and university levels, lower public transportation prices for children. Changes in W_m higher women's wages will increase the cost of mother's own time input into child quality. High wage women have more expensive children and here will be a tendency for more educated women to spend more time in market work and less time in caring for her children.

The induced substitution effect may be sufficiently large to produce a decline in fertility when income increases. It may therefore appear that the income elasticity is negative, even through children are 'normal goods' in the sense that parents want more of them when income increases.

THE ECONOMIC THEORY OF FERTILITY OF THE MYRDALS

The main elements of modern economic theory of fertility are present in 'Crisis in the Population Question'; there is a discussion of the quality of children (Q) in previous section. There are discussions of the costs of goods and services (X_c) in earlier section and how there costs could be lowered by social policies. There are also discussions of the time or opportunity costs of having children the (W_m t_{mc}) above and how these costs could be decreased by social policies. In the following I will discuss the theory of fertility of the Myrdals using this framework.

In 'Crisis in the Population Question' (1934) the Myrdals use to establish that the population goal is a no decreasing population, that there are currently 30 per cent fewer births, than necessary to achieve this goal, and that a forecast for the future points to still fewer births because people aspire to increase their standard of living. Further parenthood should be voluntary, and because people do not wish to have as many children as to warrant a non decreasing population, it is necessary to find out, what the costs of children are and by social planning and subsidies to families with children tip the balance of costs over, so that young couples can afford to have children. The normal family size ought to be 3 children per family, which is required for a constant population. Alva Myrdal (1944) computes that each woman for a constant population to result needs to have 2.21 children on average, and if only those who marry have children, it requires 2.95 children per married woman. If we deduct those marriages, that are resolved before the end of the fecund period of the woman, the number required is 3.14.

The Myrdals created their theory for the purpose of arguing for social reforms. It is also from the 'Crisis in the Population Question' (1934) and 'Nation and Family' (1941) which delved into the idea, that a demographic situation that needs more children is an opportunity to get feminist policies accepted; policies that allow women to combine work and family.

Quantity and Quality of Children

Because each child has become more costly through expenditures for all sorts of education, the budget of families is used for fewer children of better quality rather than for many children of low quality. This in turn makes a country leave the status of underdevelopment and enroll on a path of economic development. In 'Crisis in the Populations Question' a whole chapter is devoted to the quality of the people:

'The modern society, the 1930s in comparison to the 19th century, requires people of better quality because work intensity and work efficiency is outrageously raised in most industrial workplaces' (Myrdal and Myrdal 1935).

The Myrdals worry, that inefficient people and partially productive people will be left over by this productivity development to a much larger extent than in the agricultural society of past times. Their conclusion is, that there must be public policies to increase the quality of people, so that not so many risk being sorted out by the increased demands:

'Unemployment leads to future unemployment and particularly youth unemployment is dangerous. It is socially and morally demolishing. Unemployment must be removed. We must also find ways to employ partially employable people both for their own life satisfaction, but also because it is not economically efficient, that these people produce nothing instead of a partial production' (Myrdal and Myrdal 1935).

Later Alva Myrdal was a member of the Government Committee for Partially Employable People 1943-1947, where she worked out these ideas in practical policies.

In the 1930s, there was much discussion of racial issues and sterilizing people, who were antisocial, was seen as a means of racial hygiene. The Myrdals are very skeptical to such thoughts and judge that, it cannot be expected, that by sterilizing mentally ill people the frequency of mental illness will decrease. There is too little knowledge of to what extent mental illness is genetic and if so whether illness will break out in any given individual. Increasing the quality of the people is much more a question of giving children better food, better housing, better health care, better parents by parental education and better opportunities for social upward mobility.

Costs of Market Goods and Services for Children

Myrdal and Myrdal (1935) is a shocking description of the low standard of living of ordinary Swedish people in the 1930s. Particularly the housing standards were very low by necessity, because the incomes of ordinary people did not allow better homes. The most common family home consisted of one room and a kitchen. An analysis of the housing standard in 55 Swedish towns showed, that 40 per cent of all apartments for rent were one room and a kitchen and about 40 per cent of the population in the 55 towns lived in such an apartment. The average number of people living in an apartment of one room and a kitchen was 3.4 people (Myrdal and Myrdal 1935). But the spread around the average is even more telling. Seven people or more in one room and a kitchen was the case for 7 percentage points out of the 40 per cent and about 17 per cent of the total population lived with seven or more people in one room and a kitchen. In many cases a family could not afford to pay the rent but in addition to husband, wife and children, there would also be paying lodgers who slept in the home. The Myrdals calculation on the basis of an investigation of housing standards in Gothenburg that the average space for each family member among families living in one room and a kitchen was only 5 square meters.

In Myrdal (1944) the 1933 general housing investigation is available. It shows among other things (Myrdal 1944) that more than 66 per cent of families with 3 or more children were living in overpopulated housing more than 1.5 person units per room and that for 47 per cent of such families more than 2 person units per room was the case. A child is counted as half a person unit so that 2 person units mean four people: father, mother and two children. But housing standards were not better among workers on the farms (Myrdal and Myrdal 1935).

'The negative effects for children of growing up in these 'sleep and cook' places with always many adults and adult activities around them cannot be exaggerated. Particularly dangerous it is for the infants who catch diseases much more frequently if they live in such overpopulated homes, for school children, who have no quiet place to do their home work, and for teenagers in the transition to young adults, who have no opportunity to be alone or bring friends to the home. Teenagers therefore spend their time in parks, on the street, in cafes and on out door dancing floors creating the 'the dancing floor misery' (Myrdal 1944).

However, housing standards measured as number of people living together in one room had increased a little between the 1920s and the 1930s, not because housing had improved, but because the number of children per family had decreased. The workers could improve their housing standards by having fewer children.

In addition to a decent housing standard, good nutrition is essential for a child. Also in this respect young workers did not have enough income to supply sufficient food for their children. The Myrdals point to the big differences in the share of the income that is spent on food when comparing social classes. In 1923 the food expenditure share for production workers was 45.5 per cent, for lower salaried employees, 39.5 per cent and for the middle class 26.9 per cent (Myrdal and Myrdal 1935). For the Myrdals the conclusion is clean. There must be social policies to increase living standards of families with children. The children are the future of our nation and therefore people with few or no children must contribution by paying taxes, the receipts of which can be used to lower costs of children to parents, so that more children will be born. A list of necessary reforms is supplied (Myrdal and Myrdal 1935) and includes:

- Housing subsidies for large families
- General and free health care for all children
- Free school lunch for all children

- Price discounts for some food for children
- All costs for schooling removed, free books, free material, free school busses
- Free day-care
- Free education stipends for talented youth.

Almost all of these suggestions have been carried out in Sweden making child costs to parents perhaps smaller than in any other country. In the most recent decades the trend has been to rather decrease the real value of subsidies for children.

TIME COST OF CHILDREN

Alva Myrdal thought a lot about the opportunity cost of having children for the woman. By the industrial revolution the woman had lost her productive work and become locked into a miniature apartment with no stimulation. Already in Myrdal and Myrdal (1935) she notes that there are increasing numbers of wives, who have difficulties finding full employment. They have a very small family and a small apartment. She says 'normal young women want to marry and have children; nobody doubts that. But they want to and also need a job. We cannot accent these circumstances that now to an increasing degree force women to infertility in order to get a job. Reforms on the labour market have to be carried out which makes it possible for them to have children without having to leave their job entirely. They must be given a lawful right to a decent absence of leave, to reemployment etc. The question on creation of increased opportunities for part-time work must be researched, also the major problem how a woman after a few years of absence during a period of child bearing and child rearing should find her way more easily back to market work' (Myrdal and Myrdal 1935).

One could take a text written by a European Union official today in 2005 and find almost the same wording. The means Alva Myrdal suggested to decrease the opportunity costs of children was publicly organized collective childcare. This would also improve the situation for the children by giving them access to professional pedagogies, space for their playing activities, play mates of their age, at least one nutritionally well-composed cooked meal per day etc.

Hirdman (1992) speculates that for Alva Myrdal the population crisis was the means to achieve feminist goals and for Gunnar Myrdal the population crisis was the real threat and feminism one of the many means to bring a halt to the threatening depopulation of Sweden. Bok (1987) describes how Gunnar from an early age was accustomed to see himself as special. He was allowed to study in the best room of his parental home and his sisters and mother were waiting on him. He expected and got a similar kind of service from his wife Alva according to Bok (1987). Alva Myrdal on the other hand was an active feminist. She was deputy chair of the Swedish Association of Professional Women 1932-1935 and chair of the same organization 1936-1938. Further she was deputy chair 1938-1947 of the International Federation of Business and Professional Women. Ever since Alva Myrdal, population issues can be used fruitfully as arguments in feminist action.

'The fertility argument was taken from the hands of the antifeminists and became instead a new and efficient weapon in feminist action. The previous debate on the married woman's right to work was transformed into a fight for the workingwoman's right to marry and have children' (Myrdal 1944).

Whether such policies ultimately result in higher fertility is still an open question (Gustafsson and Jacobsson 1985; Gustafsson 2001) but is has certainly resulted in more equality between women and men.

The Swedish childcare system is one of the most important reasons for an international large degree of equality between women and men in Sweden. The United Nations Human Development report (1995) places Sweden as the number one country according to the gender empowerment measures as the most gender equal country in the world.

Child care centers in the year 2005 in Sweden are like Alva Myrdal planned them, available to all children whose parents want a place, close to the child's home, open to accommodate parents working hours, state subsidized, have out door play grounds and include children from the middle class as well as children of parents, who work as production workers. This has been achieved gradually and only in the 1990s, one can say, that there are enough spaces for all children. It was legislated to be a lawful must for the communities to supply day care for all its children in 1996, but some local authorities, where the population is increasing have difficulties to provide the necessary child care spaces.

CONCLUDING REMARKS

In this paper it is argued that the fertility theory of Alva and Gunnar Myrdal in many ways pioneers modern economic theory of fertility although it's never referenced as such. The fertility theory of Alva and Gunnar Myrdal develops from the idea that deciding for a child is a rational choice determined by the costs and benefits of having children. In this way the theory of the Myrdal is similar to modern mainstream economics of fertility developed by Gary Becker and others. This paper shows how similar the fertility theory of' 'Crisis in the Population Question' is to modern neoclassical theory of fertility. It is similar in discussing money and time costs of children and in the discussion of the quantity-quality tradeoff. It is also similar because both rely on the assumption that people are rational. If costs of children can be decreased, people can afford to realize their natural desire for having children. Policies suggested by Alva Myrdal have become government policy in Sweden and decreased costs of children to parents perhaps more than in any other country. Also both theories point to the idea that having a child is a deliberate decision.

REFERENCES

Becker, G. (1965), The Theory of the Allocation of Time. *The Economic Journal*, 80: 493-517.

Becker, G. (1981), *A Treatise on the Family*. Harvard University Press.

Bok, S. (1987), *A Woman's Life*. Bonniers, Stockholm.

Caldwell, J. C. (1980), Mass Education as a Determinant of the Timing of Fertility Decline. *Population and Development Review*, 6(2): 225-255.

Cigno, A. (1991), *Economics of the Family*. Clarendon Press Oxford, United Kingdom.

Cutler, D. M., Poterba, J. M., Sheiner, L. M., and Summers, L. H. (1990), An Aging Society: Opportunity or Challenge? *Brookings Papers on Economic Activity* (1): 1-73.

Easterlin, R. (1980), *Birth and Fortune: The Impact of Numbers on Personal Welfare*. Basic Books, New York.

Ermish, J. F. (2003), *An Economic Analysis of the Family*. Princeton University Press, Princeton.

Fölster, K. (1992), *The Three Leaves: A Postscriptum of the Myrdals*. Bonniers, Stockholm.

Gustafsson, S. S. and Jacobsson, R. (1985), Trends in Female Labour Force Participation in Sweden. *Journal of Labour Economics*, 3(1): 256-274.

Gustafsson, S. S. and Stafford, F. (1992), Daycare Subsidies and Labour Supply in Sweden. *Journal of Human Resources*, 27(1): 204-230.

Gustafsson, S. S. (2001), Optimal Age at Motherhood: Theoretical and Empirical Considerations on Postponement of Maternity in Europe. *Journal of Population Economics*, 14: 225-247.

Hirdman, Y. (1992), *The Socialistic Housewife and other Women's Histories*. Carlsson Publishing Company, Stockholm.

Hotz, J. V., Klerman, J. A and Willis, R. J. (1997), The Economics of Fertility in Developed Countries. In: R. M. Rosenzweig and O. Stark (eds.). *Handbook of Population and Family Economics*. Elsevier, Amsterdam.

Malthus, R. (1798), *An Essay on Population*. Everyman's Library, London.

Mincer, J. (1962), *Labour Force Participation of Married Women: A Study of Labour Supply in Aspects of Labour Economics*. A Report of the National Bureau of Economic Research, Princeton University Press, Princeton.

Myrdal, A. and Myrdal, G. (1935), *Crisis in the Population Question*. First Edition Published in 1934, Bonniers, Stockholm.

Myrdal, A. (1944), *Nation and Family*. First Edition Published in 1941, KFs Publishing Company, Stockholm.

Myrdal, J. (1982), *Childhood*. Nordstedts, Stockholm.

Myrdal, J. (1984), *Another World*. P. A. Nordstedt and Söners Förlag, Stockholm.

Schultz, T. P. (1985), Changing World Prices, Women's Wages and the Fertility Transition: Sweden 1860-1910. *Journal of Political Economy*, 93: 1126-1154.

United Nations Development Program (1995), *Human Development Report 1995*. Oxford University Press, New York.

World Bank (2001), *Engendering Development through Gender Equality in Rights, Resources and Voice*. World Bank and Oxford University Press.

APPENDIX 1

Alva Myrdal a Role Model and Her Children's Writings about Her

In 1982, Jan Myrdal, son of Alva and Gunnar, since long a famous writer, published his book about his childhood. Jan Myrdal's childhood books detonated like a bomb in Sweden. Here was this famous couple, both of them Nobel Prize winners: Gunnar received the Prize for Economies in 1974 and Alva received the Peace Prize for 1980. Their son accuses them for having neglected their children. He himself, at publishing his book childhood in 1982, had not seen his parents for 15 years. I was horrified, a 55 years old person, who does not see his parents, who does not try to understand and forgive. Alva was 80 and Gunnar was 84. Why did he not wait until they were gone? I talked a lot at home about how I experienced Jan Myrdal's books. One citation in Jan's book (1982) is, that Jan accuses his mother of having cold fingers and not liking dogs. I have never been a 'dog person' myself and my fingers were often cold. My son Magnus, then 17 used my worries in a formulation that he repeated jokingly in various situations: 'Be kind to me, behave mother, if not I will write a book about you when I turn 55'. After Jan Myrdals books also his sisters Sissela Bok (1987) and Kai Fölster (1992) published books about their parents and their childhood. Their books have different characters but they confirm that the children felt neglected by their parents. Jan Myrdal (1982) thinks that his parents were normal parents for his sisters but not for him. Fölster (1992) envies her brother, because there were many letters from Gunnar Myrdal to his son about his writings and other things, but there were only three small letters to her in the collection of personal letters that was given to Föister after Alva's death. Her father did not come to see her and her family, when he traveled to Germany. Her mother Alva Myrdal always did. Föister (1992) also explains how Alva Myrdal usually brought one of her three children at a time to do nice things with, so that there could really be time to talk, and there would not be any rivalry between the children. But the Myrdal family never had vacations together like other families.

Sissela Bok (1987) says that Alva Myrdal always thought that there were more important things that required her attention, so that it would not be useful to spend time writing memoirs. To be useful is something that was important to Alva Myrdal. Sissela Bok (1987) writes a warm and close story, as a daughter, who experienced her mother's death, and who experienced like so many daughters, that this was the last opportunity to ask about important things. Sissela asked and Alva answered for all of us who admired her. Both Bok (1987) and Fölster (1992) give warm pictures of their mother and they both think, that their father was impossible and if Alva had chosen a different man as a father of her children, they could have been a normal family. Fölster (1992) also gives the blame to her brother, who was a terribly dominant person, insensitive to how his little sister experienced him. It is evident in Jan Myrdal's childhood books, that he reflects very much on, how he experienced, what other people said and did to him, but he never reflects upon how his parents and sisters and teachers must have experienced his behavior. An adult person writing about his childhood should be expected to have done that. Did Alva enjoy her children? Bok (1987) cites a diary notation by Alva from 1927 when her son Jan was recently born where she expresses her joy and thankfulness of having had a child. Also in Myrdal (1935) she says: Normal young woman want to marry and have children nobody doubts that.

The more surprising is the severe criticism from Alva's children because she had so much knowledge of child psychology. Alva studied child psychology and wrote many articles about how parents should behave. She contributed a lot in this field. A citation (Bok 1987) is that Alva's studies in 1929 made her a pioneer to free children from the demand of child physicians, who said that infants should be breast fed only after 4 hours. 'Let them cry', do not take them up was what they taught.

Alva's insights from 1929 had not yet gotten acceptance among those, who gave advice to new mothers in the 1960's. I experienced how I tried to keep to the 'four hours rule' in 1965 and 1969 when my sons were born. Between 1996 en 2003 I have been blessed with five grandchildren. The insights that children should be given food and attention, when they need, is common knowledge and given as advice to new parents. My sons and daughters in law have commented on the old-fashioned four hours rule. I think it is symptomatic of Alva Myrdal that she was so modern and so much before her time in so many respects. She said the right thing and it took 60 years before her insights had become common knowledge.

Having read the childhood books of Jan Myrdal (1982 and 1984) one may draw the conclusion that Alva Myrdal did not have time to enjoy her children. What were the benefits of children to her? The stories of his sisters Bok (1987) and Fölster (1992) however witness, that Alva spent much time and energy on her children, and that she had wanted more than three children but several miscarriages prevented that. However, all three children agree, that Gunnar Myrdal showed no interest whatsoever in his children, and saw them merely as competing demands on Alva's time. Fölster (1992) witnesses that Gunnar Myrdal was also not interested in his adult daughter and did not visit her when he traveled through Germany. Was Gunnar Myrdal worse than other fathers of his generation? Perhaps. In Alva's writings there is however no criticism of the role of fathers. Having read some of Alva's work I am struck with how modern she was, how provident she was and I am proud of being one of many who are inspired by her work and continue her work based on her intellectual legacy.

APPENDIX II

The Style of Working in 'Crisis in the Population Question'

Reading 'Crisis in the Population Question', which was published in 1934 when Alva was 32 years old. The youthful enthusiasm and optimism that characterizes this book first strike me. Alva wrote this book together with her husband Gunnar who was then 36 years old. The final work was done while they had rented a cottage in the Norwegian mountains and could discuss the text, something that Alva enjoyed very much (Bok 1987).

The second thing that thumps me is that the book is like the front cover picture of Hirdman (1992). It shows a portrait of a young man and a young woman who have a common vision, that is only three eyes are shown. The left eye of the man is also the right eye of the woman and his face translates into her face but we do not know where the border is. When I read the first few chapters of the 'Crisis in the Population Question' I think about Gunnar Myrdal and when I read the last few chapters I think about Alva Myrdal and I do not know where it changes. There is no visible border.

The third thing that smacks me is that the language is varied and amazing, a language which is not any more used by economists today. Economists today aspire to transmit their message in as few words as possible to the group of international expert colleagues.

A fourth characteristic of the book is that it uses a biting irony, which I experience as unpleasant. There are many eyewitnesses that Gunnar Myrdal felt devalued by his economist colleagues. Mary Jean Bowman, one of the few female professors of economies the university of Chicago told me in 1979 about a meeting she had experienced in Chicago with the Myrdal couple: only wanted to speak about how little appreciation, he got from his colleagues in Stockholm although we, at the university of Chicago, knew about the Myrdals contribution to family economic and had wanted to hear about that. This would have been shortly after the publication of the second edition-of 'Nation and Family' with the preface of Moynihan in 1968. However, irony is seen by many as a fine weapon. On the back cover Myrdal and Myrdal (1935) the famous professor of political science and Journalist Herbert Tingsten praise 'Crisis in the Population Question' because 'the analysis is a masterpiece of controlled irony'. About his economist colleagues Gunnar says (I cannot think that Alva says this) 'during the recent past, the social political discussion in Sweden, some very loose and scientifically unfounded international comparisons have been used as weapons in the discussion, usually in the sphere of economies and by people who do not lack theoretical education' (Myrdal and Myrdal 1935). Further in the same page research of professor Brisman is ridiculed for drawing conclusions for Sweden by some findings from England, where he has neglected the fact, that in England there are many war widows, which is not the case in Sweden in the 1930's. This ironic tone against everyone who thought differently than Gunnar Myrdal, particularly his economists colleagues makes the first part of the book sound more like written by Gunnar than by Alva.

2

TECHNOLOGY, ECONOMIC OPPORTUNITIES AND WOMEN EMPOWERMENT

N. NARAYANA

INTRODUCTION

Information and communication technologies (ICT) provide a great development opportunity by contributing to information dissemination, providing an array of communication capabilities and increasing access to technology and knowledge. ICT have become a potent force in transforming social, economic, and political life globally. There is a wide consensus that ICT are central to the emerging global knowledge-based economies. It plays vital role in accelerating growth, in promoting sustainable development and eradicating poverty in developing countries as well as the transitional economies by effectively integrating them into the global economy.

The rapid growth of the information and communications systems is increasingly recognized as most important, in terms of its overall economic impact and spillover effects, than any of the major technological revolutions of the past two centuries. ICT are permeating all aspects of business and, increasingly, the wider society. It is emerging as one of the engines of economic growth and wealth creation by raising productivity levels and allowing markets to work more quickly and efficiently. By reducing costs and increasing the speed of communications, it is now playing a major role in globalizing production of goods and services as well as financial markets. Its broader adoption and application has already had a dramatic impact on employment patterns and skills requirements in the job market. In the long run, the significance of the new information system is likely to be even greater since it opens unprecedented opportunities for connecting and unleashing the creative potential of much larger groups of people than has been the case up to now. This, in turn, is profoundly influencing the life styles of people in general and women in particular.

However, access to and the costs of ICT continue to be a major development obstacle in the context of empowerment of women, particularly in the developing world. In semi-urban and rural areas where a great majority of population lives, ICT policy and programmes have to become a means for improving economic conditions of women. More concern is being shown about the impact of those left on the other side of the digital divide as most women with in developing countries are in the deepest part of the divide. If access to and the use of these technologies is directly linked to social and economic development, then it is imperative to ensure that women in developing countries understand the significance of these technologies and use them. This also helps to stop further marginalization of women from the mainstream of their countries and of the world.

It is essential that gender issues be considered early in the process of the introduction of information technology in developing countries and not as a corrective afterwards. The United Nations Organization places the information technology as the third most important issue facing women globally, after poverty and violence against women. It is time to ensure that women in developing countries can enter the information age. In general ICT offers many new possibilities for women since it is a lifeline for economic, social, and political empowerment and can certainly contribute to finding solutions for fulfilling women's basic needs and access to resources.

This paper examines the importance of information economy in terms of ICT development and analyses women's access to ICT and how ICT provides enabling environment and offers diversified opportunities for economic empowerment of women and their promotion in developing countries. As women are regarded as agents and beneficiaries of change, investing in women's capabilities and empowering them to exercise their choices is not only valuable but also the surest way to contribute to economic growth and all round development.

EMERGING INFORMATION ECONOMY

Information and communications system is penetrating into all aspects of human life and everything seems to be happening much faster today (Pyramid Research 1999). Majority of the world's poor living in rural areas do not have access to a reliable information and communications infrastructure (DOT Force 2001). Those who suffer from chronic hunger and poverty are obviously not covered by these communication facilities (United Nations Development Programme 2000). As we know, the poor not only need food but also a combination of basic education and skills together with information and communication infrastructure so as to derive the full effects of market forces that raise their income level.

Knowledge and information and communications systems are interdependent in the process of development. The link between knowledge and its diffusion and economic growth are the subject of a large body of literature. Schumpeter (1943) made the distinction between the creation of knowledge and its diffusion. Arrow (1962) linked diffusion of knowledge and growth in the learning-by-doing model. Further research into the .dynamics of the knowledge diffusion process and its relationship with growth and inequality was conducted by Davies (1979) and Grossman and Helpman (1991), and Aghion and Howitt (1998) reviewed the analysis of the origin of technological change from endogenous research and development decisions of firms including the impact of increasing returns.

Ultimately, it is the diffusion and accessibility of new information technology to a wider society determines it impact on the development of people. This diffusion process depends on a number of variables including the capacity of people to absorb new technologies and supportive policy environment. Educational levels and human resource development play vital role in this regard. But the educational attainment levels are far low in developing countries compared to industrial countries. There is close link between information and communication systems and human capital. If information system is skill-biased, then successful adoption of it depends on higher-level human capital. This has direct policy implications for developing countries (Patrinos 2000).

There are number of specific benefits that accrue from information and communications systems such as improved functioning of markets through easier and cheaper access to information on goods and services; quality improvements and frequent changes in product and process design; managerial improvements including better decisions through better and faster marshalling of information; savings on material costs, energy and inventories; and a faster and more efficient financial sector. On the face of it, it would stimulate the process of accumulation of human capabilities and thereby reducing the productivity gap between advanced and developing countries.

With some 1.2 billion, or over 20 per cent of the world's population living in absolute poverty at less than US $1 a day, the question is whether humanity can harness the new capabilities of information and communications technology to reduce poverty and generate more equitable growth. But the rapid spread and declining costs of information offers the world's low-income countries a chance to attain a more value-added knowledge-intensive growth and to achieve social and economic equality (ILO 2001a). Development of information systems can have a far-reaching impact on the quality of life of marginalized segments of the population by providing more responsive and transparent governance as well as improving the reach and delivery of health, education and other social services. The ability of this information technology to reduce poverty and spur development will be determined by its impact on employment, as well as the creation of productive and remunerative work. Speculation abounds that the new 'knowledge economy' will trigger a 'paradigm shift' involving new approaches to development (OECD 2001). The role of information systems should therefore be regarded as significant factor in developing economies for growth and poverty alleviation.

The dramatic acceleration in the development and use of ICT in recent years has set in motion a worldwide process of transforming the present economies into information economies. As we moved into the third millennium, it is of the utmost importance to understand and to influence the fundamental changes brought about by the communication and information revolution. The complexity and interrelation of today's world problems defy traditional explanations and solutions and require a completely new approach, which must be both comprehensive and interdisciplinary.

Moreover, individuals, groups and communities will need to develop not only new tools of analysis but also very different attitudes in order to meet the challenges of the emerging new economy based on information and knowledge. Markets for new information and interactive services are being aggressively explored and developed, as information providers and carriers seek to expand their activities beyond their traditional borders. The developed countries have an overwhelming lead in all these advances.

Some of the developing countries, using information technology in education and health to help break the vicious circle of poverty and are making rapid progress by creating new sectors of sustainable economic development like software production and data processing. The major problems are posed not by the technologies as such, which can be acquired and adapted, but rather by political, social, organizational and gender issues that are involved. However, the benefits derived by the humanity from these opportunities depend on the rate at which the transfer of information technology is possible. This again depends on the efforts of the developing countries in enhancing human capabilities to make the best possible use of the available information infrastructure. On this condition, the information economy can attain its ultimate goal – empowerment of all its citizens through access to and use of this new knowledge.

USE OF TECHNOLOGY BY WOMEN

Most women within developing countries are in the genuine part of the digital divide further removed from the information age than the men whose poverty they share. If access to and use of these technologies is directly linked to social and economic development, then it is essential to ensure that women in developing countries understand the significance of these technologies and use them. If not, they will become further marginalized from the mainstream of their countries and of the world. It is imperative that gender issues be considered early in the process of the introduction of information technology (IT) in developing countries so that gender concerns can be incorporated from the beginning and not as a corrective afterwards. Many people allow to go the concern for gender and IT in developing countries on the basis that development should deal with basic needs first. However, it is not a choice between one and the other. IT can be an important tool in meeting women's basic needs and can provide the access to resources to lead women out of poverty. Getting reliable statistics on women's Internet use in developing countries is very difficult. The standard indicators are not disaggregated by sex, and the available data are not very reliable or comparable. However, it is clear that the numbers are small and the distribution limited. Most women Internet users in almost all developing countries are not representative of women in the country as a whole, but rather are part of a small, urban educated elite. In many developing countries, less than one percent of the population male or female access Internet. Most women in developing countries who use information technology use it at work. Except in upper-income enclaves, home access to a computer and the Internet is not a phenomenon. Users at work generally divide up between those who use it as a tool of production and those who use it as a tool of communication. As a tool of communication, the most prevalent application is networking for political advocacy on behalf of women. This came about because the nongovernmental organizations that promoted electronic networking and worked in political advocacy were the early adopters and is continuing users of the technology in developing countries. Also, developing country women have used electronic communication for networking to promote their enterprises interests. This area is far less developed than that of politically activist networking, but it represents an interesting area with possibilities for further development. E-mail is the major information technology application that women's organizations and individual women in developing countries use. But, time constraints as well as bandwidth limitations make Web use difficult for women. Few women are producers of information technology, whether as Internet content providers, programmers, designers, inventors, or fixers of computers. In addition, women are also conspicuously absent from decision-making structures in information technology in developing countries. A series of factors, including literacy and education, language, time, cost, geographical location of facilities, social and cultural norms, and women's computer and information search and dissemination skills constrain women's access to information technology. Information technology can be a tool for bringing education and improved health services to women. There is no longer a choice. The forces of globalization have made this one world and one economy. While there are risks in joining the global information society, the greatest risk of all is in not joining in it. The new technologies are a lifeline that can enable women in developing countries to join the conflict for economic, social, and political empowerment.

The extent of gender digital divide in developing countries can be explained in terms of women's use of new information technologies. The Internet usage is the standard indicator of the use of information and communication technologies. The figures in the Table 1 indicate women and Internet use in some of the countries. Of course, the figures are puzzling since there is no correlation between women's internet usage and other indicators such as female literacy, female GDP per capita, female representation in professional and technical jobs or even gender empowerment. The percentage of women among Internet users in the 22 countries for which data could be found ranged from low of six percent (Jordan) to high of over 40 percent (Mexico, Croatia, Brazil, Philippines and South Africa). There is no correlation in developing countries between a high percentage of users overall and a high percentage of women users, as there is in the developed world, especially in the US and Japan.

Some of the countries with high percentage of women users are countries where overall users remain limited to a very small elite (between 0.6 and 4.3 percent of the population). Among the developing countries, large countries with large absolute number of women Internet users are Brazil, China, and the Russian Federation. The number of users in China and India is expected to go up in the coming period (Bautista 1999).

Overall, there is no correlation within countries between female literacy and women's Internet use. Countries with nearly universal female literacy are found both near the upper end of percentage of female users and near the bottom (at 10 percent) in some other countries. But the Internet use by women did not correlate with percentage of female technical and professional employment. Countries where women are nearly half or more of this category are found among the high percentages of female users of the Internet as well as among the lowest. Again, no correlation exists between high percentage of female users and high female GDP per capita (ITU 2001).

Further, the figures in the table support the view that most women Internet users in most of the developing countries are not representative of women in the country as a whole, but rather are presently part of a small-educated urban population.

Table 1
Internet use by Women in Developing Countries

Country	*Women (% of Internet users)*	*Total women Internet users (in '000s)*	*Total no. Internet users (in '000s)*	*Internet Users (% total population)*	*Population (in '1000s)*	*Female professional and technical workers % of total*	*Female literacy rate*	*Female GDP per capital (US$)*	*GDP Rank 1/174*
Philippines	51.0	765	150	0.6	77 726	65.1	94.3	2510	65
South Africa	51.0	6456	1266	4.2	42835	46.6	83.2	4637	84
Brazil	43.0	175	2500	2.1	169807	63.3	83.9	3813	67
Croatia	42.0	63	150	4.3	4672	NA	96.4	3557	50
Mexico	42.0	567	1350	2.5	98553	45.2	87.9	4594	48
Russia	38.0	4560	12000	1.8	146861	NA	98.8	3503	61
Zambia	37.5	113	3	0.2	9461	31.9	67.5	753	125
Uganda	31.5	473	15	0.1	22167	NA	35	944	131
China	30.4	6840	22500	0.7	1265530	45.1	74.5	2485	79
India	23.0	115	500	0.2	983377	20.5	39.4	902	112
Poland	18.7	2956	1581	5.4	38607	61.2	99	5061	40
Ethiopia	13.9	83	6	0.1	58390	NA	29.2	349	172
Slovakia	12.0	60	500	13.0	5393	59.7	99	6366	39
Czech Republic	12.0	48	400	6.8	10286	54.1	99	7952	34
Senegal	12.0	90	7.5	0.3	9723	NA	24.8	1253	127
Jordan	6.0	37	608	1.8	4435	NA	81.8	1429	NA

Contd...

Country	Women (% of Internet users)	Total women Internet users (in '000s)	Total no. Internet users (in '000s)	Internet Users (% total population)	Population (in '1000s)	Female professional and technical workers % of total	Female literacy rate	Female GDP per capital (US$)	GDP Rank 1/174
Peru	NA	NA	200	1.5	26111	39.4	83.7	2335	71
Turkey	NA	NA	450	2.3	64567	33	73.9	4681	73
Thailand	NA	NA	200	1.3	60037	54.5	92.8	5000	58
Indonesia	NA	NA	300	0.2	212942	40.8	79.5	2359	88
Pakistan	NA	NA	619	0.1	135135	21.0	25.4	701	116
Vietnam	NA	NA	10	0.1	76236	27.6	89	1385	91

Source: http// www.isp-planet.com and http//www.nua.ie/surveys

Note: NA stands for not available.

Figures of relatively high (e.g. 30 percent or more) women's internet use as a percentage of total users per country can be misleading when internet access is confined to a small educated population of high income urban dwellers. This is the case in the Philippines, where women are 51 percent of total users, but where total users are less than one percent of the population. Similarly in India women comprise 23 percent of users, but the overall percentage of the population with Internet access is 0.2 percent or less (Joshi 1998). The low figures of overall percentage accessing the Internet are striking in comparison to the advanced countries where Internet usage now stands around 50 percent of the population with about 45 percent of those users being women (ILO 2001b).

TECHNOLOGY AND ECONOMIC ACTIVITIES

The emphasis on empowerment of women is found throughout the development cooperation policies. Empowerment is not something that can be done by outsiders to people. Development initiatives should create the conditions whereby women can become the agents of their own development and empowerment. A key aspect of empowerment of women is taking measures to ensure women's equal access to and their full participation in power structures and increasing women's capacity to participate in decision-making.

The segregation of the roles according to gender creates barriers that are difficult to overcome. This in turn explains why poverty, which is already more widespread amongst women, is still growing. The development of women will continue to be affected as long as gender discrimination exists in the distribution of work, responsibility and power. Women's empowerment and gender equality is both a matter of justice and a prerequisite for the development of harmonic and sustainable economy.

The crucial element in the empowerment of women is transforming the position of women in such a way that their advancement is sustained. Equally important is that women should themselves feel that they have been the agents of the transformation. Empowerment focuses on strengthening women's economic independence (through increased income and greater individual self-reliance), a more useful approach appears to recognize the multiple roles and interests that women have and the interrelationships between them. In fact, women work longer hours than men in nearly every country. Since the status in contemporary society is so often equated with income-earning power, women suffer a major under valuation of their economic status. If women's unpaid work were properly valued, it is quite possible that women would emerge in most economies as the major breadwinners.

There is wide range of women's activities in developing countries that creates employment to women in both formal and informal sectors as well as self-employment in agriculture, retail trading and crafts production. Increased number of women entrepreneurs operate small and medium-scale enterprises. The possibilities are many for IT to improve women's activities in these areas.

Farmers: Women farmers could greatly increase productivity using information on improved technologies, agricultural inputs, weather, and markets. The significance of information to perk up women's agriculture and rural development is stressed as it can empower rural females to participate in decision making and improving their quality of life. Radio and television broadcasting are the most accessible and potential IT sources that would be useful to rural women farmers in the absence of formal information exchange available. IT could provide women farmers with guidance on market conditions such as the availability of inputs, market price and demand and supply conditions for their produce. Besides this, women farmers need information on improved seeds, and farming techniques, cropping pattern, access to formal credit, storage facilities etc (Munyua 2000). Information agents such as extension and community workers who work at community centres to get information from international sources relay it to local women farmers. They could also assist the farmers in delivering the information, transmitting indigenous knowledge and advice received from agriculture research station. There are number of ongoing projects using

IT to bring information to rural women in Africa (United Nations Organization 2000).

Entrepreneurs: In informal sector in developing countries many women run small businesses in Asia and Africa. In the developing economies a substantial share of employment is indeed in informal category and women in all age groups depend on the informal sector more heavily than men. Women are over represented in this sector in the sense that their share in the sector is higher than their share in total labour force. Most women tend to be own account workers and only a few are heads of micro enterprises. Relatively lower level of education among women, compared to men, seems to explain, in part, this gender differential in informal employment. Women owned businesses comprise between one-quarter and one third of the formal sector business population around the world (Munyua 2000). Women entrepreneurs globally have said that access to information, especially market information, which is their first priority in accelerating the growth of their enterprises. Women entrepreneurs are less likely than men to use IT in their business although the benefits are not gender specific. Many women entrepreneurs in Asia and Africa are small-scale traders, ranging from micro trading in foodstuffs to large-scale import-export trade.

OPPORTUNITIES FOR EMPOWERMENT

Although knowledge-based manufacturing businesses are located in affluent countries, there are opportunities for women-owned small scale manufacturing enterprises in developing countries. While such business would take considerable capital, there are others that use decentralized production techniques and telecommunications technology that could be established with fairly minimal capital. Manufacture of clothing as well as some kinds of small consumer electronics and publishing fall into this category. Given the increasing number of women entrepreneurs in small scale manufacturing in developing countries, it would be very useful for women entrepreneurs to have training in using the

Internet to improve business and in identifying entrepreneurial opportunities in the new economy.

Many of these involve marketing telecommunications services, which presently are mostly phone and fax, but as technology advances and converges, many will increasingly include Internet services as well. In Ghana, a number of women-owned business centres offer fax, email, and other communications services and majority of clients are also women. India has hundreds of thousands of small communications business. The Indian equivalents are Subscribers Trunk Dialing (STD) centres, small shops that offer public telephones for long distance calls. These can be set up for capital investments of about $2500. Some 30, 000 shops have been created, employing about 600, 000 people. Women hold half of these jobs, which are found in towns and cities throughout the country (ILO 2002). Given the relatively low capital and skills requirements to set up these centres, these are businesses that are within the reach of many women entrepreneurs in developing countries. The demand for these services remains high. Such opportunities should be of particular interest in Asia and Africa.

The greatest potential for job creation globally is within the core IT sector (ILO 2001a). As IT usage is increasing in developing countries, the design and maintenance of the fundamental IT components will become the most valued occupations. Job opportunities in these sectors are already available in a few emerging market countries with sufficient IT infrastructure. A major area for new jobs is in software programming. There are areas of production, engineering, education or general services that do not include software as an integral component. India, China and Brazil are examples of countries where software industries for export have developed (ILO 2001a). There are significant opportunities for women in software, and it is seen that women are already active as software developers in several countries especially in network administration and maintenance sectors.

The international community has realized the importance of women's empowerment in national development efforts.

This is equally true in building the information system in developing countries, where wide technical and economic disparities exist between countries and within countries. Therefore, the process of development that shapes the information economy should cover the goals of achieving gender equality and women's advancement and sustainable human development. The information economy should be grounded on human right approach as a means to ensure the rights of all, including the rights to non-discrimination and the right to communicate. Communication is a basic human need, indispensable for the organization of societies, and should be the foundation for building the information society.

Women's effective participation in the information economy needs to be assured if countries have to successfully achieve their development goals and priorities. While there have been developmental efforts to increase the access and use of ICT in general, there is still a marked difference in their impact on the lives of men and women. While assessing the implications of ICT policies, programmes and projects for women and men, necessary measures that are needed to ensure women's empowerment have to be planned and implemented. It is evident that ICT can positively contribute and facilitate women's economic, social and political participation. Women can be the best agents to transform the society, as they are not just consumers of information and information products, nor just users of these technologies. More importantly, women are producers of information as well as innovators in applying ICT and their convergence with traditional media.

Women need not be confined to the lower-skilled ICT jobs related to word processing and data entry. They should make up higher percentages of managerial, maintenance and design personnel in networks, operating systems and software. Many women are software programmers but very few are in hardware design. Women comprise the majority of those employed in computer and electronic assembly manufacturing jobs. New ICT jobs for women, especially in developing countries, are in the service industries in information processing, banking, insurance, printing and publishing. But women have to reach technical, managerial and decision-making high-level positions in order to reduce the gender gap in human resource development.

The fact is that only a smaller proportion of women in many developing countries have taken advantage of ICT for their economic empowerment as many more are being left out and have not been able to benefit from and contribute to this process. It is necessary to bring women into the ICT mainstream and make them both beneficiaries and contributories to the process of economic growth.

The potential of ICT has to be utilized as a tool for enhancing women's capacities in the area of health and education, as well as their access to basic social services and information. However, in the process of marginalization of women due to lack of accessibility and affordability of ICT, women face a variety of barriers from low rates of information literacy to lack of high-skilled ICT training. The dominance of English language in ICT and software fields should not isolate women in non-English developing countries from fully participating and benefiting from the information economy. If expectations of decline in the cost of this information technology and related infrastructure were realized then the critical factor would be empowering women's ability to make use of their creative potential to the utilization of these new technologies. If this materializes, countries of the developing world can empower their women and create new value to their human resources.

The development of information and communication systems offers many new opportunities for women. But they have to be supported by deliberate policies to ensure women's participation and their training in the information economy with no gender biases (ILO 2001a). Recent employment trends show that in spite of progress in some areas, women generally continue to earn lower incomes, suffer higher unemployment, and remain largely restricted to low-skilled, part-time, informal and unstable jobs. At the same time, the proportion of women joining the global labour market is expected to rise rapidly in the coming years. A major challenge of employment policies in the global information economy is the empowerment of women by providing decent work for the female labour force, which is increasingly entering the information workforce.

NEW AVENUES AND QUALITY OF WORK

Information and communication technologies have created new types of work that favour women. This would facilitate them to carry work to homes and allow for better accommodation of work and family schedules. The most promising potential for women is in the creation of new jobs and work in data processing activities. In India, a million jobs during the last ten years were created in these activities and a huge proportion of which have gone to women (ILO 2004). In terms of numbers employed, the role of women in the information economy has become more marked in export-oriented information-processing work. Internationally outsourced jobs, such as medical transcription work or software services are making a considerable difference in the lives and career paths of women in developing countries. In the field of software, women enjoy preferences on a scale that they never experienced in any other field of engineering and science. Women in India occupy 27 per cent of professional jobs in the software industry, which is worth 4 billion US dollars annually. Women's share in the total employment in this industry is expected to rise to 40 per cent by 2005 (ILO 2002).

Information systems have enabled women to tap global markets for their products, increased their incomes and improved their economic and social status. An organization called 'Sapphire Women', created by women in Kampala, in Uganda, supports women who have lost family members to AIDS, as well as orphans created by the AIDS epidemic (United Nations Development Programme 1995). The Grameen Bank Village Phone project, which provides mobile cell phones to its mostly female members in Bangladesh, demonstrates not only the employment-generating impact of the women who collect fees for the usage of their mobile phones, but other positive spill-over effects as well. Mobile phones and access to the Internet have given rural Bangladeshi women access to learning, created new opportunities for autonomy and improved their position in community and public life. One of the India's non-governmental organizations, Self-Employed Women's Agency (SEWA), has been involving women in the informal sector since 1972, and has a membership of over 215,000, It is one of the first organizations in India to realize the potential of harnessing information infrastructure for the productive growth of the informal sector (ILO 2001a). By organizing computer awareness programmes and imparting basic computer skills to its team leaders and association members, SEWA has enabled many of its members to launch their own websites and to sell their products in the global virtual market place. These examples illustrate how information sector can improve the lives of poor women by opening up opportunities they were previously excluded from. The empowerment of women via technology in this way enables them to challenge discrimination and overcome gender barriers.

But there is possibility that the patterns of gender segregation are being reproduced in the information economy where men hold the majority of high-skilled, high value-added jobs, whereas women are concentrated in the low-skilled, lower value-added jobs. Since the diffusion of the new information has been skill-biased accompanied by wage inequalities, rising pay inequalities between men and women has been the phenomenon. Men are more likely to be found in the high-paying, creative work of software development or Internet start-ups, whereas those in the workforce such as cashiers or data-entry workers are predominantly female and low-paid. While both men and women may be users of the advanced information technology and also share experiences of improving their relative skills, only male groups appear to be occupying the positions in the organizations where use of advanced technology is accompanied by greater discretion and responsibility on the job. Although digital globalization has brought more employment opportunities to young women, new inequalities are therefore emerging between women with information communications relate skilled jobs and those without these skills. The promotion of education in general and digital literacy in particular is the huge challenge facing all countries (Jovanovich 1989). Equipping workers with information technology related skills would need to be specifically targeted to the needs of women.

Many features of the information economy can offer women the potential to strike a better balance between work and family responsibilities, or work and leisure. The increasing knowledge content of work has to favour the equality of women and men in the workforce (UNESCO 2000). Intelligence and creativity are also evenly distributed between men and women, or between able and people with physical disabilities. The potential of the information economy to improve the quality of work and life of people is the genuine concern of the developing countries. However, there are negative effects on the quality of working life of women. Far from adjusting working needs to the requirements of family life, there can be increasing pressure for women to work everywhere and all the time. While teleworking has certainly created new employment opportunities for women, the downside is that women can be excluded from better career possibilities instead of finding a balance. Family responsibilities can be combined with paid work, so that women end up acquiring new tasks on top of the old.

Studies reveal that women in Malaysia and India are reluctant to opt for home-based telework. But they have welcomed the opportunities of employment afforded by call centres because it combines the advantages of interaction with those of being close to home. Yet they are concerned about possible health hazards brought about by repetitive work in high-pressure working environments. Overall, the work in the information economy can be an effective tool for enhancing gender equality. But the direct intervention of the governments in developing countries is essential to remove the existing inequalities and also to safeguard the needs and rights of the women workers involved. The focus should be on empowerment of women as the creation and loss of jobs for women, the content and quality of their work, the nature of their employment and the skills required for women, the organization of work and the functioning and effectiveness of worker and employer organizations are affected by the emerging information economy.

COMPREHENSIVE POLICY

To create an enabling environment that supports women's participation in information economy and thereby to enhance economic empowerment of women through ICT, the following measures have to be incorporated in ICT policy in developing countries:

- Integrating gender perspectives in the development and implementation of national ICT policies, programmes and strategies
- Allocating resources in the national budgets to support strategies to increase women's participation in the information economy, including funding for Non-Governmental Organizations to strengthen opportunities for women's empowerment through ICT
- Recognizing ICT as public goods and develop gender-responsive policies and programmes that promote universal access and affordability, especially for rural communities
- Strengthening national machineries for the advancement of women, particularly through increased financial resources and technical expertise that can facilitate their advocacy role and collaborative action amongst government bodies
- Increasing existing funding mechanisms to support women's initiatives in ICT-based entrepreneurship and other economic activities
- Encouraging greater participation of women in the ICT industry by addressing gender-based inequalities and instituting gender-sensitive employment policies
- Implementing the measures to ensure women's equal access to ICT education, training and literacy

- Integrating ICT education in school curricula based on gender equality
- Encouraging the ICT industry to provide ICT education and training, particularly to disadvantaged women and girls, especially in rural areas

Besides the above policy measures, many economic and institutional arrangements must be revamped to extend more choices to women and men in the work place. Efforts should be made to target the programmes that enable women to gain greater access to economic opportunities through information and communications systems. Remunerative employment opportunities in ICT are the key to empowerment of women. But not all of them need to be in the formal, organized information sectors of the economy. What is most essential in this regard is encouraging women to participate in information economy by creating favourable environment.

CONCLUDING REMARKS

At a wider level, the ICT will play an important role in empowering women in developing countries. With the development of world economic market, the benefits of the information economy should reach equally among different sections of people, especially women. The real constraint is the capacity of the developing countries to keep pace with the information revolution and to face the potential repercussions in the labour markets. The gender gap in access to information and communications technology has to be narrowed down in order to ensure the positive impact of ICT on economic growth and development through its linkages with the creation of knowledge.

Government policy is required to contribute to advancing the gender equality through all means of mass communication. This is needed to promote the free flow of ideas, to increase and diffuse knowledge, and to give fresh impulse to spread the new culture. With the advent of the ICT, these tasks of empowering women have to be taken up as a matter of urgency. Once accessible to all, irrespective of gender, occupation or social status, information and communication technologies in developing countries can be instrumental for achieving a truly women centered development.

Developing countries should create an enabling environment to tap the benefits of information economy. An enabling environment includes national ICT policies that promote women's empowerment and gender equality. In most of the countries, the existing national ICT policy frameworks and strategic plans are generally silent on gender and women-focused concerns. This lack of gender analysis in the development of ICT policies results in the failure to realize the potential of ICT to transform gender and power relations as evidenced by successful initiatives of the governments of developing countries. Therefore, in reviewing and developing policies and formulating corresponding strategies and programmes, it is critical to ensure that the issue of empowerment of women is properly addressed.

A new world order that would embrace full equality of opportunity between women and men should emerge to eliminate the prevailing gender disparities and create an enabling environment for the full flowering of the productive and creative potential of women.

REFERENCES

Aghion, P and Howitt, P. (1998), *Endogenous Growth in the Global Economy*. MIT Press, Cambridge.

Arrow, K. J. (1962), The Economic Implications of Learning by Doing. *Review of Economic Studies*, 29(3): 155-173.

Bautista, R. O. (1999), Staking Their Claim: Women, Electronic Networking and Training in Asia. In: Wendy Harcourt (ed). *Creating New Cultures in Cyberspace*. Zed Books, London.

Davies, S. (1979), *The Diffusion Process of Innovations*, Cambridge University Press, Cambridge.

Digital Opportunities Task Force (DOT) (2001), *Digital Opportunities for All: Meeting the Challenge*. Report of the Digital Opportunities Task Force, New York.

Grossman, G.M. and Helpman, E. (1991), *Innovation and Growth in the Global Economy*. MIT Press, Cambridge.

ILO (2001a), *Life at Work in the Information Economy*. World Employment Report 2001, Geneva.

ILO (2001b), *Information Technology and Development: New Key to Development*. Press Release, Geneva.

ILO (2002), *World Employment Report 2002*. Geneva.

ILO (2004), *World Employment Report 2004*. Geneva.

International Telecommunication Union (ITU) (2001), *World Telecommunication Indicators Database*. Geneva.

Joshi, I. (1998), India: Towards Women Friendly Communications Technologies. In: Ila Joshi (ed.). *Asian Women in the Information Age: New Communication Technology, Democracy and Women*. Asia Media Information and Communication Centre, Singapore.

Jovanovich, B and Rob, R. (1989), The Growth and Diffusion of Knowledge. *Review of Economic Studies*, 56(4): 569-582.

Munyua, H. (2000), *Application of Its in Africa's Agricultural Sector: A Gender Perspective*. Oxford University Press, London.

OECD (2001), *The New Economy: Beyond the Hype*. Report on the OECD Growth Project, Executive Summary, Organization for Economic Cooperation and Development (OECD), Paris.

Patrinos, H. A. (2000), *The Changing Role of Government Education*. Paper Presented at the Adam Smith Institute, London.

Pyramid Research Group (1999), *Will the Internet Close the Gap?* Report on Info-Development, Washington D. C.

United Nations Development Programme (1995), *The Revolution for Gender Equality*. Human Development Report, New York.

United Nations Development Programme (2000), *Human Rights and Human Development*. Human Development Report 2000, New York.

Schumpeter, J. A. (1943), *Capitalism, Socialism and Democracy*. George Allen and Unwin, London.

UNESCO (2000), *World Education Report*. UNESCO, Paris.

United Nations Organization (2000), *Report of the High-level Committee on the Review of Technical Cooperation among Developing Countries*. New York.

3

Women in Watershed Development

Falendra K. Sudan

INTRODUCTION

Many reports on women have brought together considerable data on the work and lifestyles of women workers, their invisible contribution to the economy, states of consciousness, and nascent efforts to organize them (GOI 1974, GOI 1988a, GOI 1988b). There is growing recognition that women would be in no position to absorb developmental inputs unless they themselves participate in the developmental process. Rapid changes in technology, automation and the curtailment of employment have drastically reduced their opportunities for work in the organized sector. It is in the unorganized sector that the overwhelming presence and struggles of women are manifest. The National Commission on Self-Employed Women estimates that 94 per cent of the total female workforce is found in this sector (GOI 1988c). They have a noticeable presence in several segments of the unorganized sector. They participate extensively in agriculture, animal husbandry, dairying, social and agro-forestry, fisheries, handicrafts, *khadi* and village industries, handloom weaving and sericulture. Their work ranges from wage employment at one end to self-employment, family labour and piece-rated works at the other (SEWA 1988). In addition to all this, women also put in much longer hours of work. This is primarily because of the nature of their labour. They work with the lowest forms of technology and carry out the least skilled jobs. They also have to combine gainful labour with childbearing, child rearing and the performance of domestic chores. Quite a lot of their time is taken by domestic work involved in the collection of food, fuel, water and fodder. Putting together these basic necessities is back breaking labour for great many women. A further discriminating feature is differential wages.

Several policy documents, in particular the *Report of the Committee the Status of Women in India: 1974* (GOI 1975) and *National Plan of Action for Women: 1976* (GOI 1976), brought pressure on the Government to recognize them as active participants in development and introduced numerous schemes like the Integrated Rural Development Programme (IRDP), the Development of Women and Children in Rural Areas (DWCRA), and National Rural Employment Programme (NREP). The government has come under heavy weather because of the ineffectiveness of most schemes. In Jammu and Kashmir, three programmes (land reforms, the IRDP and the NREP) have been tried on a large scale to help alleviate rural poverty and raise the status of rural women. These were not generally targeted to improve productivity of marginal lands in *Kandi* (watershed) areas, and therefore have not resulted in sustained increase in rural incomes and failed to improve the status of rural women and due to soil erosion and water-runoff, the land and water resources have been declining fast. With this backdrop, the main objectives of the present study are to analyze the existing pattern and extent of women work participation and their role in decision-making in two sub-watersheds of Akhnoor and Ramnagar in Jammu and Kashmir; to investigate the level of skill possession by women in different activities and their educational attainment to ascertain scope for income generating activities (IGAs); to investigate the factors which hinder the promotion of IGAs for women; and to suggest measurers for incorporating gender issues in watershed development.

RATIONALE FOR PARTICIPATORY WATERSHED DEVELOPMENT

The human ability to sustain the pace of development critically depends upon the status of natural resources of soil, water, vegetation, livestock and genetic diversity. Unfortunately, the methods and approaches adopted to maintain this pace often lead to over-exploitation of these resources resulting into loss of valuable natural resources. Land degradation and soil erosion, especially of village commons, roadsides, tanks and other such open-access lands, was attributed to the tragedy of the commons' phenomenon, where exploitation is by all, but maintenance by none. In the past, the problem of degeneration of village lands was seen as arising from people's demands for fuel wood and fodder, resulting in over-exploitation. However, actually the loss of soil from such lands was due more to a lack of control of rainwater runoff. It was not so much a problem of demand as one of land management, especially of common lands. Without controlling runoff, it was not possible to stabilize water regimes even for croplands, and thus it was a mistake in *Kandi* areas to look at the degradation of common lands in isolation from the other issues of low cropland productivity. It is difficult to rehabilitate degraded lands without introducing moisture – conservation and water-harvesting measures. Such measures are, in fact, needed for all *Kandi* areas put to biomass production, and not just uncultivated lands.

The best measure for restoring the degradation of natural resources has been found to be the watershed approach. The approach has found a prominent place in the development strategy of the country since Fifth Five-Year Plan. Several area development programmes have emphasized the adoption of watershed as a unit of development. The Central and State governments, NGOs, and development activists have launched several watershed projects, from which valuable experiences have been learnt. Realizing the importance of rehabilitating micro-watersheds, from 1990 onwards the Government of India (GOI) set aside substantial budgetary provisions for a programme called 'National Watershed Development Programme for Rain-fed Areas' (NWDPRA). It focused mainly on the delivery of technical inputs through government machinery on agricultural lands, but without linking these with uncultivated lands and without sound people's participation. The overwhelming evidence from natural-resource-management projects is that without people's involvement, the benefits are not sustainable in the long term. After funds from the government or donors dry up, conservation structures disappear, committees are disbanded or abandoned, and the livelihood base of the people remains only marginally improved, if at all.

Fortunately, these shortcomings were taken care of, to some extent during the implementation of Integrated Watershed Development Programme (IWDP), Hills-I, Jammu and Kashmir (Sadhu and Sudan 1999). IWDP (Hills I), Jammu and Kashmir was implemented for soil and water conservation in the watershed areas aiming at proper land use according to land potential, protection of land against all kinds of deterioration, building and maintaining soil fertility, conserving water for farm use, proper management of water for drainage, flood protection, sediment reduction and increasing productivity from all kinds of land uses. Besides improved vegetative coverage of treated areas, increased community participation and formulation of engaged village users group, increased crop yields, milk production and horticulture products and increased household incomes of marginal and small farmers, the landless and the women, were included as major objectives of IWDP, Hills I (World Bank 1998). However, this project has made only a modest impact and it cannot be denied that as it has been the first phase of this experiment, some shortcomings were bound to remain, but, at the same time, it must have enriched the experience of project authorities which should equip them to carry out their role more efficiently in the second phase (Sadhu and Sudan 1999).

IWDP, Hills-II, Jammu and Kashmir is an effort to arrest natural resource degradation of the *Shivaliks* and *Karewas* watersheds, to benefit the local communities and to protect the environment. The key performance indicators of the projects are: increased availability of surface and ground water, reduced soil erosion as measured by silt observation posts, improved vegetative cover of treated areas, increased community participation and formulation of engaged village users' groups, increased crop yields, milk production and horticultural products, upgrading the existing road links to markets, and increased household incomes of marginal and small farmers, the landless and women (World Bank 1999). All these would be achieved by a variety of methods accompanied by strong stakeholders' participation including a number of mechanical and vegetative measures for watershed development and protection improve livestock management, rural road rehabilitation and institutional strengthening.

Watershed management in India has been defined as a rational utilization of land, water resources for optimum and sustained production with minimum hazards of natural resources. It essentially is related to soil and water conservation meaning thereby, the proper land-use, protecting lands from all forms of degradation, building and maintaining soil fertility, conserving water for agricultural use, proper management of water for drainage, flood protection, sediment reduction and increasing the productivity of land uses. Benefits from the watershed approach can be obtained only through integrated watershed management. Integrated watershed is the process of formulating and implementing a course of action involving economic and institutional factors operating within the watershed area. Typically, this process includes: establishing watershed management activities, formulating and evaluating alternative resource management actions, choosing and implementing a perfect course of action and thorough monitoring of activities and outcomes (Easter, Dixon and Hufschmidt 1986).

The main objective of IWDP (Hills II), J&K is to restore the productive potential of the project area using watershed techniques and participatory planning and local institutional development. The project will facilitate formulation of village Development Committees (VDCs) to plan, implement and manage assets through preparation of Village Development Plan (VDP) using participatory approaches. VDPs prepared, appraised and analyzed jointly with the communities will be the building blocks that will create community capacity for sustainable investment of the development of the region (World Bank 1999). People's participation in watershed management reduces the cost of the project, increases the benefits to people participating in the programme, corrects the mistakes made by the project authorities, designing various structures, increase the level of political awareness of the people, decrease the perpetual dependence of the people on government and thereby making the programme self-sustaining. Mobilization of local resources and project implementation becomes easier and smooth as a result of participation of local people including the vulnerable groups, the landless and the women.

One of the major reasons for deterioration in the ecological balance has been the excessive pressure of population on land. With the increase in population, marginal lands were brought under cultivation and pastures and forests encroached upon. Therefore, unless alternative sources of income are provided to the population, any attempt to promote optimum use of land and water cannot succeed in spite of the improved dry land agricultural practices. The problem of employment has to be tackled by covering opportunities in the secondary and tertiary sectors. To attain the philosophy of the project IWDP-II and to make the targeted group self-reliant on a sustainable basis, skill impartation and/or creation/ starting of viable IGAs need to be taken up in the project area. Women have traditionally been at the fag end of the development conduit and hence there is an urgent need to bring them in the mainstream of the society through their capacity building.

OBJECTIVE AND METHODOLOGY

The main objectives of the present study are:

- To analyze the existing pattern and extent of women participation in agriculture, cattle rearing, fodder and fuel wood collection, casual labour, domestic chores and other activities and their existing role in decision-making matters in the family and outside;
- To investigate the level of traditional/technical skill possession by women in different activities such as rope making, mat weaving, handling machinery, bee-keeping, dairy technology, etc; and their educational level to ascertain scope of planning training programmes for income generating activities;
- To investigate the factors which impede the promotion of income generating activities for women and the scope of marketing of goods and services generated through viable IGAs; and
- To suggest measurers for incorporating gender issues in watershed development and promoting IGAs and improving the existing marketing network and intervention.

The primary data has been collected using structured questionnaires and by adopting participatory appraisal techniques. The study was confined to the Sub-Watersheds (SWs) of Akhnoor in Jammu district and Ramnagar in Udhampur district of Jammu and Kashmir State, India. The data has been collected on the basis of three-stage random sampling procedures. Selection of administrative block forms the first stage and the selection of villages form the second stage and respondents constitute the third stage of the survey. The data and information was collected from 10 villages each from the selected SWs and the sample was restricted to 144 and 70 women respondents from Akhnoor and Ramnagar SWs respectively. Besides, information has also been collected through informal interviews with various stakeholders together with project functionaries. The data has been analyzed using descriptive statistics.

WOMEN WORK PARTICIPATION AND DECISION MAKING

The type of economic development, which we are witnessing, is inimical to the poor and weak. It is leading to environmental degradation, food insecurity, and demographic pressures and growing inequality and impoverishment. The contribution of women to development is comparatively new area. Women's involvement in the economic and social development process in the country has remained comparatively neglected area, which shows that our society has hardly bothered to pay due attention to its women folk. The economic development has not been an unmixed blessing for women and it has worsened their lot. Women are seen working even longer hours. They are forced to walk greater distance to get firewood and water or work extra hours in other's field. They have no time to produce the surpluses that women have traditionally produced to pass on to the next generation. The question of rural women's contribution acquires more importance because in this sector women contribute sometimes more than men, particularly when we consider their contribution in kind. Moreover, they exercise no control over their earnings, an example of social discrimination practiced for a long time. Naturally, women are also either by-passed or denied the benefits of the economic development. Rural women contribute in multidirectional ways viz. as workers, labourers, producers and traders and also as housewives performing all kinds of so-called non-productive household duties.

Unfortunately due to high illiteracy, rural women are subjected more than urban women to the common social evils affecting women adversely. The spread of education has not been always positively correlated with higher work participation due to the influence of family taboos. Deforestation, soil erosion, etc. have also adversely affected women more as their main household duties usually consist of collecting fuel, fodder and water, all of which had become more scarce as industrialization gathered momentum. Not only this, the effects of improved technology have not been neutral to rural women. More alarming is the fact that women work participation declined more in rural areas thus seriously affecting the already very poor standard of living of the rural poor women in general. It should not be forgotten that employment to rural women also gives her strength of fight against all kinds of oppression. Women generally accept family taboos to forego employment opportunities. Due to poverty and other adverse conditions, rural women are vulnerable to sexual exploitation too. Among rural women again perhaps the old and the disadvantaged appear to be the most destitute among all segments. The scheduled caste (SC) women are subject to double exploitation as both weaker sex and low caste. They actually share the major burden of performing the task of agricultural labourers; the incidence of indebtedness also is much higher among the scheduled caste women agricultural labourers. However, the women labour participation rate among SC women is nearly double than that of non-SC women. All these observations point to the need for watershed development, which may serve as a key to a number of problems including the problems of, disadvantaged women. These special problems and dimensions should attract more attention of the planners for the formulation of future watershed development plans.

Age Specific Work Participation

Age specific distribution of women workers (respondents) shows that the highest number of women workers is from the reproductive age group of 25-44 years. The proportion of women workers to total workers increases from the lower proportion in the age group 15-24 years to increasing proportions in the age groups 25-34 years and 35-44 years and thereafter it records a steep fall for the subsequent age groups. This is highly undesirable, as women are at the peak of their work only for a period of 20 years i.e. the age groups of 25-34 years and 35-44 years. This is the age group, in which the burden of performing the reproductive functions is the highest and under normal conditions, women may like to devote themselves to look after the children rather than seeking employment. Thus, the process of aging, particularly with reference to employment starts too early and grows too fast in the case of women. It is pertinent to note that data presented in table 1 reflects no women work force participation in the age group below 15 years, which is primarily due to the fact that only adult female respondents were selected for collection of data and information. During the course of this investigation, it has been revealed that young girls are mostly engaged in the task of collecting firewood and fodder, fetching water, washing utensils, tending animals, and looking after young siblings besides attending other domestic chores. It has affected their schooling after primary or middle standard and dropout rates are quite high in case of girls.

Table 1
Age-specific Women Workforce Participation

Age groups	*Age specific participation*			
	Akhnoor		*Ramnagar*	
	Number	*Percentage*	*Number*	*Percentage*
15-24	13	9.0	9	12.85
25-34	38	26.38	13	18.57
35-44	57	39.58	24	33.80
45-54	36	25.00	24	33.80
Total	144	100	70	100

Pattern of Work Participation

A very less percentage of women in the sample sub-watersheds received from their husbands everything they needed-food, clothing and some cash and only a few of them did no work other than domestic activities. A large majority of them are working and many-helped husband on his farm, in addition to their own work and domestic duties. Most of these workingwomen had to provide at least part of the food for the family as well as clothing and cash out of their own earnings. They performed domestic duties for the husband and majority of them also helped him on his farm. Further, it has been observed that in the sample sub-watersheds, the upper caste women with better economic status took least part in outside activities and many observe *purdah*, i.e., they never left the house unveiled. Their husband's agricultural work is restricted to the supervision of those who performed the actual manual work. However, opposite is true of the selected respondents from landless and disadvantaged group. The women of land-owning families are occupied mainly with domestic duties and dairy and poultry keeping. In the category of disadvantaged groups, women assisted their husbands in the fields and they also went to the market. They work mainly within the family framework and in their own fields, although they might work for a wage (mostly in kind) in busy season on other's land or households. However, a significant percentage of women from the landless and disadvantaged groups are expected regularly to seek paid work for the support of their families. The same is true of women-headed households in the case of widow; destitute, deserted women and where male migration has taken place.

Table 2
Exiting Pattern of Women Work Participation

Status	*Pattern of women work*			
	Akhnoor		*Ramnagar*	
	Number	*Percentage*	*Number*	*Percentage*
Veiled and non working	102	70.83	54	77.14
Contributing very little to farming	84	58.33	38	54.28
Carrying large share of family burden	38	26.38	44	30.55
Fend independent for own and family	12	8.33	8	11.42
Taking part in trade and craft	12	8.33	9	12.85
Unpaid family work	127	88.19	59	84.28
Exchange of goods and services in kind	17	11.80	11	15.71
Total	144	100	70	100

The Table 2 gives the data on women work pattern in sample sub-watersheds. From this table, it is clear that a majority of the women (above 70 per cent) in sample sub-watersheds are veiled and working. Further, less than 60 per cent are housewives and contributing very little to farming. The percentage distribution in terms of active female workers and carrying large share of family burden is 26 per cent in Akhnoor. A significant percentage of women headed households in the sample area are a clear indication that they must fend independent by for their own support and to family. Similarly, the percentage distribution of women respondents taking part in trade and craft is 8 per cent in Akhnoor. Thus, it is not wrong to infer that due to technological change, women are replaced from the fields and are looking for one or other type of viable income generating activity to assist their family earnings.

Participation in Domestic and Other Specified Activities

The data relating to women employment are startling. Under sheer force of compulsion and urge to survive, they are confronted with multiple employment status, which varies from mainly unpaid family work to wage-labour outside home and rendering of services in exchange of goods and services in kind. On the whole, unpaid family work constitutes the major source of women work force participation in the selected sub-watersheds (Table 3). Not only this, there is high degree of multiplicity in the nature of employment of women workers. Their employment varies from work to work and also within the same work. Although unpaid family works in the watershed areas claim a vital part of their engagement. The largest concentration of unpaid family workers have been found in the selected sub-watersheds in agricultural operations followed by collection of goods, particularly fuel and fodder and domestic services. As a percentage of total women workers, a significant percentage of them are engaged in wage labour (mostly in kind) outside home in others field and households during peak agricultural seasons. Besides above, a smaller percentage of women workers are engaged in exchange of goods and services in kind mainly in collection of fruits and seeds.

Table 3
Women Participation in Domestic and other Specified Activities

Domestic and other specified activity	*Akhnoor*		*Ramnagar*	
	Number	*Percentage*	*Number*	*Percentage*
1. Maintenance of kitchen, garden etc.	26	18.05	58	82.85
2. Work in household poultry	32	22.22	12	17.14
3. Work in household dairy	122	84.72	62	88.57
4. Any of the activity 1 to 3	126	87.05	62	88.57
5. Free collection of firewood and feed	46	31.94	29	41.42
6. Any of the activity 1 to 5	126	87.05	62	88.57
7. Husking paddy	14	9.72	8	11.42
8. Grinding of food grains	36	25	42	60
9. Preparation of cow dung cakes	32	22.22	48	68.57
10. Sewing and tailoring	29	20.13	36	51.42
11. Tutoring of children	18	12.05	8	11.42
12. Bringing water from outside	78	54.16	29	41.42

Pattern of women work (spanning header above Akhnoor and Ramnagar)

Participation in Domestic Duties

Domestic duties have been of feminist concern although it is a neglected issue in the domain of public policy. The nature of housework that women largely perform varies not only across societies and over time, but also within groups in a society at a point in time. Such variations in the housework that women do, are to a large extent determined by the economic status of the household, the socio-demographic characteristics of the household, the prevalent cultural norms on the division of labour in households and above all the characteristics of the economy itself. In poor agrarian watershed economies with a significant component of non-market activities, the range of what constitutes housework is different from those of the advanced market economies. Boundaries of housework and economically gainful work are difficult to draw in watershed areas where non-market activities predominate. There is an overwhelming consensus that there are limits to the domestic drudgery that women can bear and that women's bargaining position in households has to be strengthened by making resources and income accessible to them, A large proportion of women mainly participate in the household activities. The proportion of women engaged in domestic duties along with the free collection of goods (vegetables, roots, firewood, cattle feed), sewing, tailoring, weaving for household use, is several times more than males. Some prominent activities in which females attending household duties in watershed areas are engaged include: work in household dairy, bringing water from outside the household premises, free collection of firewood and cattle feed, work in household poultry, grinding of food grains and maintenance of kitchen garden, orchards etc.

Participation in Unpaid and Paid Work

There is some arbitrariness in the classification of borderline activities that are 'economic' and those that are 'not economic but beneficial' to the household. For instance, free collection of firewood, etc, is considered economic, preparation of cow dung cakes is considered only beneficial, although both these activities fulfill the household's fuel requirements. The women participation in paid work presents a complex picture. Poor women workers, on account of the high incidence of actualization, intermittency of work and erratic availability of work are generally engaged in a multiplicity of activities. Along with multiplicity of activities, they are confronted with multiple employment status which varies from unpaid family work to wage labour outside home (mainly in other fields and households) and in this case they receive wages in kind, and rendering of services in exchange of goods and services. Besides, in the sample sub-watersheds a smaller proportion of the women workers are engaged in skill activities, salary workers as clerks/typists and non-farm, self-employed vocations (Table 4). It has been observed that women workers are engaged in paid agricultural activities mainly as agricultural labourers during the peak seasons. In the sample area, other activities in which women are mainly concentrated include livestock production and household chores.

Table 4 presents the percentage of female respondents engaged in food preparation, fuel collection, water collection, cloth washing, looking after cattle and attending pre-and-post

Table 4
Extent of Women Participation in Unpaid and Paid Work

Unpaid work	*Akhnoor*								*Ramnagar*							
	Below 25		*25-50*		*50-75*		*75-100*		*25*		*25-50*		*50-75*		*75-100*	
	No.	*%*	*No.*	*%*	*No.*	*%*	*No.*	*%*	*No.*	*%*	*No.*	*%*	*No.*	*%*	*No.*	*%*
Food preparation	2	1.38	6	4.16	4	2.77	132	91.66	2	2.85	5	7.14	3	4.28	60	85
Attending bazaar	79	54.86	29	20.1	17	11.80	19	13.19	32	45.7	16	22.85	16	22.8	6	8.5
Water collection	3	2.08	7	4.86	20	13.88	114	79.16	3	4.28	6	8.57	19	27.1	42	60
Fuel collection	28	19.44	42	29.1	36	25	39	26.38	7	10	16	22.85	18	25.7	29	41
Utensils washing	1	0.69	2	1.38	19	13.19	122	84.72	-	-	3	4.28	8	11.4	59	84
Cloth washing	11	7.63	5	3.47	14	9.72	114	79.16	12	17.1	5	7.14	8	11.4	45	64
Looking after cattle	42	29.16	45	31.2	27	18.75	30	20.83	14	20	16	22.85	10	14.2	30	42
Pre-harvest	23	15.97	53	36.8	51	35.41	17	11.80	23	32.8	33	47.14	6	8.57	8	11
Post harvest	29	20.13	56	38.8	27	18.75	32	22.22	26	37.1	27	38.57	17	24.2	-	-
Paid work																
Skilled/trained	11	7.64	-	-	-	-	7	4.86	8	11.42	-	-	-	-	-	-
Clerical /typists	-	-	-	-	-	-	3	2.08	-	-	-	-	-	-	-	-
Salary worker	-	-	-	-	-	-	7	4.86	-	-	-	-	-	-	-	-
Agricultural	14	9.72	-	-	-	-	-	-	13	18.57	-	-	-	-	-	-
Non Farm (Self)	4	2.77	-	-	-	-	-	-	5	7.14	-	-	-	-	-	-

harvest operations. In this case too, there are noteworthy differences in the extent of women participation in unpaid activities in the sample sub-watersheds of Akhnoor and Ramnagar. The data presented in table 4 reveals that food preparation; water collection and utensils washing are the dominant unpaid female work in the sample sub-watersheds. Women's participation in post-harvest operation is restricted to the extent of less than 75 per cent in the sub-watershed of Ramnagar. Thus, it is not wrong to infer that a large proportion of the respondents spend most of their days in unpaid domestic activities to a greater extent in terms of time. Such a heavy involvement in domestic duties is likely to discourage women from labour market participation.

Extent of Participation

Women work for longer hours and contribute more than men in terms of total labour energy spent by the household members. On account of deeply entrenched social customs, taboos and prejudices, women's work continues to be invisible and confined to non-monetary activities like agriculture and household (Table 5). The data presented in table 5 makes it clear that average hours of unpaid work done by women in agriculture and household are far more than non-agricultural activities whether paid or unpaid. Apart from the domestic duties, women engaged in agricultural operations on an average of 4 to 6 hours on farm and in taking care of cattle at home.

Work Participation and Income Status

By and large, earnings of women workers in sample sub-watersheds are extremely low. This is not surprising, as the employment opportunities are meager. In the case of the women workers engaged in unorganized occupations or self-employed (running small petty shop/trade with their husband and/or alone), the level of earnings is quite low and there are glaring differences in average earnings per worker in case of organized and unorganized workers. It is common knowledge that the unprotected female workers in the unorganized sector

Table 5
Extent of Women Participation and Average Daily Time Spent on Work

	Akhnoor		*Non -*				*Ramnagar*		*Non-*			
	Agriculture		*agriculture*		*Household*		*Agriculture*		*agriculture*		*Household*	
	No.	*%*	*No.*	*%*	*No.*	*%*	*No.*	*%*	*No.*	*%*	*No.*	*%*
Less than 4	98	68.0	15	10.4	105	72.9	26	37.1	13	18.5	37	52.8
Between 4-6	32	22.2	26	18.0	24	24	12	17.1	14	20.0	12	17.1
Between 6-8	14	9.7	-	-	15	15	24	34.2	-	-	18	25.7
Between 8-12	-	-	-	-	-	-	-	-	-	-	3	4.2
Total	144	100	41	28.4	144	100	62	88.5	27	38.5	70	100

receive wages, which are less than half the wages of males (whether paid in cash or kind), and the earnings of self-employed females are still more depressed. It is high time that the potential of poor labouring women be harnessed to give them dignity and equality in the economic sphere. The data presented in table 6 makes it evident that even with low earnings; the contribution of an individual female worker to the family income is quite significant. The study of percentage distribution of respondents in selected sub-watersheds by broad income ranges presents an appalling picture.

Table 6
Women Workforce Participation and Income Group

Income group (Rs.)	*Akhnoor*		*Ramnagar*	
	Number	*Percentage*	*Number*	*Percentage*
Below 500	12	37.50	8	47.05
501 - 1000	5	15.62	5	29.41
1001 - 1500	6	18.75	4	23.53
1501 - 2000	2	6.25	-	-
Above 2000 - 2500	7	21.87	-	-
Total	32	-	17	-

Contribution to Family Income

Women are undoubtedly engaged in several activities, which add to household incomes but are totally outside the sphere of the market economy. There are numerous activities like free collection of fodder and fuel, maintaining of dairy, poultry and animals, vegetable growing, food processing, sewing, weaving etc. in which women are engaged and increase the household command over the necessities. The household would have to spend a lot of money in procuring these services, if women do not render them. If the proportion of women engaged in these activities is added to the conventional workforce participation rate, the extended workforce participation rate of women increases markedly and gets much closer to that of males. Under the present socio-cultural pressures, women are burdened with heavy domestic duties and childcare. A significant proportion of them try to add something to the family's real income by engaging themselves in market oriented or non-market oriented household activities, as is clear from data presented in table 7.

It is significant to note that out of total women respondents engaged in paid work, as many as 9 per cent of them are contributing between 60-70 per cent to their total family earnings in the sub-watershed of Akhnoor. Again 9 per cent of the females are contributing to total family earnings to the tune of 50-60 per cent in sub-watershed Akhnoor. On the whole, a significant proportion of the women are contributing more than 40 per cent to the family income. The quantitative contribution of poor females to their family income is not only highly significant but the qualitative contribution is also of immense value to their families. Unlike the males who spend a portion of their earnings on themselves, the poor female workers hardly spend anything on themselves. Their entire earnings are spending on the up bringing and the betterment of the family members.

In nutshell, poor women in the sample sub-watersheds are not a homogeneous group. They are divided on various grounds like caste, class and employment activity. What they have common is deprivation and discrimination. They have poorer access to development. They are discriminated against in the family itself, in terms of distribution of income, consumption and assets. Consequently, poverty affects women with lower consumption levels, poorer health and lower education. The women-headed households in sample area have a higher incidence of poverty. A majority of the women particularly of disadvantaged groups are landless, they work in fields, they look after the animals, and they are actively involved in food production, food processing and other manual works. They work in other households and engage in petty trade and vending along with their husbands or alone. In addition, they have the burden of bearing and rearing children, collecting and fetching water, gathering firewood, cooking and cleaning activities, which consume much time and energy. Although women work for longer hours and contribute substantially to the family income, either the women do not perceive them as workers themselves or their male counterparts. In a significant percentage of cases, women are the major earners for their families, which also go unrecognized.

Table 7
Share of Women Earnings in Family Income

Contribution to family income (%)	*Akhnoor*		*Ramnagar*	
	Number	*Percentage*	*Number*	*Percentage*
Below 20	8	25.00	4	23.53
20-30	6	18.75	3	17.65
30-40	5	15.62	4	23.53
40-50	7	21.87	6	35.30
50-60	3	9.37	-	-
Above 60	3	9.37	-	-
Total	32	100	17	100

The women respondents in the sample area often argued that the approach of the government to women's development is one of adhocism leading to marginal benefits and blamed that the government programmes designed for them have not been proportionate either to their needs or their numbers. As far as labouring women are concerned, there has been no thrust to improve their lot by concerted efforts. However, it is significant to note that the women in the sample area were found to be engaged in agricultural production, livestock rearing, food processing etc. Apart from these activities, they spend almost 10-14 hours per day doing household chores, including fetching of water and gathering of fuel. Large number of female workers is engaged in marginal occupations in order to supplement the family income by collection of firewood, cow dung, maintenance of kitchen gardens, tailoring, weaving, knitting and spinning. It has been observed those new technologies in watershed agriculture and allied occupations have displaced rural women from many of the traditional activities. The incomes of the poor households are increased by women, although they have to face many problems due to family responsibility, limited mobility and social restrictions. Though many of the tasks performed by males are getting mechanized, the women continue to toil in labour intensive jobs, like rice transplantation, cleaning and storage of grain in post harvest operations, picking of leaves and fruits, picking out common seed, etc.

Decision Making in Family and Outside

The data presented in table 8 makes it clear 'how many' female respondents participate in decision-making process in the family in the sample sub-watersheds. A perusal of table 8 makes it quite evident that a majority of female respondents takes part in decision-making in terms of daily expenditure, education and marriage of their children, but there are significant variations across selected sub-watersheds in this regard. It is significant to note that girl child does not get adequate nourishment or medical care. More male children are brought to clinics or hospitals for medical treatment. The girls are brought for treatment only when the ailment is too serious. Girls are discriminated in the matter of education and food too. For instance, they are breasts fed for shorter periods, and weaned earlier than boys. Thus, it is not wrong to infer that it is mother who discriminates against her daughters in preference to sons in every respect; it is she who neglects her nutrition, health and education. It is women who are willing, many even anxious, to abort female foetus and nurture only male offspring.

Table 8
Female Decision-making in Family

Female decision-making	*Akhnoor*		*Ramnagar*	
	Number	*Percentage*	*Number*	*Percentage*
Daily expenditure	135	93.75	46	65.71
Agriculture	84	58.33	32	45.71
Education of girls	111	77.08	47	67.14
Education of boys	107	74.03	49	70.00
Marriage of daughter	85	59.02	40	57.14
Marriage of son	85	59.02	39	55.71
Dowry	74	51.38	19	27.14
II. Type of work				
Ploughing	9	6.25	11	15.71

Contd...

Female decision-making	*Akhnoor*		*Ramnagar*	
	Number	*Percentage*	*Number*	*Percentage*
Sowing	33	22.09	21	30.00
Bunding	73	50.69	15	21.42
Weeding	7	4.86	5	7.14
Manufacturing	27	18.75	19	27.14
Irrigating	1	0.69	3	4.28
Harvesting	47	32.63	20	28.57
Threshing	2	1.38	2	2.85
Hoeing	2	1.38	1	1.42
Carrying	3	2.08	-	-

Table 8 further reveals that women contribute mainly in labour intensive tasks in agriculture like sowing, bunding, manuring, harvesting etc. In certain cases women performed their marriages by personal choice. However, such cases were not much in number, but the performance of marriage without the approval of the parents or only on the basis of the self-choice is itself an index of a trend of change. In other words, a process of rationalization has started in the village community at ideological level though its impact on actual life is still insignificant. In spite of having a rational approach in respect of performing marriages, most of the sample women are opposed to inter caste marriages. It means that caste exogamy is not favoured even at ideological level and the majority of the respondents are opposed to it.

But in respect of performing marriage, the dominant opinion appears to be rational because a significant percentage of the women respondents have preferred modern ways of performing marriage. The traditional and luxurious forms of marriage performance are not favoured in general. The respondents desired that marriage performance should be simplified, rationalized and modernized and a number of traditional usages and practices should be abandoned.

Women Awareness and Perception

The participatory appraisal exercises reveals that the traditional economic relations found in the form of *jajmani* system and based on caste relationships are still persisting in the selected sub-watersheds but the importance of these relations is gradually declining. Even the *jajmani* relations have themselves undergone considerable changes and modifications in the present age according to the demands of the existing economic system in the village. In this way, the traditional economic ties are gradually weakening, but these are still regulating economic relations and patterns of economic activities in the village life. Moreover, the system of cultivation has also undergone considerable changes in the present age. The women are acquainted with agricultural innovations like tractors, tube-wells, threshers, chemical fertilizers and insecticides. Those who can afford are utilizing these agricultural innovations. The use of chemical fertilizers is very common in the selected sub-watersheds. Thus, significant changes are taking place in the system of cultivation and the adoption of agricultural innovations suggests a significant change in their attitude and outlook because they are switching over from traditional system of cultivation to modern and scientific system of cultivation.

Another index of modernization and change in attitude and outlook of women is found in respect of preference regarding saving. In the past, the form of saving in village community was either ornament or landed property. But now, they have started opening accounts in banks and post offices. In this way, banking system has been introduced in the village and they have accepted the modern system of saving and investment. It is obvious that the question of having bank deposits and/or post office deposits arises only in case of those families, which are rich and wealthy. As most of the families in the sample sub-watersheds are not rich and wealthy, these families do not have any considerable bank deposit or a deposit in the post office. In respect of education, the women respondents appear to be quite rational and in general all irrespective of caste, economic condition and family background favours education. The poor and downtrodden families are not in a position to educate their children, but these families also have a desire for educating their children and in case the economic condition has improved in some of these families, the education of children has started in those families. Further, the women respondents were found significantly in favour of education of girls. The favourable attitude towards education is also reflected from the viewpoint that 'one should not receive education with the aim of earning livelihood rather with the objective of advancing knowledge, broaden outlook and develop social personality.' The study further reveals that occupational mobility is not the established rule and those who are still engaged in their traditional occupations are doing so because they prefer to remain in the same occupation or because they do not have any alternative for earning livelihood.

The occupational and social mobility generated under the impact of different forces in the present age has also resulted in a change in the pattern of social stratification. However, caste differentiation and caste distinction have not been abolished in the village community. The caste affinity and caste solidarity are more obvious on the occasion of marriage and organization of functions in the families. When any function is organized in the family, the respondents in sample sub-watersheds extend the invitation to caste people in general and in certain cases members of other castes are also invited. Some degree of inter-caste invitations and common participation is found between the families of upper caste and lower castes but these interactions are also at a limited level. The women respondents admitted that in spite of caste mobilization, they vote not exclusively on the basis of caste consideration but also on the basis of the capability and suitability of the candidate party and other factors.

The sampled women can neither be placed in the category of extremely conservative and orthodox nor in the category of those disbelieving in religion or showing disrespect to religious faith and observances. The majority of women respondents have a respect for religion and religious sanctions, but they do not blindly follow and observe all the norms and sanctions prevalent in the traditional society in the name of divine decree and religious rules. The analysis of the degree of political socialization and political participation reveals a complete ignorance of political developments and political events is not found among the women respondents. But, at the same time, it has come to light that a fully developed political consciousness is still lacking. Some degree of political awareness is found among the villagers but most of the people are not properly acquainted with some of the terms like mid-term poll, bye-election, president's rule, etc. It means that political socialization is taking place among the rural women folk, but the degree of political socialization is still relatively lower. This fact is also evidenced from the finding that excepting congress (I), Bhartiya Janata Party (BJP), Bahujan Samaj Party (BSP) and National Conference (NC), very few women respondents were acquainted with the symbols of other national parties contesting elections in their constituency. It is obvious that this lack of acquaintance with the symbols, programmes and manifestoes of different political parties is due to a lower degree of political socialization and political awareness.

Thus, it may be concluded that due to modernization and change, social structure of rural life is in the state of transition and the traditional social structure has neither completely vanished nor it is operative in its full strength and potency as far as women are concerned. Although the importance of increasing women's participation in watershed development is recognized, and efforts are being made to sensitize and train government functionaries to facilitate women's participation in watershed projects, it is also important to ensure equal division of benefits to women within the household and community. Equal division of benefits for women can be achieved only if the women participate in decision-making. In fact, better and more effective participation of women in community activities may improve intra household benefit sharing as well.

In order to facilitate the participation of women user-groups in the decision-making process, the objectives of the government agency and the plans for intervention in the watershed should be made available to them from the very beginning. This could be done through village-based organizations, in which 50 per cent attendance of women should be made compulsory. In addition, these plans should be discussed separately with the women in smaller groups to obtain the viewpoints of different categories of resource users. Although watershed development may be the aim of the project, it is extremely important to prioritize the needs of different groups within the community, and deal with them in order to develop mutual trust between the project implementing agency and the community. In the long run, this is what will ensure effective use of public interventions.

Type of Work Acceptable

In the selected sub-watersheds, a greater proportion of the women are engaged in domestic duties as their principal usual status. Some of them do engage in economic work as their subsidiary status. Out of those who are engaged in domestic duties, a greater proportion of them indicated their willingness to accept work in their household premises. Among the activities, dairy is the most desired as the returns on it are considered to be higher if the venture is successful. Tailoring is the second most desired. Similarly, handicrafts, mushroom cultivation, poultry, manufacturing of cane products spinning and weaving, and horticulture related activities are other desired occupations. It is pertinent to note that due to multiplicity of responses (i.e. preference for more than one viable income generating activity) the total percentage distribution is exceeding 100 (Table 9). However, there are considerable differences across the selected sub-watersheds. While 76.37 per cent in Akhnoor have a markedly higher preference for dairy, and 81 per cent in Ramnagar have a markedly higher preference for tailoring. The data suggests that greater efforts should be made in the coverage of various watershed development schemes to reach out to those women who are primarily housewives and have indicated a preference for some income generating activities in their home premises. There must be more imaginative efforts in identifying a set of unconventional occupations as supplementary activities for rural housewives that are specific to particular sub-watershed or micro watershed.

Table 9
Engaged in Household Duties and Willing to Accept Work at their Residence

Type of work acceptable	*Akhnoor*		*Ramnagar*	
	Number	*%*	*Number*	*%*
Dairy	97	76.37	39	66.1
Poultry	28	22.04	32	54.24
Other animal husbandry	24	18.89	46	77.96
Spinning and weaving	48	37.79	38	64.4
Manufacturing and cane products	57	44.88	24	40.67
Tailoring	82	64.56	48	81.35
Leather goods manufacturing	2	1.57	2	3.39
Handicrafts	43	33.86	37	62.71
Horticulture	46	36.22	27	45.76
Mushroom cultivation	42	33.07	36	61.01

Extent of Likely Participation

A greater proportion of rural housewives have expressed willingness to accept work in their household premises. Not surprisingly, the proportion of women in the younger age group (up to 35 years) who are willing to accept work in the household premises are higher than those in the old age-group (above 35 years). More than one-third of those willing to accept work wanted only part-time work, but they wanted work to be regular. This shows that their engagement with domestic duties did not permit them to engage in full-time economic work, although their desire for regularity of part-time work suggests their need to have access to a regular income stream. Here too, there are variations between the selected sub-watersheds in terms of their likely participation in various viable income generating activities. Those women who have indicated their preference regarding handicrafts, spinning and weaving and horticulture related activities, a higher proportion of women preferred full-time work.

Training Skill Required

The unskilled working population in both sub-watersheds expressed the type of assistance in the form of training skills; they would require in order to taking up viable income generating activities (Table 10). A significant percentage of unskilled skill working population including the women, land less and disadvantaged groups wanted training assistance. At the same time, it is significant to note that a large proportion of them, who are willing to accept work, stated that they already possessed necessary skills. An activity-wise break-up of skills possessed by the targeted group shows that dairy ranked the highest with greater proportion of targeted group claiming that they have the necessary skills for it. Similar is the case of poultry and tailoring.

Table 10
Training Skills Required for Income Generation

Training skills required	*Akhnoor*		*Ramnagar*	
	Number	*%*	*Number*	*%*
Poultry production	19	17.11	20	32.78
Live stock production	58	52.25	30	49.18
Agricultural services	41	36.93	25	40.98
Manufacturing of food products	16	14.41	5	8.19
Manufacturing of carpet/ wool products	42	37.83	24	39.34
Manufacturing of wood and cane products	3	2.70	-	-
Horticulture	10	9.00	16	26.22
Sericulture	6	5.40	3	4.91
Pisciculture	-	-	2	3.27
Mushroom cultivation	34	30.63	32	52.46
Food preservation and canning	4	3.60	6	9.83
Tailoring	47	42.34	49	80.32
Medical and health services	3	2.70	-	-
Recreation and cultural services	4	3.60	3	4.92
No skill working population	11	-	61	-

Besides these, the other predominant type of assistance they sought is financial assistance, including initial finance on easy terms to start the work activity, and subsequent working finance facilities. There are no significant inter-sub-watersheds variations regarding the requirement of initial finance on easy terms. Other unspecified assistance which needs to be taken into account in the framing of policies for annihilating viable IGAs for the women are easy availability of raw-materials and an assured market for products which are generally perceived as problems faced by home-based producers. What needs to be underlined is that due to wide-spread poverty and deprivation, not even a single woman-willing to accept work-stated that they needed no assistance, most by all of them wanted some kind of assistance. However, it is pertinent to note that the village leadership in general is interested in initiating various viable IGAs on cooperative basis with greater assistance from government, for which they too are willing to mobilize the requisite financial and manpower resources from within their respective villages. Such cooperative viable income generating enterprises could be located in leading villages having necessary basic infrastructural facilities and these villages should serve as nodal centres to cater to the needs of periphery villages.

In the context of women's participation in watershed development, it has been observed that a host of factors restrict their active participation. Some of them are outlined below:

Logistical Constraints: Women have longer workdays than men, and meetings are often called when they are busy with domestic chores or fieldwork. Women (especially younger ones with children) are thus rarely able to attend long meetings, unless family or friends can cover such responsibilities.

Official Male Bias: In government schemes, male functionaries rarely consult women, be it regarding the choice of trees or the village-level micro-plans for watershed development. Many women also complain that the officers 'always crosscheck with the men to verify the truth words'. And if ever there is any conflict or contradiction between the women and the men, the officials always settle the disputes in favour of the men.

Social Constraints: The social constraints includes female seclusion practices; specification of appropriate female behaviour and forms of public interaction; social perceptions, articulated in various ways, that women are less capable than men, or that their participation in public forums is not appropriate or necessary; and so on. Village women claim that the committee meetings are considered to be only for men, whose 'opinions and consent are taken as representative of the whole family'.

Absence of 'a Critical Mass' of Women: Women are often reluctant to attend meetings if there are only a few of them. Most women also feel they cannot change procedures by acting individually, and that individual women would be better able to speak up for their interests if they were present in large numbers.

Women's Lack of Recognized Authority: Many women find that when they do attend meetings their opinions are disregarded - they thus, become 'discouraged dropouts.'

What accounts for women's participation in some initiatives and not in others? What factors could make the emergent community institutions for resource management more gender equal and strengthen, in particular, women's formal involvement in the village based committees, users' groups or *Mahila Mandals.*

Gender-progressive NGO Presence: Typically a major factor facilitating women's participation and also effectiveness in committee meetings is the presence of a gender-progressive organization. There are several examples where such an NGO has explicitly brought women's concerns to the fore, and led to those concerns being addressed to some degree.

Gender-Sensitive Government Officials: A gender-sensitive functionary can also make a marked difference. Women labeled as 'offenders' becoming 'defenders' of forests through the intervention and support of watershed functionaries.

Involvement in the Initial Stages: Experiences in several watershed areas suggest that if women are involved from the beginning when the organization is formed, the chance of their sustained participation is greater. This might be both because they are more motivated as a result, and because their presence has greater legitimacy.

Critical Mass: It is emphasized that without a good majority of women present, it is impossible to express opinions, and that men would find it difficult to ignore larger numbers of women. Of course new initiatives usually involve a process of learning, and what may begin as women-exclusive initiatives can become more women-inclusive over time. But again the presence of vocal women in large enough numbers appears important.

All Women's Groups: In general, it is noted that village women are more comfortable and vocal in all-women's groups than in mixed ones. Women village leaders also argue that separate groups will enhance women's participation.

CONCLUDING REMARKS

In nutshell, women's lack of direct membership and participation in decision-making adversely affects theirs and the family's welfare, efficient functioning of the institutions, and scope for women's empowerment. In women's absence from the protection groups, the rules framed for watershed management by the all-male groups tend to take little account of women's concerns. A number of all-male youth clubs, which are protecting the forests in eastern India, for instance, have not only banned entry, they have been selling the forest products obtained from thinning and cleaning operations. Many poor households cannot afford to buy this firewood and other forest products (which they had earlier collected free), and women again have to bear most of the burden of finding alternative collection sites.

Moreover, cash generated through the sale of timber or grass from the protected sites is often put in a collective fund and used by the groups, as they deem fit. In a number of cases the money has been spent on building a clubhouse or for club functions. Even where the groups distribute the cash benefits to participating households through the male members, there is no guarantee these will be shared equitably within the family, or even shared at all. In many cases, the men have been known to use the money for gambling, liquor or personal items. Outside the context of watershed initiatives, in fact, there is a good deal of evidence that in poor households men tend to spend a significant per cent of their earnings on personal goods. In contrast, women in poor households tend to spend almost all their incomes on basic household needs. Hence, where women are not part of the formal protection committees and get excluded from receiving the benefits directly, it is not just their welfare, which gets affected adversely, but also that of the children.

Welfare apart, women's exclusion from the decision-making forums can adversely affect the long-term efficiency and sustainability of these initiatives (whatever the immediate gains). It can also obstruct the full realization of potential benefits from protection. Since it is typically women who have to collect firewood and grasses regularly, their lack of involvement in framing workable rules for protection and use can cause them to circumvent the rules in order to fulfill essential household needs. In addition, excluding women means that plantation plans lack the benefit of their particular knowledge of plants and species, which would enrich the selections, made, enhance biodiversity, and increase the overall productivity of the commons. Overall, women's absence from formal participation in these new initiatives not only reinforces pre-existing gender inequalities; it further reduces women's bargaining power within and outside the household. Thus, what initially appears to be a success story of participative community involvement in resource regeneration is found to be largely non-participatory and highly inequitable in relation to women. This highlights too the problem of treating 'communities' as engendered units and 'community participation' as an unambiguous step toward equity.

- To ensure long-term benefits to women, the women should be encouraged to take up self-employment schemes. To begin with, the women in the micro-watershed areas should be constituted into a Mahila Cooperative Society. The society should be entrusted with the task of planning a number of viable income generating activities including establishing small shops, handicrafts and spinning and weaving units, tailoring centres, sheep breeding, goat rearing, mushroom cultivation, etc. The success of the society, however, depends on the supportive climate provided by the watershed functionaries.

- While developing livelihoods to meet basic needs is a long-term effort, the women should be organized to meet their strategic needs. 'Strategic needs' are defined as enabling conditions which assist women in seeking gender justice i.e. better living conditions and genuine choice to manage their lives (the ability and possibility of attending meetings and taking decisions is an example of meeting strategic needs). The struggle to meet both basic and strategic needs should be strengthened through the watershed development intervention. A process of change towards establishing equal rights should be initiated.
- Through women's organizations, the women's needs and demands should be projected to the community and government. Men with reputation for fair dealings should be identified to support women's self-assertion. Cases of atrocities against women should be taken up by the women's organizations, and justice ensured for vulnerable women. The organization of women to enforce their own rights will give them confidence to deal with different government departments, including police. A process of change towards establishing equal rights will be initiated.
- The watershed functionaries including female coordinator, facilitators and motivators should play a significant role in molding the views of men in the community. The watershed programme is likely to be an opportunity to create gender justice. The NGOs' Commitment is essential in bringing about change.
- The women's organization should take the initiative to acquire usufruct rights for the women user's group. The allocation to a user group of the usufruct rights to government-revenue land could prove to be a model to other community organizations. The legal sanction of usufruct rights should enhance the interest and motivation of the user-group members to protect the resource.

- Essential interventions, such as soil and water conservation on the severely degraded patches, seed broadcasting, planting etc. should be carried out to speed the regeneration of the area. The users' group should develop a separate accounting system for managing the resources. After the protection and regeneration, grass should be sold locally to the milk producers and savings, after deduction of wages for women watchers, should be deposited in the bank. The deposits could be utilized for loaning purposes to the members of the users' group.
- The women organization should mobilize the whole community to establish their rights collectively as well as individually. Women should play an active role in asserting their rights and legal action should also be taken in conferring their rights. Constant discussion about gender issues and deprivations faced by women should help the community to decide that women could be given ownership rights (*pattas*).
- Women lay great importance on education for their children and the acquisition of information, knowledge and skills for themselves. The high and secondary schools and higher education centres are often located far away, limiting attendance, particularly of girls. Cultural norms and poverty require girls to do household chores and look after younger siblings. Income sources provided by the project and related developments can help reverse this situation. As watershed project work with the community, the opportunity to promote education, especially for girls, should not be missed.
- Exposure visits and training programmes should be organized on regular interval to give women opportunities to learn and express themselves in public and improve their self-confidence. As confidence increases, leadership emerges. The village women promoters should be identified by female

coordinator, facilitation and motivators and trained to conduct women's group meetings and sessions. This will ensure continuity and functioning of women's groups after the project ends.

- While watershed development can lead to an increase in groundwater levels and ensure water is available in the village for longer periods, obtaining water for household needs still consumes, in many cases, one-and-a-half hours. Water sources (especially natural springs) are often unhygienic. Women should be provided with information on the causes of water contamination, its consequences for health, and simple purification methods. Water sources that are susceptible to contamination should be protected by masonry aprons or structures. The formation of village-level committees or users'-group committees can be established to ensure that water sites are well maintained and protected.
- Women bear the burden of their family's ill health. The health and nutrition of women and girls are usually the last priority. Providing information can improve nutritional status. The female facilitators and motivators should educate the women on the topics related to health, hygiene, sanitation, family planning and nutrition. They should be encouraged to keep kitchen gardens or homestead poultry, and building latrines can help address some of these needs. Soak pits can drain away wastewater and improve the hygiene of surroundings, so reduce skin and diarrohoeal infections. Improved, energy-conserving *chulhas* (earthen stoves) and biogas units can reduce time and effort spent on fuel collection, as well as cut smoke levels in the kitchen the cause of many respiratory illnesses, where women and small children usually sit.
- Any change in gender relations must be obtained in a manner that does not threaten the harmony of their

homes or their security. To create a space for women in watershed society, sessions on gender sensitivity need to be organized for men. The approach and method adopted for awareness generation and integration should be consensual, even if at times change appears imperceptibly slow.

In rural society, the women have been given a lower economic and social status than that of other socio-economic groups. They are usually held as passive or indirect beneficiaries of the on-going initiatives. In reality, the women are strong contributors to the economic and social well being of the watershed areas-and should be regarded as such. This implies that they should be given equal representation with other socio-economic groups and should be treated at par with men on various committees dealing with watershed development and equal opportunities and wages in construction and other work. They should also be given the technical and social support necessary to allow them to play a fuller role in watershed development. The homogeneous and focused women groups need to be formed and supported if they are to develop viable income generating activities depending upon the skills they already possess and the training imparted in such activities which should be conducive to watershed development. In addition, if the women's interests are to be adequately represented, it will be necessary for the government functionaries to be sensitized to their roles and needs, and to ways of meeting those needs. Ways will have to be found of increasing the proportion of women on watershed committees. Monitoring systems must be established to assess how women's interests are being defended.

REFERENCES

Easter, K. W., Dixon, J. A. and Hufschmidt, M. M. (Eds.) (1986), *Watershed Resources Management: An Integrated Framework with Studies from Asia and the Pacific*. Westview Press, Boulder.

Government of India (1974), *Towards Equality*. Report of the National Commission on the Status of Women in India, New Delhi.

Government of India (1975), *Report of Committee on Status of Women.* New Delhi.

Government of India (1977), Report *of the Sub-group on Statistics on the Employment of Women.* Employment and Manpower Planning Division, Planning Commission, New Delhi.

Government of India (1988a), *Shramshakti.* Report of the National Commission on Self-Employed Women and Women in the Informal Sector, New Delhi.

Government of India (1988b), *National Perspective Plan for Women, 1988-2000.* Report of the Core Group set up by the Department of Women and Child Development, New Delhi.

Government of India (1988c), *Annual Report, Part IV, 1987-88.* Department of Women and Child Development, New Delhi.

Sadhu, A. N. and Sudan, F. K. (1999), *Retrospective Study: IWDP (Hills I).* Integrated Watershed Development Project, Hills II, Jammu and Kashmir, World Bank and Integrated Watershed Development Project, Hills II, Jammu and Kashmir.

SEWA (1988), *SEWA in 1988.* Mahila SEWA Trust, Ahmedabad.

World Bank (1998), *Project Concept Document: Integrated Watershed Development (Hills-II) Project.* Rural Development Sector Unit, South Asia Region, New Delhi.

World Bank (1999), *Project Appraisal Document: Integrated Watershed Development (Hills-II) Project.* Rural Development Sector Unit, South Asia Region, New Delhi.

4

GENDER, VULNERABILITY AND INFORMALITY

SIDDHARTHA SARKAR

INTRODUCTION

The term informal sector and informal economy are used interchangeably to refer to that segment of the economy and labour market, which has absorbed significant numbers of job seekers and unemployed workers outside government regulations and formal systems of labour and social protection. The informal sector is becoming gradually recognized as imperative segments of the labour market in many countries, especially developing and transition countries and thus plays a major role in employment creation, production and income generation. Research efforts in urban employment and urban labour markets have most often focused on the formal sector with an emphasis on industrial employment (Mehta 1995: 326). In countries with high rates of population growth and/or urbanization, the informal sector tends to absorb most of the growing labour force in the urban areas. Informal sector employment is a necessary survival strategy in countries that lack social safety nets such as unemployment insurance or where wages, especially in the public sector are low. In such situation, indicators such as unemployment rates and time related underemployment are not sufficient to portray the labour market situation. In other countries, the process of industrial restructuring in the formal sector is seen as leading to a greater decentralization of production through subcontracting to tiny enterprises, many of which are in the informal sector (Hussmanns 1998).

Starting from complete ignore, the phenomenon of informal economic activity has grown to be a subject of study by many researchers, both governmental and non-governmental. The nature and the means of the informal economy changed with the deregulation and liberalization while rules of competition were being set up. Informal labour obviously represents only a part of the underground or hidden or shadow or informal sector. Underground employment or informal labour may be defined as additional or primary job, which is performed through by passing regulations of the labour or tax system. Such a definition can be applied to both illegal employment between households and enterprises, irrespective of whether they are registered or not, and it also covers self-employment. This definition may also apply to outsiders and to work, which is not paid for. Informal labour can be grouped or classified according to various criteria. It may represent the principal or the additional place of employment. Underground employment may be permanent or temporary. As far as the economic sectors are concerned, illegal employment may be found in industry, construction, agriculture, transportation and services. Illegal employment may be provided by residents and non-residents of a country. The essence of an informal economy is to escape from being measured and captured, therefore both definition and methodologies shall be treated only as a way of approximation more than elsewhere in the economy in general. The informal economy is particularly flexible in reacting to changes in the regulatory framework, every groundbreaking prohibition or regulation widens its scope and size.

Though the term informal sector has been used to describe a set of economic activities that take place outside the recognized institutional framework it calls for some further elaboration and clarification. All enterprises operating on own account as well as most of the micro enterprises are assumed to fall outside the recognized institutional framework and hence belong to the informal part of the economy or simply the informal sector. It is obvious that the institutional framework is but a criterion by which the enterprises are classified into formal and informal. Redefining this criterion will no doubt affect the relative magnitudes of the two segments in an economy. But it is unlikely to influence the extent of informal employment because the fundamental causes that contribute to informality in these enterprises have not been misrepresented. It is therefore clear that the institutional framework is only a criterion by which the employment quality is reviewed; it is not by itself the cause of inferior quality. This raises the question concerning what factors contribute to informality in these enterprises? Study on the informal sector worldwide during the last three decades points out that the distinguish characteristic of these enterprises is that they operate in a different business environment than the firms in the formal sector. Fundamentally they lack free access to factor and product markets, public resources, information and opportunities as the formal enterprises carry out. Consequently they opt to operate in an informal manner, avoiding compliance with most regulations. Not only they perceive diminutive benefit from compliance, more significantly full compliance adds to the cost of running an enterprise. Lack of access to resources, markets and opportunities is in part the result of non-recognition of these enterprises by the authorities concerned. Without formal recognition few enterprises can anticipate to obtain either credit from the formal financial institutions or access to proper premises and infrastructure. It is difficult to articulate which comes first whether the lack of access to resources and markets forces these enterprises to operate outside the regulation or whether non-compliance with regulations limits their access. A self employed unit operating in an unauthorized location within the country cannot obtain legal recognition until it moves into a proper location and without recognition; it cannot expect to get a proper location from the appropriate authorities which controls the allocation of space. Similarly without adequate economic means it cannot obtain a business license and without such a license, it cannot apply for a loan. But it is clear that both lack of access and non-recognition contributes to informality. To the extent lack of legal recognition is the limiting factor; clearly modifying the institutional framework to broaden such recognition can help these enterprises by improving their access to resources and markets. It can thus contribute to a reduction in informality. But it cannot eliminate it completely. This is because there are also other factors, which contribute to informality. It is supposed that there exists an institutional bias against the vulnerable and the illiterate, who are disproportionately represented in these enterprises. The markets in developing countries, besides being deficient in many respects are also supposed to be unfriendly to them. Both the regulatory and policy environment is also understood to be unfavourable for these enterprises, origins for this bias can be traced to the mistaken perception among the authorities concerned, most believe that these tiny enterprises are only marginally productive, if not unproductive. Finally, certain social and cultural factors also induce these enterprises to operate under conditions of informality because they limit their access to resources and markets. Women entrepreneurs often cannot have access to credit without the consent of men in the household or cannot work far away from residence because of family and child care responsibilities. It is this hostile environment that distinguishes these enterprises from the formal ones. It should however be noted that the formal enterprises in developing countries are also often subjected to a variety of limitations including unfavourable policy and regulatory environment and market imperfections. But the consequences to small enterprises are overwhelming in part because of their weak economic base. Informality will persist as long as these enterprises are not fully integrated with the mainstream, i.e., the institutionalized part of the economy. One major consequence of not having free access to resources and markets is that few are able to improve upon their initial endowments in terms of physical and human capital and know how, by resorting to transactions in the market, they are obliged to rely on own savings from incomes that are already meagre. These enterprises, already disadvantaged because of the small scale of operation, are further handicapped by the unsupportive business environment. The net result of all this is to oblige these enterprises to function in a manner that is in striking contrast to those in the formal sector - besides being small in terms of output and employment, they are also labour intensive, use little capital and skills, they often operate without proper business premises, work long hours, work from locations vulnerable to harassment by police, remain invisible, beyond the recognized institutional framework – the visible physical characteristics derived from informality. These are the underlying causes of informal employment. They explain why productivity and incomes are low and the conditions of work are poor in these enterprises. Another consequence of informality is that some of these enterprises choose to avoid dealing with markets altogether by seeking to operate on a subcontracting basis albeit under conditions that are considered less than fair. What distinguishes them from other own account or micro enterprises is that they often have special relationships with their contractors which influence the way they conduct their business as well as their income. Since this class of enterprises is a sub-sector of the informal sector, employment in them also forms part of informal (Psacharopoulos and Tzannatos 1992). But the factors governing their income are different. Similarly some of those operating an enterprise on own account are labeled as home-based workers or home-workers if they operate on a subcontracting basis because they have their business premises within their home or residence, but they nevertheless also form part of informal employment as defined above. At the risk of over simplification it might therefore be stated that the term informal sector or economy refers to a segment of the economy where the agents of production are not only small in scale but also operate under conditions of informality. It thus encompasses all small scale economic activities carried out by individuals, either through enterprises established and operated independently on own account, or through micro enterprises with the help of hired workers. They also often engage family labour and apprentices. It should be evident from the above discussion that informality strikes different enterprises differently, because not all these enterprises are affected by various constraints to the same degree. Some are more informal than others, measured in terms of the deviation from the established norms. Evidence from countries show that the extent to which these enterprises have free access to factor and product markets, public resources, information and opportunities varies considerably across enterprises. Some enjoy better access to credit or premises while others do not. Similar observations hold regarding compliance with laws and regulations. Some comply with none of the regulations while others comply partially e.g., they may pay the market fees or local taxes but not registered or licensed. Regulatory and policy environment affect some more severely than others. These considerations suggest that even though the enterprises are all classified as informal, in reality, the extent of informality varies across enterprises. In other words the enterprises are subjected to different degrees of informality. Informal sector is thus far from homogeneous. This also means that the extent of informal employment i.e., low income and poor conditions of work varies considerably in developing countries. From the point of view of efficiency and equity, the loss of output and welfare resulting from the presence of informality should be obvious. These informal enterprises devote considerable part of their time and energy on how to overcome informality rather than on improving their business. No attempt however has been made in the literature to measure this welfare loss. This remains a challenge and belongs to the future research agenda. Based on evidence one can put forward some general propositions: Enterprises that are smaller, those headed by poor, less educated, women and recent migrants to cities are more likely to be informal (Sethuraman 1998).

Looking at the various qualitative assessments undertaken in many developing countries, informality could aggravate poverty, either directly or indirectly, through increasing inequality in the access to services and opportunities, increased vulnerability and human abuse. The informality is an important coping means when formal systems have collapsed or are under enormous stress. People recognize that informality is harmful to their standards of living and to the distribution of income in general, but in most cases they have no choice because there are no viable formal alternatives. In some cases, however, there is a perception that through informal means it may be possible to get better deals by performing on connections or just by appealing directly for the understanding of the service provider. Indeed, in countries where formal cost recovery for services has been imposed to try and reduce under the table payments, it is not clear that the poor have been made better off. Recent research has identified a number of potentially negative impacts that informal payments have had on health care, including decreased access to healthcare for women and the poor. These informal payments, however, also allow for services that the State cannot fund to continue to exist. The problem once again is not the informal payment but the under-funding of health services. The relationship between informal payments and access is complex. It may not make much difference to the poor whether high health expenditure is official or unofficial, as hindrances would be equal in both cases. Informal payments, however, make it impossible for the government to modulate health fees in order to facilitate access by the poor. Health indicators and anecdotal evidence suggest that the increase in out of pocket payments has substantially brought down the utilization of healthcare facilities. People tend to utilize these facilities only under exceptional circumstances. Moreover, many studies show that the poor have been forced to pay an increasingly larger percentage of their income on healthcare. On the other hand, the demand for informal payments may simply arise out of the need to survive. The introduction of health insurance systems also has a negative impact on access because of the large informal sector in developing countries. The poor in the informal sector do not have formal labour contracts, so no contributions are made by their employer or by themselves to the State pension funds or for healthcare benefits. The result is that these individuals are not eligible for those services and that little money is actually paid for health insurance. Principally, for those who are at the bottom of the socioeconomic ladder and those in rural areas without access to key infrastructure, such as water and sewage systems, health and healthcare conditions are worse. The role of education is very influential in preventing people from falling into poverty and informality. The link between education and poverty is similar to that between unemployment and poverty as unemployment rates fall with every additional level of education. The poor suffer from the larger level of bribes than the non-poor households. With the difficult economic conditions of transition, a number of people no longer value education as much as they did before the transition, their pinnacle priority is mere survival. The interaction between informality and social protection raises two very different issues. First, the poor tend to rely on informal means in the traditional areas of social protection, including help for the aged, the extended family, and the handicapped and for those in extreme poverty. The high demand for benefits from the State and the low level of public funds available for this purpose in many of the countries under review limit the effectiveness of social protection systems. Consequently, many people among the elderly from large families handicapped or others have been left with no other means than their own or family support. The second issue is that the high level of informal activities considerably limits the financing available for formal social protection, especially in countries, in which payroll taxes constitutes the largest source of funds for pensions and other forms of support, such as unemployment benefits. Analyzes of informal employment in social assessment and other qualitative studies have emphasized the insecurity, hard work, very long hours, extremely low wage rates and sometime hazardous working conditions. The unemployed rarely choose to become involved in informality, preferring the security of formal employment. Nevertheless, the lack of formal employment coupled with an inability to meet household needs in the absence of welfare benefits or because of the inadequacy of the available assistance, encourages people to turn to the informal economy in response. Likewise perceive the informal employment strategies of the unemployed as a part of a survival strategy, through which some individuals develop alternative ways of working in the face of the existing limited opportunities and the failure of the welfare system. Informality enables the unemployed poor to get some basic income, but what is more important, it may help them maintain a sense of self-confidence. Most individuals work in the informal sector only if they have to or if they can supplement their informal sector earnings with their unemployment benefits and the social services, such as health care, that are available with these benefits. First of all, for the vast majority, informal sector wages are very low. The more illegal the work, the higher the wages, as well as the higher risks and fines if caught. In turn high taxes depress economic activity and income stabilization, which brings us back to square one, making informality a mechanism of survival and coping, especially for the poor. Many poor people observe the lack of fair access to the legal system and the lack of security as major components of poverty. The lack of trust in the legal system and the possibility for people to have influence on it in a non-transparent way are major issues.

In India the informal sector employs more than 90 percent of workforce, most if not all, are covered by meaningful social security schemes. The informalised workforce is unprotected labour, which implies labour that does not have any socio-economic safety. The protection that a society provides to individuals and households to ensure access to wage and working conditions in a comprehensive sense, in matters of security of employment, health care, maternity benefits, provident fund, retirement benefits, is an essential element of the safety nets that keeps working people and their families from falling into poverty (Sarkar 2004 a: 122).

The informal sector represents an important part of the economy and certainly of labour market in many countries, especially developing countries and poses a challenge to policy makers with regard to issues relating to improvement of the working condition and social protection of the workers engaged in the informal sector. In the developing economies a substantial share of employment is indeed in informal category and women in all age groups depend on the informal sector more heavily than men. Women and children are over represented in this sector in the sense that their share in the sector is higher than their share in total labor force. Most women tend to be own account workers and only a few are heads of micro enterprises. Relatively lower level of education among women, compared to men, seems to explain, in part, this gender differential in informal employment. Discrimination in the labour market also explains in part the disproportionate concentration as it limits women's access to formal and wage employment. Women also face additional constraints because of their homemaking and childcare responsibilities, which limits their participation in formal employment. Even within the informal sector more women than men seem to be in poor quality employment. The causes for participation in the informal sector can be economic and non-economic. Economic reasons are related to unemployment and an inflexible formal labour market, a declining real price of capital and the high cost of formal production. Besides, non-economic causes are concerned with a greater flexibility and satisfaction in work, a complete use of workers professional qualifications and increased leisure time. There are two groups of factors, which determine the decision to become active in the informal sector, more specifically, the structural as well as opportunity factors. The structural factors consist of financial pressure, socio-psychological pressure and institutional constraints. The opportunity factors consist of individual background, skills, education, living condition or non-individual components, environment, values, standards etc. (Sarkar 2004 b: 366).

THE CONCEPT

The concept of informal sector is not easy to define specifically. Most often it is defined negatively by indicating the nonexistence of characteristics that belong to formal activities, of special emphasis being labour market characteristics, security or regularity of work, better earnings, existence of non wage and long term benefits, protective legislation and union protection (Papola 1980; Banerjee 1985). Since a number of activities within the formal sector are getting informalised and private, small scale manufacturing units employing predominantly women labour is growing – the borderline becomes blurred. While earnings may still be better in the emerging formal sector, its major advantages in terms of non-wage and long term benefits, security and protection of work likely to be getting diluted (Eapen 2001: 2390). At the same time, within the informal sector itself, evidence discloses that a number of self-employment activities in the form of micro enterprises are undertaken with great ingenuity and entrepreneurial spirit and therefore have a growth potential (Rakowski 1994).

The term informal sector was first initiated by Keith Hart (1970) in a study of urban Ghana. He describes the informal sector as that part of the urban labour force, which falls outside the organized labour market. The study identified a number of incomes and employment generating activities in the un-enumerated sector of urban settlements. The workers involved in the un-enumerated sector mainly served as self-employed, as against the wageworkers in the enumerated sector. The new entrants to the urban labour market particularly migrants from rural areas were forced to work in the informal sector partly on account of lack of adequate opportunities in the formal sector and partly due to the workers' lack of skills and adequate experience required for the jobs in the formal sector. Keith Hart has used the terms, namely, informal income generating activities, unorganized sector, un-enumerated sector, self-employed individuals and urban proletariat in his study more or less alternatively and interchangeably.

The concept has been further refined by a mission of International Labour Organization (ILO) (1972), which studied the employment situation in Kenya within the framework of the World Employment Programme. The ILO employment mission to Kenya adopted the term 'informal sector' for analyzing the employment situation and for working out a strategy for employment generation in Kenya. The study reveals that informal sector has the characteristics like easy entry for the new enterprises, reliance on indigenous resources, family ownership, small scale operations, unregulated and competitive markets, labour intensive technology and informally acquired skills of workers.

Mazumdar, in a World Bank paper (1975), describes informal sector as an easy entry, residual sector providing mainly services and crowded with secondary workers with low productivity and wages.

Sethuraman (1976) has defined the informal sector as consisting of small scale units engaged in the production and distribution of goods and services with the primary objectives of generating employment and income to their participants notwithstanding the constraints on capital, both physical and human.

Tokman (1976) looks at the informal sector as a self-contained sector with well-defined and significant links with the rest of the economy.

Squire (1981) defines informal sector as a sector in which wages are determined by demand and supply forces.

Papola (1981) has defined informal sector as a convenient way of designating a segment of economy having certain characteristics, which lead to unfavourable conditions for the growth of enterprises and activities operating in this segment.

Nattrass (1987) defines informal sector at the interface of formal sector, reserve army and marginal pole.

The System of National Accounts (SNA) (1993) defined the informal sector as consisting of units engaged in the production of goods or services with the primary objective of generating employment and incomes to the persons concerned. They form part of the household sector as unincorporated enterprises owned by households. They are distinguished from corporations and quasi-corporations on the basis of their legal status and the type of accounts they hold. These household enterprises do not have a legal status independently of the households or household members owning them.

The fifteenth International Conference of Labour of ILO (1993a) adopted an operational definition of the informal sector that is irrespective of the kind of workplace, the extent of fixed assets, the duration of the activity of the enterprises and its operation as a main or secondary activity. Within the household sector, the informal sector comprises of informal own-account enterprises that are single member or partnership household units that do not hire workers on a continuous basis, enterprises of informal employers are household units owned and operated by employers, singly or in partnership, which employ one or more employees on a more or less continuous basis. For operational purposes the latter may be defined in terms of either, the size of unit below a specified level of employment or non-registration of the enterprise or its employees.

Gibson and Kelly (1994) have defined informal sector as a sector that uses inferior technology. According to them, initially multiple production processes exist in informal sector but competition among informal sector units ensures survival of only the most profitable process.

According to ILO (1999) informal sector refers to activities typically at a low level of organization and technology, with the primary objective of generating employment and income. The activities are usually carried out without proper recognition from authorities and escape the attention of the administrative machinery responsible for enforcing laws and regulation.

The labour market in developing and transition countries is strikingly different from that in the developed countries. The most arresting feature of labour markets in the developing countries is its non-homogeneous character. The labour markets in these two economies diverge in its sectoral composition with the vast majority of employment being in the non-agricultural sectors in the developed countries whereas the developing countries are still predominantly agricultural. The status of the vast majority of workers in the developed countries is of wage and salary earners whereas in the developing countries there is a predominance of self-employment. This non-homogeneous character of the labour markets in developing countries also implies that the nature of employment and the manner in which it is created is different in the two economies. Almost all the employment in developed economies is created within the recognized institutional framework as the economic agents, which create these jobs, operate within the existing laws and regulation (Sethuraman 1998). These economic agents are the government, and private enterprises, including non-corporate entities, and the employment thus created is governed by the prevailing labour laws and regulations. In contrast, in the developing countries the vast majority of the population is left to fend for itself and create employment out of its own ingenuity, skills and capital. This leads to vast differences in the nature of employment and the creation of a dualistic structure of formal and informal components of the labour market. The standard textbook model assumes a homogeneous market with an inelastic supply of labour, where demand conditions alone determine the price of labour or wage. This assumption leads to thinking about an average productivity of labour for the economy as a whole. Labour market policies based on this assumption can be quite misleading if prescribed for the developing countries. The productivity differences between the various sectors of the labour market in the developing countries are of major importance for both labour market outcomes and policies. The World Development Report (1995) argued implicitly that the reasons for the growth of the informal sector in developing countries were labour market distortions, such as trade unions and government policies leading to inflexible labour markets. However, this has been contested on the ground that the informal sector existed before the growth of trade unions and the reason for the growth of the informal sector is capital market distortions. Since capital labour ratios are generally higher in the formal sector, labour productivity is higher and so are earnings in this sector. The chain of causation runs from differential capital intensity to productivity differences to wage differences. The reasons for the growth of the informal sector are important from the point of view of developing policies. Whatever the reason, the growth of the informal sector in the emerging labour market is inevitable. Women's employment in the informal sector is also likely to rise due to various reasons. With the adoption of the structural adjustment programme women tend to loose ground in the formal sectors of the economy. The growth of ancillarisation and industrial employment through sub-contracting appears to be gaining importance. Stagnating and falling incomes of households due to poor performance of the economy also leads to increased entry of women into the labour market. The process of globalization, export-oriented industrialization and relocation of industries from the developed to the developing countries also lead to the increase in the employment in the informal sector. Women's employment is often favoured in many of these industries. These factors lead to the increasing informalisation of the labour force. This informalisation takes place broadly in two ways. Work is pushed out of the enterprises and formal work situations into tiny workshops, the homes and informal situations i.e., there is an global trend in sub-contracting of work and a consequent increase in informal work, often in home working. Secondly, the workers who remain in the factories or in formal work situations are governed by looser contracts and obtain fewer social security benefits. That is, there is an attempt on the part of the employer to reduce his liabilities. The definition of the informal sector cited by ILO was descriptive. It specified a set of characteristics to distinguish informal enterprises such as small scale of operation, family ownership, reliance on indigenous resources, labour intensive and adaptive technology, skills acquired outside the formal system and operation in unregulated and competitive markets. The problem with applying such multiple criteria is that all of them could be found in units pursuing different objectives. It is also difficult to apply. In practice, most of the early ILO studies ended up using a single index of the employment size. On account of the complexity and looseness of the concept, the labour statisticians decided to distinguish one single statistical definition for the purpose of data collection from the several definitions that may vary according to the needs of the users and could be differentiated at the tabulation stage. The SNA (1993) characterizes the informal sector as consisting of units engaged in the production of goods or services with the primary objective of generating employment and incomes to the persons concerned. They form part of the household sector as unincorporated enterprises owned by households. They are distinguished from corporations and quasi-corporations on the basis of their legal status and the type of accounts they hold. These household enterprises do not have a legal status independently of the households or household members owning them. An operational definition of the informal sector that is irrespective of the kind of workplace, the extent of fixed assets, the duration of the activity of the enterprises and its operation as a main or secondary activity. Within the household sector, the informal sector comprises of informal own-account enterprises that are single member or partnership household units that do not hire workers on a continuous basis; enterprises of informal employers are household units owned and operated by employers, singly or in partnership, which employ one or more employees on a more or less continuous basis. For operational purposes the latter may be defined in terms of either, the size of unit below a specified level of employment or, non-registration of the enterprise or its employees. The SNA definition of the informal sector is based on the legal status of the enterprise. To distinguish employment in the informal sector one will have to assume that all persons working in such units are workers in this sector namely, informal employers and employees in the enterprises of informal employers, own account workers and unpaid family helps in informal enterprises. This definition of the informal sector, focusing on the enterprise, does not give us any clue about the status and working conditions of the workers in them. It will not be correct to assume that all workers in the formal sector are better off than all workers in the informal sector, or that all workers in the informal sector are equally badly off. In recent years many writings have expressed the view that such a dichotomized classification of the formal and informal sector is unrealistic and tends to hide more than it reveals. It also fails to capture three things, which are important from the point of view of social protection for workers, particularly women - the continuing process of informalisation of the formal economy; the great diversity within the informal economy itself; and the linkages between the formal and informal parts of the economy. The term informal sector is giving way to the term informal economy. Sethuraman (1998) argued that it is now widely accepted that such a dichotomy into the formal and informal is but a caricature of the real economy because both the formal and informal parts exhibit considerable diversity. Employment in the informal economy is not only inferior to that in the formal economy in terms of wages and benefits received, but also varies in terms of quality. Some jobs tend to be more informal than others in the sense that the extent of deviation from the established quality norms is greater. The dichotomous definition of the formal and informal sector actually distinguishes the status of the enterprise. This is useful for national accounts and in estimating the gross value added accruing from the two sectors. The concept of the informal economy in fact tries to characterize the workers depending on the degree of informality of their work status. This is more useful to persons concerned with wages, working conditions and access to social protection to workers. A second problem with the enterprise-based definition is when it is used in an establishment survey to distinguish the unit. This definition tends to leave out more invisible groups of own-account enterprises such as those operating on the streets or in their homes. A labour force survey with clear questions on the place of work and nature of contract may be better able to net in all such workers. It is argued that the enterprise-based dichotomous definition is important from the point of view of estimating the contribution of this sector in the gross national product. However, an additional worker based approach is required to identify the status of workers within the two sectors and invisible groups of workers often missed out through an enterprise approach (Unni 2001).

Thus, the informal sector is its identification with pre-capitalist mode of production, own account of workers and no access to the benefits of social security and is characterized by low capital intensity, low level of productivity, a tiny and usually poor clientele, a low level of formal schooling, intermediate technology, preponderance of family labour and ownership, ease of entrance and last but not least, lack of support and recognition from the government.

BASIC CHARACTERISTICS

The rapid rise in research focusing on the urban informal sector in developing countries has led to a greater vagueness and inconsistency of definition of the term informal sector. Obviously, the major reason behind this state of affairs is the lack of a 'clear empirical basis' for the concept (Mehta 1985:327). However, several scholars have attempted to make generalization of the salient characteristics of group of activities and workers in the informal sector. The identification of characteristics of the informal sector has mostly been derived from the various empirical studies conducted in developing countries. The following are the basic characteristics of informal sector in studies on the subject:

(a) Ease of Entry: The informal sector is characterized by its fluidity and mobility of its labour. It is the entry point to the city for immigrants who left their native villages in the aspiration of urban income higher than their poor agricultural income. New entrants depend on their friends and relatives already settled down in the city to support them financially and search for job opportunities (Romatet 1983: 2115)

(b) Autonomy and Flexibility: Many informal sector participants in developed countries choose to participate in the informal sector because they find more autonomy, flexibility and freedom in this sector than in the formal sector.

In other words, participants have the freedom of operation they can use and developed their creativity (Gerxhani 1999).

(c) Small Scale of Operations: Informal sector generally comprises with tiny establishments. The sector may be single worker establishments and those with only self-employed and own account workers form (Bienefeld 1974; Breman 1976:1873; Hart 1973: 66). Small scale of operation is considered a necessary condition for inclusion of an enterprise in the informal sector, because 'smallness' is usually accompanied by several other attributes, which make such enterprises disadvantaged (Sethuraman 1976:76). The small size indicates a relatively small size of employment with low capital intensity and low rate of return on capital employed.

(d) Family Ownership of Enterprise: In informal sector, functional division of labour and specialization is limited and most of the managerial and administrative functions are to be performed by the owner. The family labour is extensively used in the sector. These all features are not necessarily found to go together. Small size itself makes it possible to run an enterprise without a structural division of labour and management hierarchy. The organizations with wider ownership and using hired labour may disclose these feature if their scale of operation is small. On the contrary, large even family owned organizations cannot be run on the basis of informal and un-structural organization and undefined functional division of labour. Thus, structure of organization is mainly a function of size and is not necessarily related to the pattern of ownership (Papola 1981).

(e) Labour Intensive and Adaptive Technology: The informal sector units use labour intensive, predominantly manual, low productivity techniques of production. According to John Week (1975:2), informal sector is characterized by small-scale operations labour intensive techniques, low levels of income and indigenous ownership. Informal sector may not adopt capital-intensive modern technology, either because it does not have access to it or because it does not suit the sector in the given relative cost position of capital and labour is hired at a much lower wage rate than the formal sector.

(f) Lack of Support and Recognition from the Government: Informal sector activities have grown without any government support. The organized capital market, bank finance, foreign technology, imported raw materials, protection from foreign competition etc. are not available to the informal sector enterprises on account of meagre material resources. Sometimes the informal sector units are found to engage in certain activities requiring legal permission without obtaining it or to acquire certain inputs requiring license from the illegal market, as a consequence of official limitation of access to the formal sector (Week 1975:3). The government's attempts to enforce certain regulations are naturally considered by these enterprises as 'hostile' conditions making their operations difficult (Sethuraman 1977: 198).

(g) Competitive and Unregulated Product Market: The informal sector in developing countries is generally found to have competitive and unregulated market. It is not always true that the informal sector produces goods and renders services of general use, while the formal sector enterprises predominantly cater to the demand of high income group of population and foreign market nor do all informal sector enterprises operate in a competitive market and all formal sector enterprises in a oligopolistic and protected market (Joshi and Joshi 1976; Weeks 1975:3).

(h) Unprotected Labour Market: The labour market in the informal sector is supposed to be unregulated and highly competitive because of absolute freedom to entry in the sector. The supply of labour in the informal sector consists of mostly new entrants in the labour market in-migrants or young persons entering the labour force. Since the opportunities for getting a job in the formal sector become restricted, they move towards a small establishment in the informal sector. As a result situation of underemployment and depressed wages prevail in the informal sector (Mazumdar 1977).

(i) Unreported Income or Tax Evasion: The informal sector is described as the sum of all taxable money income left unreported with the intension to evade taxes (Feige 1990). There is no record of monetary transaction, therefore the

income is not reported for taxation. The subject becomes more complex while market activity is categorized into taxable and non-taxable activity. A classification system for viewing this distinction is presented in Table1 (McCrohan *et al.* 1991).

(j) Legal or Illegal: Within the framework of informal sector activities may be legal or illegal. Economic activities may be classified by the manner in which goods and services are produced or exchanged. Income generated by economic activity may be segregated by the legality of the production or provision of goods and services and the legal status of goods and services themselves.

On the whole, these characteristics of informal sector may be grouped into three broad categories as follows (Mehta 1985:328):

- Those related to the characteristics of the enterprise, like size, family ownership, source of inputs, labour intensive technology etc. In this category, the emphasis is on the context within which people work, the stress being placed on the mode of production.

Table 1
Relationship between Taxable and Measured Market Income

	Taxable	*Not taxable*
Measured	Legal source market income: Informal economy Example: Payment to contractor, bartering of vehicle repairs for services	Legal source market income: Informal economy Example: Lawn cutting done by a teenager
Not Measured	Illegal source market income: Illegal sector of informal economy Example: Sale of drugs, sale of stolen automobiles	Intra-sector transfer Example: garage sale, sale of used refrigerator to a neighbour

Source: McCrohan *et al.* [1991]

- Those related to the nature of exchange relationship with the State and the rest of urban economy like unregulated and competitive markets, lack of support and recognition from the government, lack of structural organization, unregistered nature of enterprises etc.

- Those based on the employment situation or labour market processes like ease of entry, self-employed or casual nature of work, lack of formal contractual arrangement for employment etc.

CAUSES AND MOTIVES

The causes for participation in the informal sector can be economic and non-economic. Economic reasons are related to unemployment and an inflexible formal labour market, a declining real price of capital and the high cost of formal production. Besides, non-economic causes are concerned with a greater flexibility and satisfaction in work, a complete use of workers professional qualifications and increased leisure time (Gerxhani 1999). There are two groups of factors, which determine the decision to become active in the informal sector, more specifically, the structural as well as opportunity factors. The structural factors consist of economic pressure, socio-psychological pressure and institutional constraints. The opportunity factors consist of individual background, skills, education, living condition or non-individual components, environment, values, standards etc. The fundamental reasons to participation in the informal economy may be cited as:

- As a consequence of stagnation, unemployment and depreciation of capital stimulate participation in the informal activities. Thus, economic recession is the foremost cause of informalisation.
- The tax evasion is another cause to participation in the informal economy that has recently gained much more attention amongst the economists.
- Governmental excessive regulation of the market sector through the various legislations related to labour conditions, quality regulation and production limits tend to a larger informal sector. This type of over regulation enhances the transaction costs of the participants in the formal economy, so that it becomes relatively more appealing to shift to the informal economy.

The main causes of informal labour may be divided in three main groups such as economic, institutional and social. This classification can be instrumental for the adoption of policy measures addressing the issue of informal labour. The main economic reasons of informal labour are the following:

- Lack of legal jobs
- Lack or insufficient level of legal income
- Higher remuneration if the job is done without registration
- Strong and unfair competition, which may prompt firms to look for cost reduction, including through informal labour

Economic transition has brought new phenomena such as unemployment, poverty and large income disparities. This has been instrumental for many people to accept jobs in the informal sector. Fast changes in income distribution may create incentives for the losers to accept additional informal jobs. Strong competition from firms, which benefit from the informal economy, including from black labour, may create pressure for other firms to do the same (a mimic effect). The institutional environment, in which firms, workers and households operate, is usually considered as a major cause of informal labour. This environment includes:

- High taxation on labour
- High unemployment benefits
- Complicated procedures for getting unemployment benefits (how easy it is to get benefits, their time-span, methods of skill assessment, rules of registration of temporary job contracts by retired and unemployed people, etc.)
- Other specific labour markets regulations, such as rules of hiring and firing employees, including temporary and seasonal workers
- Size and capacity of the tax administration

High income taxes create large disparities between legal and informal wages and incentives to go informal. Empirical studies suggest that labour supply (the number of hours worked) is strongly correlated with the pay rates in both legal and informal labour markets. This means that a reduction of the divergence between the pay rates for legal and illegal work will lead to a decline of the volume of informal work. Low unemployment benefits create incentives for taking informal jobs. In addition, relatively high unemployment benefits do not motivate towards searching for jobs (this is the poverty trap). Barriers to registration of temporary labour contracts by employers may lead to increase of informal labour. Inflexible labour regulations also provide incentives to go informal. High firing costs, such as obligatory severance pay, do not encourage employers to hire workers legally. This is certainly obvious for small firms. Transformation has also brought new challenges for the administration in general, but both fiscal and labour administration can be instrumental for controlling the size of informal sector, although it takes a long time to build their capabilities. The third group of causes of informal activities consists of psychological and cultural motivations to go informal:

- Social tax morality (i.e., the acceptance of black labour and tax evasion by society)
- Risk-adverse or risk-taking attitudes in society
- Willingness to work on a permanent labour contract

In developing countries most of the people engage in the informal economy. They do so for a variety of reasons. For some it is an economic inevitability, their only resort or a better alternative to other low-wage formal employment available. Others are involved in informal work for personal fulfillment, social obligation or as a means of supplementing their primary income. The majority of informal economy participants are employees, working for others, in sweatshops or out of their homes in contract relationships to producers. But, many are also self-employed. The very nature of being a micro or very tiny activity lends itself to operating in the informal economy. These enterprises are largely invisible or operate at low levels of visibility. They may or may not have licenses, and are often engaged in casual hiring, non-reporting of income and other informal labour practices. They can be easily moved, opened or closed and thus, can hide from regulation. Finally, it is important to note that the formal and informal economies are connected. Participants may combine earnings from informal self-employment with wages from formal employment or transfer payments, such as public benefits or investment income or savings or, they may be employed both formally and informally at the same time. They engage in these activities to generate extra income in low-wage markets and to create an economic buffer to cover periods of unemployment. Informal work arrangements may also be a strategy imposed from the outside as big enterprises restructure and outsource functions to subcontractors both to minimize costs and maximize flexibility. Under these arrangements, they push workers out of the formal economy into the informal economy where they suffer without protections of the legal system. Workers are found who move fluidly back and forth between the two economies, some by necessity, and others by choice. While the factors above influence the size of the activity, entrepreneurs cite additional reasons for keeping the segment informal:

- Perhaps most importantly is the attitude of the individual toward the activity itself. Looked at as something that matches within other economic activities that they do, it is seen less as an enterprise than as just another way one works to make a little money. As one more patch in a complex of economic endeavors, it is not perceived as something that needs to be any more structured than the work itself requires and if it demanded more rigors in paperwork and other requirements, it would lose its value to the entrepreneur and his/her family.
- Often the activity is so small-scale (or occasional or erratic) that it is not worth reporting as far as the entrepreneur is concerned.
- There is a tradition of exchange and while these exchanges may be calculated in rough terms to ensure

that the trades are even rarely are records kept of these valuations. Rather the exchanges represent important inputs into households that can operate quite invisibly to the outside world and are attractive for that reason.

- Finally, in a few cases, the activity is new and being tested to overview if it is worth converting into a larger or more formal operation. The entrepreneur will increasingly move to following more of the rules of the game as the potential of the business becomes clearer.

TYPOLOGY

All informal activity has one common feature namely the entrepreneurs who works in the informal economy perceive the benefits of doing so to offset the costs of going formal. Recent studies have identified a number of reasons why some entrepreneurial activity may take place in the shadows. The most important determinants are the prevalence of burdensome and costly government regulations and the level and administrative complexity of taxation. Informality comes at a cost, the inability to use government and some private sector services available to firms that fully comply with regulations. In countries entrepreneurs may well opt to be formal, even if regulations are many and taxes are high. In contrast, entrepreneurs in countries where the quality of public services to enterprises is poor have a much easier choice. In the absence of discernible benefits of going formal, they prefer to save their time and money and stay informal. Many transition economies have experienced surging share of entrepreneurial activity in the informal sector. Some of this activity is illegal. Such activity will not become formal, regardless of improvements in the enterprises climate. Other activities, like small production units operate merely for the subsistence of their owners and do not generate enough revenue to make their inclusion in the tax base meaningful. However, there exists a considerable share of entrepreneurial activity that is semi-formal e.g., the organization is registered but most changes. Informal activities usually fall into three broad categories namely employees are not, and can become formal with appropriate policy underground enterprises, subsistence enterprises and unofficial enterprises. Subsistence enterprises result from coping strategies adopted by families to compensate for low wages or external shocks e.g., unemployment etc. Unofficial enterprises generally result from the desire to escape or avoid the administrative and/or financial burden of regulation e.g., license and permit regimes, taxes, labour regulations etc.

CLASSIFICATION OF PARTICIPANTS

Following the worker approach workers in the informal economy can be broadly distinguished into wage employment and non-wage employment, each consisting of the components of own account workers, employers/owners of informal enterprises with at least one hired worker; unpaid family helpers in both types of informal enterprises, employees in the enterprises of informal employers, outworkers or home workers (persons working at home, or on premises of his choice other than the employer's, to produce goods or services on a contract or order for a specific employer or contractor), independent wage workers not attached to only one employer and providing services to individuals, households and enterprises, e.g., maid servants and watchmen working for households and informal employment in formal sector enterprises (workers whose pay and benefits do not conform to existing labour regulations). This categorization is similar to that developed by Sethuraman (1998). In the literature the first four categories are generally taken to represent employment in the informal sector. The need to distinguish the category of independent wageworkers can be debated. In many Latin American

countries domestic helps are distinguished in the national surveys and together with independent wageworkers are added to the informal sector (Sethuraman 1998). The first process of informalisation of the labour force, pushing work out of formal work situations, leads to an increase in the first component, non-wage employment. It can also lead to increase in the first two varieties of the second component i.e., informal wage employment. The second process of informalisation, resulting in looser contracts and fewer benefits, leads to an increase in the last category of workers, informal employment within the formal enterprises as defined by the enterprise-based approach. Obviously it is not easy to obtain empirical estimates of these categories of workers from the national official labour statistics. However, an approximation of the first component of the informal economy can be arrived at, non-wage employment or self-employment, by the addition of employers, own account workers and unpaid family helpers in the activity status classification of the national labour force survey. While it may be relatively safe to assume that own account workers and unpaid family helpers are part of the informal economy, this assumption may not be very accurate for the category of employer. Employers, however, form a very small proportion of the workforce. The second component of the informal economy is even more difficult to demarcate from the official data since there is really a continuum in the degree of informality in the employer-employee relationships. The official data distinguish only employees. The Indian labour force surveys further classifies them into casual and regular. All regular workers do not necessarily belong to the formal economy, as they often do not receive a variety of benefits due to the formal worker such as provident funds, paid leave etc. An approximation of the second component of the informal economy can be made by assuming that all casual employees definitely constitute a part of the informal economy since they are least likely to obtain any of the benefits accruing to formal economy workers. Another indicator or measure of the nature of informality of the work status or sector is the earnings differentials. The informal economy can be distinguished by the inferior quality of work and inferior terms of employment, both remuneration and benefits. Among the non-wage component inferior technologies lead to low productivity and hence to low earnings or incomes.

Since informal sector is very diverse and it covers many types of work, so it is difficult to classify it into a specific group as uniform. However, the workers in the informal sector may be classified broadly into four categories as under:

(i) *Home Based Workers*: The workers in this category carry out their activities using their traditional skill and labour. The majority of the home based workers work in the privacy of their homes and they are invisible. This category of workers engages in earthen pots making, rural artisans etc.

(ii) *Self Employed or Own Account Workers*: Self-employed or own account workers are those who do not have any permanent place for carrying out their activities. Some of them have to change their place of activity almost on a daily basis. In this category of workers includes street vendors, hawkers, rag pickers, rickshaw pullers, sex workers etc.

(iii) *Piece Wage Workers*: There has been a tremendous growth of private informal manufacturing such as garment making, knitting etc. These categories of workers are employed by entrepreneurs. They are usually employed on a piece rate basis. This type of workers carries out their work independently, but employers exercise control over them by supplying raw material and sometimes advancing minimum cash. This kind of labour is often found in beedi making, carpet and mat weaving, lace industry etc.

(iv) *Time Wage Workers*: This type of workers sells their labour power in exchange of a low paid time rate of wage. The most of the workers in this category are quasi permanent. These workers are placed in a most disadvantageous position. Their activities rely heavily on manual labour. This category includes gardeners, cleaners, sweepers, construction labourers, bricks workers, agricultural labourers, domestic servants etc.

PAID-UNPAID ECONOMY

In economy two types of work exist namely, paid work and unpaid work. While a worker is engaged for performing chore on the basis of an agreed wage payment, the activities carried out by the concerned worker may be termed as paid work. On the other hand, the time spent by a worker in several activities in domestic sector may be termed as unpaid care work. In economy unpaid work is often informal while paid work may be formal or informal. The connections between the unpaid care economy and the paid economy (Himmelweit 2002) are represented in Figure 1, which shows the flows of the characteristic net contribution of each sector to the rest of the economy. The unpaid economy consists of the domestic sector that contributes to individual socialization and to the production and maintenance of human capabilities. The paid economy contains both the social and economic infrastructure and producing sector. However, each sector may and does make other outputs.

Gender impact analysis must examine the effects of any economic policy on both the paid and unpaid economies, disaggregating these effects by gender. The most significant gender division of labour is that between the two economies. Women still devote the majority of their working time to the unpaid economy and men devote theirs to the paid economy in both developed and developing countries (United Nations Development Programme 1995). Given this disparity, the overall distributional effect of policies that improve the conditions of paid work over unpaid work will be to worsen gender inequality, unless those policies are specifically targeted on improving women's situation. Thus there are two aspects to the gender division of labour between paid and unpaid economies. It is not only that woman overall tend to do more unpaid caring work than men. It is also that an inside division of labour within households allocates that work and if a woman shares her household with another member, it is likely that that other member does less unpaid caring work than she does. This is not of course exact for women who share their household with other women, although the allocation of caring work may in practice still be unequal. A woman or anyone doing the bulk of caring work can lose bargaining power because her contribution of unpaid labour is less visible than her counterpart's economic contribution.

A United Nations (1991) report on women's work patterns based on surveys made across countries of the world gives a summary of women's devotion of time to both paid and unpaid economic activity. The findings are as follows:

- Women spend more of their time working than men folk in all developed and developing regions except northern America and Australia where the working hours are almost equal.
- In developing countries women spend more time in the labour force than their household work. Men by contrast are spending less amount of time working in the labour force than before in all developed regions and slightly rising amounts of time in household in northern America and Western Europe.
- In Africa, Asia and the Pacific women as on average 12-13 hours more than men per week.
- Men in developing regions generally do more household chores than men in the developed regions.
- Women everywhere in the world have nearly total responsibility for housework. While men help out women keep the responsibility of housework.

Figure 1: The Interdependence of the Paid and Unpaid Economies

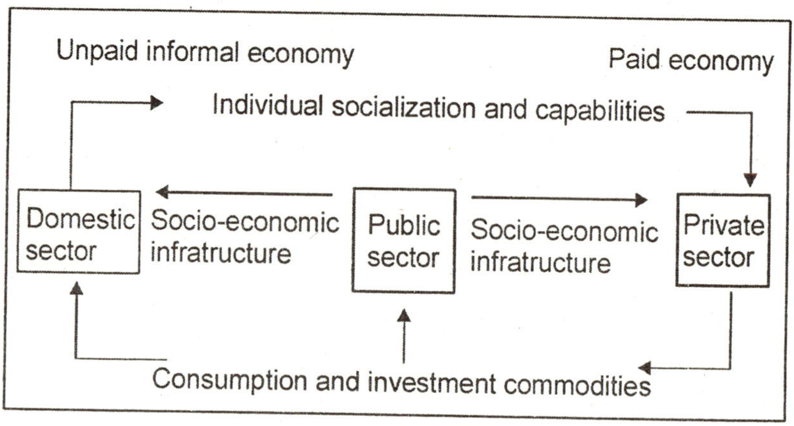

Source: Himmelweit [2002]

FORMAL -INFORMAL DICHOTOMY

(A) *Contrasting Characteristics*: The most commonly used classification is the one, which segregates the economy into formal and informal sectors. As a classification of economic activities, one would intuitively assume that distinction refers to the fact of formal or informal character of producers. However, it has not meant so, the distinction has been made on the basis of certain empirical facts of size, nature of market and relation with the State (Papola 1981). Various empirical studies highlight distinguishing characteristics of formal and informal sectors.

Joshi and Joshi (1976) have laid down the distinguishing characteristics of the two sectors. According to them, informal sector contains large manufacturing firms operating in oligopolistic markets sheltered from foreign competition by high tariffs and quantitative restrictions, selling their product mainly to middle and upper income groups. On the other hand, informal sector contains a very large number of small producers operating on narrow margins in highly competitive product markets, selling a variety of goods and services mainly to low-income groups. They also added that while formal sector uses capital intensive, imported technology, the informal sector adopts labour intensive indigenous technology.

In John Weeks (1975) study, on analytical base to the descriptive nature of the distinction between formal and informal sectors is found. According to him, formal sector is characterized by privileged access to resources, large scale of operations, capital-intensive techniques, high wage rates and salary packages. Besides, informal sector is characterized by deprived of privileged access to resources, tiny scale of operations, labour intensive techniques, low level of earnings and indigenous ownership.

Mazumdar (1977) has explained the distinction sharply focusing on the fact that entry into the informal sector labour market is unrestricted, while that in the formal sector labour market is restricted by artificially raised hiring standards, norms and producers.

Thus, the distinguishing characteristics of the two sectors may be summarized from the various studies as shown in Table 2.

(B) *Linkages:* Apart from the contrasting characteristics of formal informal sector, it is worthwhile to identify the nature of linkages between the two sectors or among the various economic activities in the urban economy. The linkages may initially be classified as direct and indirect. The direct linkages may be in terms of resource inputs from formal to informal sectors or technology and market linkages (Bose 1978). On the other hand, indirect linkages refer to the demand of goods and services generated in the informal sector by a clientele whose income is dependent on the formal sector.

Table 2
Distinguishing Characteristics of Formal and Informal Sectors

Formal sector	*Informal sector*
(a) Difficult to entry	(a) Ease of entry
(b) Legal form of enterprises, corporate ownership	(b) Cottage enterprises, family ownership
(c) Large size of operations	(c) Small size of operations
(d) Capital intensive and foreign technology	(d) Labour intensive and indigenous technology
(e) Regulated and restricted competition	(e) Unregulated and high competitive product market
(f) High level of earnings	(f) Low level of earnings
(g) Formally acquired skill	(g) Skill acquired through on the job training
(h) Less chance of exploitation of labour for existence of trade union	(h) More chance of exploitation of labour for non-existence of trade union
(i) Access to government favours	(i) Development of activities without government support
(j) Definite structure	(j) Structure less
(k) Permanent and stable	(k) Temporary and instable
(l) Official channels of communication	(l) Own communication, commonly known as grapevine

Many of the research studies have identified the nature of direct relationships between formal and informal sectors. Bienefeld's (1975) study in Tanzania with a tentative framework assumes that many small scale operators are engaged in a process of production and of technological development but their ability to develop cumulatively over the terms of trade, by their dependence on large scale industry for inputs (often illegally obtained) and by the fact that when the markets they serve grow beyond a certain size this will not be a gradual but accelerating stimulus to further will not be a gradual development of the forces of production. Instead it will trigger a discontinuous shift to international technology, which will incorporate this market by virtue of its efficiency and / or its market power the latter based on effectively unlimited access to capital and on the establishment of brand name products through heavy advertising (Bienefeld 1975:56). Thus, exploitative character of linkages has been identified by Bienefeld.

Bose (1978) in his study explains the exploitative character of linkages in the urban economy of Calcutta. According to him, the informal sector enterprises perform two basic functions. First, they produce cheap goods for rural and urban poor, who are finding it increasingly difficult to purchase high cost, standard industrial goods. This is based on the low wages in this sector. The second function is to supply the large units with huge trading profit through an unequal exchange relationship. Thus, the poor in the informal sector operate in a separate market both for resource inputs and outputs, which is highly unfavourable to them, the gains being appropriated by the large sector.

Other studies including Bose's shows that official programmes which aim at stimulating industry in the informal sector are of little use in practice.

Breman (1976:1874) explains that neither can increase aid by the State be expected as long as the political system is dominated by interests, which are linked to the formal sector.

Papola (1979) identifies the informal manufacturing activities, which are linked up vertically to the formal sector through market and technology linkages. He concludes that although the informal sector provides a significant part of goods and services in the urban economy and generates employment to practically the entire residual labour force, its growth largely depends on the fortunes of the formal sector.

Jagannathan (1987) focuses on the direct linkage between formal and informal sectors in developing countries are the result of the existence of a large parallel urban informal sector.

In Datta Choudhury's (1989) formulation, formal and informal sectors are linked together because capital costs and wages differ between them. Informal sector will exist as long as these differences exit. If cheap credit is provided to informal sector, it will in due course of time specialize in producing intermediate products. It may even completely take over their production from formal sector.

Peattie (1980) in her study of small manufacturing enterprises in Bogota, Colombia finds that these enterprises served two distinct types of clientele. Firstly, enterprises were producing on inferior and cheaper product in a way, which makes it accessible to persons who can neither buy in large quantities nor transport for long distances. The other type served a small and individualized market (as in custom made furniture and shoes) or where a great deal of flexibility in marketing is advantageous (as in street vending and illegal occupations).

Operations Research Group (1980) in their study of informal sector in Madras looks at the backward and forward linkages for informal enterprises in manufacturing, trading and service activities. They find that it was more in terms of resource inputs that a variety of linkages with large dealers were common. However, the activities on the whole were more individual customer oriented. Only the craft based items, there were some links with other dealers.

Stark (1982) has extended Harris-Todaro model by incorporating a linkage coefficient to denote the connection between formal and informal sectors. The coefficient can assume both positive and negative values. Thus, expansion of formal sector can lead to both expansion and construction of informal sector. One more possibility is considered, viz., if rural migrants take up informal sector jobs, a negative signal about their human capital acquisition is flashed and their future employment and earning prospects are harmed. Therefore, the journey from formal sector to informal sector is easy but not vice versa. The model disposes that the dominance of formal sector cannot be presumed in migration decisions. It arrives at the result that the determinants of informal sector growth originate in formal sector but the role of informal sector in urban growth cannot be predetermined analytically.

So far as the indirect linkages are concerned, it refers to those generated by the goods and services produced in the informal sector for a clientele whose income is dependent on the formal sector. The activities namely building and furnishing of middle class houses, repairs and maintenance services, trading of fresh vegetables, fish, fruits etc. and of course are dependent on the income of a clientele who in turn is dependent on formal sector activities. Thus, a growth in the formal sector productivity and wages obviously creates the additional demand for these activities.

Besides, these types of direct indirect relationships, there also exist social dependency linkages, which have their basis in the lack of economic security. A complete lack of public welfare or unemployment compensation, coupled with a highly irregular and insecure nature of income, forces these people into either social dependency relationships or petty entrepreneurships (Mehta 1985:329).

Therefore, it can be concluded that the informal sector is in no way an independent and exclusive entity rather it is linked to the formal sector and the rest of the economy.

The possibility of growth and expansion of the sector largely depends on the nature and type of linkages that are prevailing in reality.

INFORMAL VS HOUSEHOLD AND UNDERGROUND ECONOMY

While the divergence between informal and underground activities is the subtlest, it is also imperative to discriminate between other forms of non-measured, non-taxed, and/or non-regulated activities. Several scholars have argued that a distinction can be made between households, informal, underground and illegal activities (ILO 1993b; Thomas 1992). In fact, as much of the research in developing countries has revealed there is a continuum, not only between informal and formal activities, but also between household, informal, underground and illegal activities. However, for policy, measurement and analytical purposes it is important to distinguish between them. Initiating with the household sector, the informal sector could be defined as the set of activities, enterprises, income or persons, which satisfy certain characteristics and which are by definition, not part of the household sector, and so on.

The term hidden economy refers to the output from all productive activities, enterprises, income or people, which are unmeasured in gross domestic product and/or untaxed and/or unregulated. Thus the hidden economy comprises a wide range of productive activities from housework to organized crime. These can be grouped into four main categories namely, the household sector, the informal sector, the underground sector and the illegal sector.

Add to, the household sector as the set of household productive economic activities that produce goods and services for own consumption within the same household and which are unmeasured and/or untaxed and/or unregulated because they are outside the SNA production boundary. The household sector includes those activities that fall within the general production boundary but not within the SNA production boundary. Some scholars have argued for the inclusion of non-quantitatively significant household activities in the SNA, particularly in developing countries where they may contribute considerably to livelihoods . In developing and transition countries where social services are extremely limited and incomes are very low, household activities are an important source of income and employment for a significant share of the population.

The informal sector is defined as the set of productive economic activities, which fall within the SNA (1993) production boundary and are unmeasured untaxed and/or unregulated, not because of deliberate attempts to evade the payment of taxes or infringe labour or other legislation, but because they are undertaken to meet basic needs. The ILO (1993b) and SNA (1993) also argue for the need to distinguish informal sector activities from underground activities on the basis that the former are not necessarily performed with the deliberate intention of avoiding the payment of taxes, social security contributions or complying with certain legal standards, while the latter are. The ILO (1993b) defines the informal sector as the set of units engaged in the production of goods or services with the primary objective of generating employment and incomes to the persons concerned. Production units of the informal sector are defined as a subset of household unincorporated enterprises. Household enterprises are units engaged in the production of goods or services which are not constituted as separate legal entities independently of the households or household members that own them, and for which no complete set of accounts are available which would permit a clear distinction of the production activities of the enterprises from the other activities of their owners and the identification of any flows of income and capital between the enterprise and the owners. Indeed, since its conception the informal sector has been of interest in developing countries because it is an important source of income and employment for the poor. It is a survival strategy in countries where there is insufficient formal employment opportunities, where wages may be too low to cover the cost of living and where social safety nets such as unemployment or pension benefits are either lacking or also insufficient to cover the cost of living. As such, it should include all productive activities, which generate income and employment for the poor, and not just those that take place in household enterprises with certain characteristics.

The concepts of underground and illegal production as defined in the SNA (1993) consists of legal productive economic activities that are part of the production boundary and are unmeasured and/or untaxed and or unregulated because they are deliberately concealed from public authorities for the following kind of reasons to avoid the payment of income, value added or other taxes; to avoid the payment of social security contributions; to avoid having to meet certain legal standards such as minimum wages, maximum hours, safety or health standards, etc. to avoid complying with certain administrative procedures such as completing statistical questionnaires or other administrative forms.

The illegal sector consists of productive activities that generate goods and services forbidden by law or that are unlawful when carried out by unauthorized producers. There are two types of illegal activities: those that produce goods and services whose sale, distribution or possession is forbidden by law, and activities which are usually legal, but become illegal when carried out by unauthorized producers (SNA 1993). Furthermore illegal activities are included in the SNA production boundary if the transactions involved are based on mutual consent.

It is observed that the borderline among household, informal, underground and illegal sectors may not be very clear and activities may often belong to more than one sector. The Figure 1 illustrates how these sectors are interrelated (Bernabè 2002). It may not be obvious whether an activity is part of the household or informal sector (area A in figure 2). Subsistence farming, for instance, may be considered part of the household sector if it is not quantitatively significant in respect to total agricultural production (as may be the case in many developed countries), whereas it may be part of the informal sector if it is quantitatively significant (as may be the case in many developing and some transition countries). Similarly, it may be difficult to determine whether an activity is part of the illegal, household, or informal sectors (area B). The boundary is similarly difficult to define between informal and underground and between underground and illegal activities. Thus, construction activities undertaken by unregistered construction workers, for instance, may be considered informal or underground (area C), depending on whether or not they are deliberately concealed and whether they are undertaken to meet basic needs (they could of course be both). Finally, as highlighted in the SNA (1993), production that does not comply with certain safety, health or other standards, for instance, could be described as either underground or illegal (area D).

Figure 2: The relationship among Informal, Household, Illegal and Underground Economy

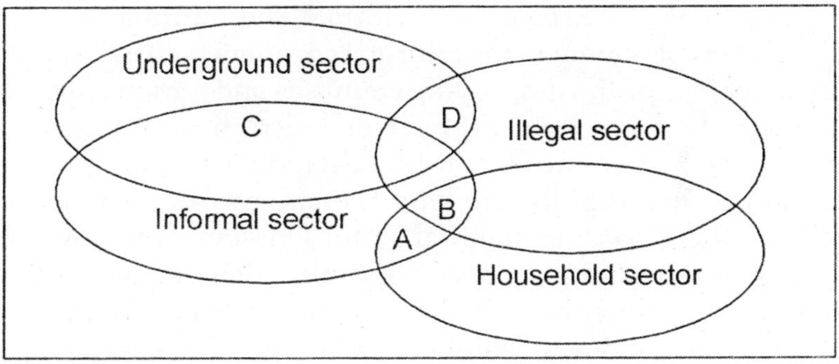

Source: Bernabè [2002]

CONCLUDING REMARKS

The term informal sector was first used by Keith Hart (1970) in a study of urban Ghana and it has been further refined by ILO (1972) while studying the employment situation in Kenya. The informal sector is characterized by ease of entry, small-scale operations, family ownership of enterprise, labour intensive and adaptive technology, lack of support and recognition from the government, competitive and unregulated product market, unprotected labour market, undisclosed income or tax evasion etc. In addition to these, the other characteristics include deplorable working condition and low level of wage, low capital accumulation and reinvestment, insecure and temporary nature of employment etc. Besides, the informal sector may be classified into four categories on the basis of their nature of works namely, home based workers, self-employment workers, piece wageworkers and time wageworkers. The causes of informalisation may be of economic recession, evasion of tax as well as excessive governmental regulation of market sector.

The urban economy can be classified broadly as formal and informal sectors. As far as the contrasting characteristics of the two sectors are concerned, the entry into the informal sector labour market is unrestricted and level of earning is also very low, while that in formal sector labour market, entry is restricted and level of earning is high. Apart from the distinguishing characteristics, there exist strong direct and indirect inter-linkages between formal and informal sectors.

The employment in the informal economy has risen rapidly in all regions of the developing countries and various forms of non-standard employment have emerged in most regions of the developed countries. In the developing economy, it was only the once rapidly growing economies that experienced substantial growth of modern sector employment. However, in the wake of the recent economic crisis, most of these countries experienced a substantial decline in formal wage employment and a concomitant rise in informal employment. How many retrenched workers have been reinstated in formal jobs as these economies have begun to recover from the crisis is not yet known. Why has the informal economy continued to expand and grow? There is no simple answer to this question as different causal factors are at work in different contexts. However, some mix of the following sets of factors would explain the persistence or expansion of the informal economy in most countries, regions, or industries. The first set of factors relates to the pattern of economic growth. Some countries have experienced little or no economic growth, while others have pursued capital-intensive growth or what some observers call jobless growth. In both such contexts, not enough jobs are created for all those seeking work. Many frustrated formal job seekers find employment or create their own work in the informal economy. Another pattern of economic growth namely high tech growth tends to create more high-skill service sector jobs than lower-skill manufacturing jobs. In such contexts, those without the skills to compete for high-tech formal jobs find work or continue to work in the informal economy. There is another, more optimistic, scenario namely, growth from below. In some countries the tiny business and micro-business sectors are more dynamic and create more jobs than the formal sector. The second set of factors has to do with economic restructuring and economic crisis. Available evidence suggests that during periods of economic adjustment whether due to economic reforms or economic crises, the informal economy tends to expand. This is because retrenched workers move into the informal economy when public enterprises are closed or the public sector is downsized. This is also because households need to supplement formal sector incomes with informal earnings in response to inflation or cutbacks in public services. The third set of factors relates to the globalization of the world economy. Global trade and investment patterns tend to privilege capital, especially companies that can move quickly and easily across borders and to disadvantage labour especially lower-skilled workers that cannot migrate easily or at all. To enhance their global competitiveness more and more investors are moving to countries that have low labour costs or shifting to informal employment arrangements. Furthermore, there has been a radical restructuring of production and distribution in many key industries characterized by outsourcing or subcontracting through global commodity chains. The net result is that more and more workers are being paid very low wages and many of them have to absorb the non-wage costs of production. Globalization also tends to privilege large companies who can capture new markets quickly and easily to the disadvantage of small and micro entrepreneurs who face difficulties gaining knowledge of much less access to emerging markets. In sum, globalization puts pressure on low-skilled workers and petty producers by weakening their bargaining power and subjecting them to increasing competition. Why should the persistence or expansion of the informal economy be of interest or concern? There is a link between working in the informal economy and being poor. Average incomes are lower in the informal economy than in the formal sector. As a result, a higher percentage of people working in the informal economy, relative to the formal sector, are poor. However, there is no simple relationship between working in the informal economy and being poor or working in the formal sector and escaping poverty (Sethuraman 1998 and Thomas 1995). The relationship between informal employment and poverty appears only when informal workers are classified by employment status and by industry or trade. Informal incomes worldwide tend to decline as one move across the following types of employment: from employer to self-employed to informal and casual wageworkers to industrial outworker. The link between working in the informal economy and being poor is stronger for women than for men. A higher percentage of women than men worldwide work in the informal economy. Moreover, there is a gender gap in incomes and wages in the informal economy. This is because women worldwide are under-represented in higher income employment statuses in the informal economy (employer and self-employed) and over represented in the lower income statuses (casual wage worker and industrial outworker). Available evidence suggests that globalization of the economy tends to reinforce the links between poverty, informality and gender. This is because global competition tends to encourage formal firms to shift formal wageworkers to informal employment arrangements without minimum wages, assured work, or benefits and to encourage informal units to shift workers from semi-permanent contracts without minimum wages or benefits to piece-rate or casual work arrangements without either assured work, minimum wages, or benefits. This is also because globalization often leads to shifts from secure self-employment to more precarious self-employment, as producers and traders lose their market niche. With these shifts, and as more and more men enter the informal economy, women tend to be pushed to the lowest income end of the informal economy. But globalization can also lead to new opportunities for those who work in the informal economy in the form of new jobs for wageworkers or new markets for the self-employed. However, a collaborative effort on the part of grassroots organizations of those who work in the informal economy with sympathetic representatives of non-governmental, research, government, private sector and international development organizations is needed to enable the most vulnerable segments of society to seize these opportunities. There needs to be a much more detailed interpretation of who is in the informal economy and what they are doing, as well as a more comprehensive analysis of how globalization, particularly trade and investment policies, are affecting the employment arrangements and income sources of those who work in the informal economy.

REFERENCES

Banerjee, N. (1985), *Women Workers in the Unorganised Sector*. Sangam Books, Hyderabad.

Bernabè, S. (2002), *Informal Employment in Countries in Transition: A Conceptual Framework*. CASE Paper 56, Centre for Analysis of Social Exclusion, London School of Economics, London.

Bienefeld, M. (1975), The Informal Sector and Peripheral Capitalism: the Case of Tanzania. *Institute of Development Studies Bulletin*, 6: 53-73.

Bose, A. N. (1978), *Calcutta and Rural Bengal, Small Sector Symbioses*. Minerva Publications, Calcutta.

Breman, J. (1976), A Dualistic Labour System? A Critique of the Informal Sector, Concept I: the Informal Sector. *Economic and Political Weekly*, XI (48): 1870-1875.

Datta Choudhuri, T. (1989), A Theoretical Analysis of the Informal Sector. *World Development*, 17 (3): 351-355.

Eapen, M. (2001), Women in Informal Sector in Kerala: Need for Re-examination. *Economic and Political Weekly*, XXXVI (20): 2390-2392.

Feige, E. L. (1990), Defining and Estimating Underground and Informal Economies: the New Institutional Economic Approach. *World Development*, 18 (7): 989-1002.

Gerxhani, K. (1999), *The Informal Sector in Developed and Less Developed Countries*. Tinbergen Institute Discussion Paper No. 1999-083/2, Tinbergen Institute, The Netherlands.

Gibson, B. and Kelly, B. (1994), A Classical Theory of the Informal Sector. *The Manchester School of Economic and Social Studies*, LXII (1): 81-96.

Hart, K. (1970), Small-Scale Entrepreneurs in Ghana and Development Planning. *The Journal of Development Studies*, 6 (4): 104-120.

Hart, K. (1973), Informal Income Opportunities and Urban Employment in Ghana. *Journal of Modern African Studies*, 11 (1): 61-89.

Himmelweit, S. (2002), Making Visible the Hidden Economy: the Case for Gender Impact Analysis of Economic Policy. *Feminist Economics*, 8(1): 49-70.

Hussmanns, R. (1998), *Developments in the Design and Implementation of Informal Sector and Similar Surveys: A Review of National Practices and Experiences*. DOC.ICLS/16/RD2, International Labour Office, Geneva.

International Labour Organization (1972), *Employment, Income and Equity: a Strategy for Increasing Productive Employment in Kenya*. Geneva.

International Labour Organization (1993a), *Highlights of the Conference and Text of the Three Resolutions Adopted*. Report of the XVth International Conference of Labour Statisticians, 19-28 January, Geneva.

International Labour Organization (1993b), *Resolution Concerning Statistics of Employment in the Informal Sector*. Geneva.

International Labour Organization (1999), *Employment in the Global Economy: How Training Matters*. World Employment Report, Geneva.

Jagannathan, N. V. (1987), *Informal Markets in Developing Countries*. Oxford University Press Inc., New York.

Joshi, H and Joshi, V. (1976), *Surplus Labour and City: A Study of Bombay*. Oxford University Press, New Delhi.

Mazumdar, D. (1975), *The Urban Informal Sector*. World Bank Staff Working Paper No. 211, World Bank, Washington DC.

Mazumdar, D. (1977), Notes on the Urban Informal Sector. In: Subbiah Kanappan (ed.). *Urban Labour Market Behaviour in Developing Countries*. International Institute of Labour Studies, Geneva.

McCrohan, K., Smith, J. and Adams, T. (1991), Consumer Purchases in Informal Markets: Estimates for the 1980s, Prospects for the 1990s. *Journal of Retailing*, 67(1): 22-50.

Mehta, M. (1985), Urban Informal Sector: Concepts, Indian Evidence and Policy Implications. *Economic and Political Weekly*, XX (8): 326-332.

Nattrass, N. J. (1987), Street Trading in Transkei: A Struggle against Poverty, Persecution and Prosecution. *World Development*, 15 (7): 861-875.

Operations Research Group (1980), *Informal Sector Enterprises in Madras: A Profile and Strategy*. Mimeo, Madras.

Papola, T. S. (1979), *Informal Sector in an Urban Economy: A Study in Ahmedabad*. Giri Institute of Development Studies, Mimeo, Lucknow.

Papola, T. S. (1980), Informal Sector: Concept and Policy. *Economic and Political Weekly*, 15 (8): 817-823.

Papola, T. S. (1981), *Urban Informal Sector in a Developing Economy*. Vikash Publishing House, New Delhi.

Peattie, L. R. (1980), Anthropological Perspectives on the Concepts of Dualism, the Informal Sector and Marginality in Developing Urban Economies. *International Regional Science Review*, 5 (1): 1-31.

Psacharopoulos, G. and Tzannatos, Z. (1992), *Women's Employment and Pay in Latin America: Overview and Methodology*. World Bank Regional and Sectoral Studies, Washington DC.

Rakowski, C. A. (1994), Convergence and Divergence in the Informal Sector Debate: a Focus on Latin America, 1984-92. *World Development*, 22 (4): 501-516.

Romatet, E. (1983), Calcutta's Informal Sector: Theory and Reality. *Economic and Political Weekly*, 18 (50): 2115-2128.

Sarkar, S. (2004a), Extending Social Security Coverage to the Informal Sector in India. *Social Change*, 34 (4): 122-130.

Sarkar, S. (2004b), Theorising in Informal Sector: Concept and Context. *Social Action*, 54(4): 356-373.

Sethuraman, S.V. (1976), The Urban Informal Sector: Concept, Measurement and Policy. *International Labour Review*, 114: 69-81.

Sethuraman, S. V. 1998. *Gender, Informality and Poverty: A Global Review*. World Bank, Washington DC.

Squire, L. (1981), *Employment Policy in Developing Countries: A Survey of Issues and Evidence*. Oxford University Press, New York.

Stark, O. (1982), On Modeling the Informal Sector. *World Development*, 10 (5): 413-416.

System of National Accounts (1993), *System of National Accounts, 1993*. World Bank, Washington DC.

Thomas, J. (1992), *Informal Economic Activity*. Harvester Wheatsheaf, Hemel Hempstead.

Thomas, J. J. (1995), *Surviving in the City: the Urban Informal Sector in Latin America*. CT: Pluto Press, East Haven.

Tokman, V. E. (1978), An Exploration into the Nature of Informal-Formal Relationships. *World Development*, 6 (9-10): 1065-1075.

United Nations (1991), *The World's Women 1970-1990*. New York.

United Nations Development Programme (1995), *Human Development Report 1995*. Oxford University Press, Oxford.

Unni, J. (2001), Gender and Informality in the Labour Market in South Asia. *Economic and Political Weekly*, 36(26): 2360-2377.

Weeks, J. (1975), Policies for Expanding Employment in the Informal Urban Sector of Developing Economics. *International Labour Review*, 3 (1): 1-13.

World Development Report (1995), *Workers in an Integrating World*. World Bank, Washington DC.

5

FARMERS COMMITTING SUICIDE

G. SREEDHAR & K. DASARATHARAMAIAH

INTRODUCTION

There have been an escalating number of farmers committing suicide in different parts of India during the last decade. It has widely been noticed that the farmers committed suicide primarily on account of indebtedness, attributed to losses in the cultivation of commercial crops triggered by various causes ranging from the use of fake seeds and spurious pesticides or insecticides to the lack of access to timely and adequate institutional credit and marketing, and absence of remunerative prices for the agricultural produce. Despite the technological advancements made in agriculture, it needs to be admitted that these are largely confined to the irrigated regions and agriculture is still a gamble with monsoons in many arid and semi-arid zones. In the event of crop failure during successive seasons, the farmers are invariably forced to fall into the clutches of indebtedness. The Royal Commission on Agriculture rightly pointed it out way back in 1927 that 'the Indian farmer is born in debt, lives in debt, dies in debt and bequeaths debt'. Indebtedness has been the part and parcel of the life of farmers in India. On account of their gullible nature, illiteracy and ignorance, the farmers have been an easy prey to the moneylenders and traders who exploit them in many ways. Besides, the agro-economic characteristics of the country such as the excessive dependence on monsoons, large number of small and uneconomic holdings, and lack of access to institutional credit and marketing also contribute to growing indebtedness among the farmers. Perhaps, there would be no farmer, whether small or large, without any debt. Then the question arises as to why only a tiny number of farmers are resorting to suicide under conditions of severe socio-economic distress, reportedly due to losses in agriculture. Since the macro level situation pertaining to a particular area or crop is common to all farmers, the reasons for farmers' suicides must be specific to the individual farmers, which need to be probed in greater detail. A glance at the available literature[1] reveals divergent views, which necessitates more number of micro-level studies to understand the dynamics of the issue.

In this backdrop, it becomes pertinent to examine the following questions. What are the specific circumstances under which the farmers have committed suicide? To what extent these could be attributed to agriculture-related indebtedness? What other factors are at work in driving the farmers towards suicide? What is the nature of relief and rehabilitation measures initiated by the government and their effectiveness in providing succour to the families of the deceased farmers? This study seeks to provide answers to these questions based on empirical evidence from Anantapur district of Andhra Pradesh, which occupies a prominent place in the state in terms of the number of farmers committing suicide during the last decade.

Anantapur is the largest district in Andhra Pradesh in terms of geographical area accounting for 19130 sq kms comprising a population of 36.39 lakhs according to 2001 Census. The district receives the lowest average annual rainfall of 544 mm in the state and is known for recurring droughts and large-scale seasonal migration to the neighbouring districts / states. The district is relatively backward in terms of literacy rate at 57 per cent when compared to the state average of 61 per cent for the population aged 7 years and above according to the 2001 Census. The district has a thin forest cover (about 10 per cent of the geographical area), and the net irrigated area formed hardly about 14 per cent of the net sown area. The main source of irrigation is wells/bore wells, accounting for about 72 per cent of net irrigated area, followed by canals 22 per cent and ponds/tanks and other sources the rest (Government of Andhra Pradesh 2001:63-64, 66 & 110). Groundnut is the principal crop grown in the district accounting for over 71 per cent of the gross cropped area. The other principal crops of some significance are paddy (5.7 percent) and jowar (3.2 per cent). Besides groundnut, the other important commercial crops grown in the district are mulberry, sweet orange, papaya, pomegranate, guava and mango. The district experienced recurring droughts as a result of both scanty and erratic rainfall, leading to crop loss in respect of all the major crops. The agricultural economy of the district essentially revolves around groundnut cultivation. There has been a failure of groundnut crop for four successive years from 2000-01 to 2003-04 due to capricious and/or scanty rainfall[2], causing untold miseries to the farming community. In addition, the water table levels have gone down considerably, and the farmers have gone for more and more number of bore wells to save the standing commercial crops on which they pinned their hopes. There has been some respite for the farmers during 2004-05 as they obtained relatively good crop of groundnut in many mandals of the district, even though the actual rainfall was deficient when compared to the normal rainfall[3].

It appears that farmers' suicides have become an all-pervasive phenomenon in the district, with 60 out of 63 revenue mandals having reported such cases. It is unfortunate that the number of farmers committing suicide has not come down, despite the efforts of the state government to establish a 'help line' at the district headquarters to prevent the farmers in economic distress from committing suicide. According to the information furnished by the district administration, 276 farmers committed suicide from July 1998 to April 2005 in Anantapur district in respect of whom the relief and rehabilitation measures were initiated, even though the unofficial figures compiled by other sources based on media reports and their own studies were much higher[4]. Of these, 66 farmers (24 per cent) resorted to suicide after formation of the present government in the state in May 2004. In accordance with the Government Order (GO) Ms. No.421 of the Revenue (DA-II) Department dated 1-6-2004 issued by the Government of Andhra Pradesh outlining the economic support and rehabilitation package to the families of the deceased farmers, the district administration has taken steps to provide financial assistance to the tune of Rs.1 lakh as ex-gratia to the family / next of kin of the deceased farmer as an economic support, besides loan settlement up to a ceiling of Rs.50000 as one-time settlement to the creditors. In addition, the rehabilitation package envisaged the admission of children in social welfare hostels, allotment of houses under the Indira Awaas Yojana (weaker sections housing scheme of the Government of India), provision of economic support and old age pension under government schemes to the dependents of the deceased farmers as a measure of social cushion.

OBJECTIVE AND METHOD USED

The main objective of the present study is to identify the factors forcing the farmers to commit suicide. Besides, it seeks to determine to what extent these could be attributed to agriculture-related indebtedness. It also examines the utility of the relief and rehabilitation measures initiated by the government and comes out with suggestions to implement the GO in this regard in an effective manner. Based on the findings, the study would throw light on the measures required to prevent farmers' suicides.

For the purpose of the present study, the official list of 276 farmers who committed suicide between July 1998 and April 2005 in Anantapur district was taken as the universe. The study was conducted on a sample of 30 deceased farmers' households, drawn on the basis of stratified proportionate sampling method, giving proportionate representation to the three revenue divisions in the district. The three revenue divisions in the district, viz., Anantapur, Dharmavaram and Penukonda, accounted for 137, 56 and 83 cases of farmers' suicides respectively during July 1998-April 2005. Accordingly, the sample was drawn choosing 15 households from Anantapur, 6 households from Dharmavaram and 9 households from Penukonda. In each revenue division, two or three revenue mandals were chosen keeping in view the number of cases to be covered. The sample chosen for the study constitutes about 11 per cent of the universe, and is considered as a large sample in statistical terms based on which valid inference could be drawn. The sample is also representative in nature as it is spread over 26 villages in 8 revenue mandals from all the three revenue divisions of the district. Case study method was followed for eliciting information from the sample households regarding the factors responsible for the suicide of the deceased farmers, the nature of relief and rehabilitation measures initiated by the government and their effectiveness. The information provided by the respondents was crosschecked with the secondary data available with the district administration. Where necessary, this information was also crosschecked with a few villagers to ascertain the truth. The field study was undertaken during May 2005.

RESULT AND DISCUSSION

The results of the study are presented in four sections, viz., basic characteristics of the sample deceased farmers, their land particulars and indebtedness, chief reasons for their suicide, and relief and rehabilitation measures initiated by the government and their utility.

Basic Characteristics of the Sample Deceased Farmers

The basic characteristics of the sample deceased farmers such as the sex, age, education and caste along with their household size, dependency ratio and visual rating of poverty of their households are shown in Table 1. It may be noted that out of 30 sample deceased farmers, there was only one female. All but two of them were aged below 60 years, implying that they belonged to economically productive age

Table 1
Basic Characteristics of the Sample Deceased Farmers

Case number	*Sex*	*Age*	*Education*	*Household size**	*Dependency ratio*	*Caste-category*	*Visual rating of poverty*
9	F	45	Illiterate	4	1.00	OC	Non-poor
8	M	35	High school	3	2.00	BC	Non-poor
7	M	40	College	4	3.00	BC	Poor
6	M	50	Illiterate	3	0.50	OC	Poor
5	M	50	Illiterate	4	1.00	BC	Poor
4	M	40	Illiterate	4	3.00	BC	Very poor
30	M	45	Illiterate	8	7.00	OC	Non-poor
3	M	75	Illiterate	5	4.00	OC	Very poor
29	M	58	Illiterate	6	1.00	OC	Non-poor
28	M	45	High school	7	2.50	SC	Very poor
27	M	37	High school	4	3.00	OC	Non-poor
26	M	50	Middle school	3	2.00	OC	Non-poor
25	M	45	Illiterate	5	1.50	BC	Poor
24	M	60	Illiterate	6	2.00	BC	Poor
23	M	45	Illiterate	4	1.00	OC	Poor
22	M	55	Illiterate	5	4.00	ST	Non-poor
21	M	38	Illiterate	6	2.00	BC	Poor
20	M	38	College	4	3.00	OC	Non-poor
2	M	35	Illiterate	4	1.00	OC	Poor
19	M	50	Middle school	5	1.50	BC	Poor
18	M	32	Illiterate	4	3.00	SC	Very poor

Contd...

Case number	*Sex*	*Age*	*Education*	*Household size**	*Dependency ratio*	*Caste-category*	*Visual rating of poverty*
17	M	55	High school	8	1.67	OC	Poor
16	M	35	Middle school	3	2.00	OC	Poor
15	M	54	College	5	4.00	OC	Poor
14	M	40	Primary	5	1.50	BC	Poor
13	M	50	Illiterate	5	1.50	OC	Poor
12	M	50	Illiterate	4	3.00	OC	Poor
11	M	55	High school	4	3.00	OC	Poor
10	M	24	College	3	0.50	OC	Non-poor
1	M	49	Illiterate	3	2.00	OC	Non-poor

* Including the sample deceased farmer.

group. The average age at the time of death of the sample deceased farmer worked out to 46 years. Even though 17 out of 30 sample deceased farmers were illiterate, there were nine sample deceased farmers who had high school/ college education. Only six households had 6 members or more, with the average household size for all the sample households being 4.5. Thus, most of the sample deceased farmers had small households and killed themselves at a prime age. A considerable proportion of them (30 per cent) had reasonably good education (high school level and above). However, the dependency ratio (number of dependents per earning member) was considerably higher among the sample households. One-third of the sample households had a dependency ratio of three or more. Only one-fifth of them had a dependency ratio of one or less. On the whole, there were more dependents per earner in a vast majority (80 per cent) of the sample households. The deceased farmers belonged to all the caste groups in the district, with a majority of them belonging to the other castes (OCs), followed by the backward classes (BCs), the scheduled castes (SCs) and the scheduled tribes (STs). Regarding the visual rating of poverty of the sample households, a majority were poor (53.3 per cent) or very poor (13.4 per cent). One-third of the sample households were, however, non-poor.

Land Particulars and Indebtedness of the Sample Deceased Farmers

The land particulars, amount of debt and reasons for indebtedness of the sample deceased farmers are presented in Table 2. It could be seen from Table 2 that the sample deceased farmers owned a total of 137.97 acres of agricultural land, out of which 95.9 acres (70 per cent) was unirrigated and 42.07 acres (30 per cent) irrigable dry (irrigated under wells / bore wells). All but one household had own land. Besides, six deceased farmers had leased-in 27.2 acres. The total land cultivated by the sample deceased farmers stood at 165.17 acres. The average landholding per deceased farmer worked out to 4.6 acres (own) and 5.5 acres (cultivated). A vast majority

Table 2
Land Particulars and Indebtedness of the Sample Deceased Farmers' Households

Case number	*Land owned (Rain fed)*	*Land owned (Irrigable dry)*	*Land leased -in*	*Total land cultivated*	*Debt (Rs.)*	*Major reasons for indebtedness*
1	1.96	0.00	0.00	1.96	52500	Crop failure+ House construction
2	0.00	3.00	0.00	3.00	84200	Failure of bore wells + Lack of remunerative prices#
3	0.00	2.00	0.00	2.00	65000	Ill-health of wife and self
4	2.00	0.00	0.00	2.00	60000	Ill-health of wife and self
5	6.00	0.00	0.00	6.00	70000	Crop failure + Marriage + Bad habits
6	3.50	3.10	0.00	6.60	147000	Failure of bore wells + Crop loss + Cheating by traders#
7	0.00	1.94	0.00	1.94	200000	Failure of bore wells + Crop loss#
8	2.00	2.00	0.00	4.00	196000	Crop failure + Ill health
9	0.00	0.00	3.80	3.80	42000	Domestic expenses*
10	3.50	2.50	0.00	6.00	165000	Crop failure + Domestic expenses*
11	7.00	0.00	3.90	10.90	210000	Crop failure + Marriage + Domestic expenses
12	2.13	0.00	0.00	2.13	80000	Domestic expenses
13	3.31	0.00	2.00	5.31	170000	Crop failure + House construction + Ill health
14	0.00	3.50	0.00	3.50	250000	Failure of bore wells +Crop loss +house construction
15	7.00	1.53	0.00	8.53	245000	Crop failure + loss in business+ domestic expenses*
16	0.00	3.67	0.00	3.67	130000	Failure of bore wells + Crop loss#
17	3.00	2.00	0.00	5.00	80000	Failure of bore wells + Crop loss#
18	1.75	0.00	3.50	5.25	70000	Crop failure + Ill health
19	3.00	2.00	0.00	5.00	52000	Failure of bore wells + Crop loss#
20	0.50	2.50	0.00	3.00	90000	Crop failure + Marriage + Involvement in politics

Contd...

Case number	*Land owned (Rain fed)*	*Land owned (Irrigable dry)*	*Land leased -in*	*Total land cultivated*	*Debt (Rs.)*	*Major reasons for indebtedness*
21	3.00	0.00	0.00	3.00	114000	Gambling + Addiction to alcohol
22	4.41	0.00	0.00	4.41	92000	Loss in business + Domestic expenses + Education
23	2.50	0.00	0.00	2.50	100000	Gambling +Addiction to alcohol
24	6.50	0.00	4.00	10.50	400000	Crop failure +Domestic expenses
25	6.20	0.00	0.00	6.20	175000	Crop failure + Loss in business + Marriage
26	0.00	11.00	0.00	11.00	250000	Crop loss due to fake seed +Failure of bore wells#
27	6.14	0.00	0.00	6.14	135000	Crop failure+ Non-payment by sharecroppers#
28	7.50	0.00	0.00	7.50	36000	Crop failure + Addiction to alcohol
29	3.00	1.33	10.00	14.33	189000	Crop failure + Loss from leased-in land + Ill health#
30	10.00	0.00	0.00	10.00	135000	Crop failure + Domestic expenses*
Total	95.9	42.07	27.2	165.17	4084700	

* Debt amount and reasons for indebtedness are not genuine

Exclusively related to agriculture

of them were marginal, small and medium farmers, with only one-sixth of them cultivating more than 10 acres.

The sample farmers reportedly had a total debt of Rs.4084700, the average per head being Rs. 137157. About 47 per cent of them had a debt of Rs. 1 lakh or less, 37 per cent Rs. 1-2 lakhs, and only 14 per cent more than Rs. 2 lakhs. There were more reasons than one for the indebtedness of the deceased farmers. The chief reason for indebtedness was exclusively agriculture-related in respect of only nine farmers (30 per cent), as presented in Box 1. It may be seen from Box 1 that all these farmers landed themselves into debt due to severe losses in agriculture mainly on account of failure of bore wells and the resultant crop loss. In the case of five farmers (16.7 per cent), the reasons stated and the debt amount were reported to be not genuine, including the case of a person who encountered a failure in love affair and suspected to have AIDS, while there were three cases (10 per cent) where the deceased persons committed suicide on account of vices like addiction to alcohol and gambling or involvement in extra-marital affair (for details, see Box 2). Thus, the cases that are not genuine constituted over one-fourth of the sample deceased farmers. This is vindicated by a higher proportion of non-genuine cases out of the total cases of farmers' suicides reported in Andhra Pradesh both during the Telugu Desam Party (TDP) regime from 1999 to 2004 and during the 14 months Congress regime since May 2004, according to the findings of the Commission of Inquiry into the Farmers' Suicides in Andhra Pradesh[5]. In all other cases, the main reasons for indebtedness include, besides losses from agriculture, house construction, marriage of children / siblings, domestic expenses, and loss in business. However, it needs to be borne in mind that even though the sample farmers borrowed for other than agricultural purposes, they had no other source of income and pinned their hopes on the anticipated income from agriculture to repay such loans.

It was noted that all but one of the sample deceased farmers were owner-cultivators. A majority of them took to agriculture seriously and took decisions on their own with regard to use of seed, fertilisers, pesticides/ insecticides, and the loans made, without consulting or revealing the details to their family members. In most cases, the survivors informed that the deceased farmers did not disclose the details of the amount and source of borrowing to any of the family members. It appears that they took on themselves the entire burden and sole responsibility of running the household and to meet their expenses including those for agricultural purposes by making necessary borrowings with the fond hope of repaying them from out of agricultural income. The inability to derive sufficient income from agriculture due to successive crop failure seems to have pushed these farmers in economic distress. Since they did not share their burden with other family members, this might have caused severe stress on their minds forcing them to take the extreme step of ending their lives.

Box 1

Cases of Sample Deceased Farmers with Exclusively Agricultural Indebtedness

Case 2: The deceased farmer grew sweet orange, chillies, flowers and groundnut. When the well dried up, he dug as many as four bore wells together with his brothers but failed. Later two more bore wells were dug. The losses to his share worked out were Rs.30000. He took a crop loan from the bank, which got accumulated to about Rs.50000 and the bank obtained a decree from the court to auction the land. He had debts from other sources in the tune of Rs.35000. He also suffered losses due to absence of lucrative prices for chillies. He was put into intense pressure from the bank and other creditors to repay the loans. He committed suicide on the day of harvest of groundnut because he felt that income from the crop would hardly be sufficient to redeem his debts.

Case 6: To save the standing crop of sweet orange, the deceased farmer dug four bore wells out of which three failed and one bore well yielded about an inch of water. Crop loss and failure of bore wells landed him in a debt amounting to Rs.80000 with the banks, Rs.90000 for which documents were available and hand loans of Rs.45000. It was reported that he also suffered losses due to hoaxing by the traders in marketing of sweet oranges. The creditors heaped insults on him and one creditor went to the extent of manhandling him. This incident seems to have spurred him to commit suicide.

Case 7: To save about 190 orange trees that were 12 years old due to drying up of the open well, the deceased farmer dug three bore wells, but each of them worked for only 3-4 months. The total loss due to the failure of the bore wells was about Rs.1 lakh. The farmer was expecting an amount of Rs.2 lakhs from the crop by which he could repay the debts. But, the bore wells failed and the crop also, resulting in a severe loss to him and forcing him to commit suicide.

Case 16: The farmer grew drumstick trees in 2.5 acres and chillies in 0.5 acres. He dug three bore wells to save his crops, but failed to carry out the venture, thereby incurring a loss of Rs.45000 apart from the loss of standing crop. It was informed that he spent about Rs.60000 on medical treatment to his mother. He had a total debt of Rs.155000 out of which Rs.55000 was due to the bank and Rs.1 lakh to the farmers, and unable to clear off these debts he decided to end his life.

Case 17: When the open well went dry, the deceased farmer along with his brothers dug an in-well bore but did not achieve. They dug two more bore wells but became unsuccessful again. His debts amounted to Rs.4.5 lakhs, of which Rs.2 lakhs was with the bank/society and the rest with the farmers. He was growing groundnut on dry land and paddy on the irrigated land. His wife noticed that he never used to disclose anything to her or children. She told that after separation from the joint family, the agricultural holding became unviable, water declined and crops failed leading to the death of her husband.

Case 19: The farmer had an open well. He dug an in-well bore and three bore wells, but all of them failed. Only one bore well-yielded 0.5 inches water for six months and failed thereafter. This resulted in a loss of Rs.60000. The groundnut crop failed during four successive years. He had a debt of Rs.52000. He owed Rs.30000 to a farmer who fixed a date for repaying it. Unable to mobilise the money and fearing humiliation, he was reported to have committed suicide one day before that date.

Case 26: The farmer had an open well. He went for an in-well bore, which failed. He dug a bore well which yielded some water. He grew papaya but failed on account of fake seed, resulting in a loss of Rs.80000. Later, he suffered losses in papaya cultivation due to lack of water. Due to failure of bore wells and losses in agriculture, his debts accumulated to Rs.2.9 lakhs. Unable to bear the losses, he seems to have ended his life.

Case 27: The farmer had leased out 6 acres on sharecropping basis. The important crops grown were Bengal gram and groundnut. It was reported that due to successive crop failure, the sharecroppers did not pay him anything, and therefore he suffered heavy losses. Even the profits from business were invested in agriculture and this money was also lost. He had a total debt of Rs.1.35 lakh. Unable to bear this loss, he consumed pesticide to end his life.

***Case 29**: The farmer had invested Rs.80000 to purchase 1.33 acres land and dug a bore well. He cultivated about 15 acres dry land on lease basis and 7 acres on sharecropping basis due to which he suffered a loss about Rs.90000. He spent Rs.30000 towards the treatment of his daughter. He had a total debt of Rs.2.25 lakhs. Unable to bear the burden of debt, he seems to have ended his life.*

Box 2

Cases of the Sample Deceased Farmers who Died on account of Vices or where the Reasons for Indebtedness were not Genuine

Case 5: The farmer was reported to have a debt of about Rs.2 lakhs at the time of his death (as per present records, it was Rs.70000) on account of crop failure, huge expenditure on the marriage of his daughters and his own bad habits including addiction to alcohol. It was informed that in a drunken position he consumed pesticide and collapsed at once on the way to the hospital.

Case 9: The husband of the deceased female farmer had taken to the habit of gambling and used to always move around in the name of some business or the other, leaving the responsibility of running the household on her shoulders. Both the husband and wife used to quarrel with each other frequently on the issue of responsibility of the household and the marriage of their two daughters. One day, they had a quarrel while applying pesticide to the crop when she got desperate and consumed the pesticide in her hand and collapsed before taken to hospital.

Case 10: The deceased person used to stay with his parents. It was noticed in the village that he had encountered a disappointment to his love affair and he was also suspected to have got AIDS. Because of these two factors, he committed suicide at own house.

Case 15: The deceased farmer allegedly had major clash with his wife. He used to spend money lavishly which his wife did not like, and as a result she did not cooperate with him. Due to frequent quarrels with his wife, he got habituated to alcohol. He was reported to have renewed his crop loan just before his demise, out of which he spent Rs.1000 for himself over which there was continuous squabble in the house with his wife and children, who together went to the extent of manhandling him. This incident seems to have spurred him to buy pesticide the very next day and consume it on the way to the village. According to one of the villagers who knew him personally, all the documents regarding his borrowings from private sources were fictitious.

Case 21: The deceased farmer had 5.2 acres of dry land, but he did not cultivate that land for nearly three years before his demise. He had been working as a carpenter. He had a total debt of Rs.114000. He got habituated to involve in daily gambling and drinking alcohol. In a drunken state, he used to beat his wife and children frequently. His wife got dejected and left for her parents' home. He went and quarrelled with her to come back but she declined. In a state of anger, he ended his life.

Case 23: The deceased farmer had met with an accident long time back and underwent treatment at NIMHANS, Bangalore. He was accustomed to the habit of gambling and consuming alcohol. He had a total debt of about Rs.1 lakh. Unable to bear the burden of debts, he seems to have killed himself.

Case 28: The deceased farmer's elder daughter loved a boy of another caste and married him. His wife used to support that family by way of supplying provisions and meeting the expenses for which he used to beat her in a drunken state. Unable to bear the frequent beatings from her husband, she consumed poison. Immediately afterwards, he also consumed poison and both of them collapsed. The villagers informed that he did so, because he feared that his in-laws would not leave him if his wife dies.

Case 30: It was stated by villagers that the deceased farmer had an illegal contact with a lady in the neighbouring village. One day he was reportedly beaten up by the people of that village. Unable to withstand the humiliation, he seems to have ended his life the next day.

Suicide of Sample Deceased Farmers: Major Reasons

An attempt is made here to trace the chief reasons that drove the sample deceased farmers towards suicide. For the sake of understanding the overall picture at a glance, the information pertaining to the chief reasons for suicide of the sample deceased farmers along with other details such as the year of suicide and mode of suicide are presented in Table 3.

Table 3
Chief Reasons for the Suicide of the Sample Deceased Farmers

Case number	*Year of suicide*	*Mode of suicide*	*Chief reasons for suicide*
1	2001	Poison	Family disputes
2	2003	Poison	Pressure from creditors#
3	2002	Hanging	Poverty and Ill-health

Contd...

4	2004	Burning	Ill-health
5	2000	Poison	Addiction to alcohol
6	2000	Poison	Humiliation from creditors#
7	2003	Poison	Crop failure#
8	2002	Poison	Ill-health
9	2001	Poison	Family disputes
10	2001	Poison	Failure in love + Ill-health
11	2004*	Poison	Crop failure + Domestic expenses#
12	2004*	Hanging	Pressure from creditors
13	2004*	Poison	Ill-health
14	2004*	Poison	Crop failure#
15	2004*	Poison	Family disputes
16	2004*	Poison	Crop failure+ Family disputes#
17	2000	Poison	Crop failure#
18	2004	Hanging	Family disputes
19	2003	Poison	Pressure from creditors#
20	2001	Poison	Pressure from creditors#
21	2002	Poison	Addiction to alcohol + Family disputes
22	2002	Poison	Family disputes
23	2000	Poison	Addiction to alcohol and gambling
24	2003	Hanging	Crop failure + Domestic expenses#
25	2000	Poison	Pressure from creditors
26	2004*	Poison	Crop failure#
27	2004*	Poison	Crop failure + Family disputes#
28	2004*	Poison	Addiction to alcohol + Family disputes
29	2002	Poison	Crop failure#
30	2002	Poison	Extra-marital affair

Attributable to losses in agriculture
* During the tenure of the present government

It may be noted from Table 3 that the sample farmers committed suicide during 2000 – 2004. There were nine sample farmers (30 per cent) who committed suicide after the formation of the present government in the state. A vast majority of the sample farmers (83 per cent) ended their lives by consuming poison, with four cases of hanging and one case of burning/self-immolation. It was painful to note that those who consumed poison used pesticides distributed free of cost by the government in most cases. Only one farmer bought a pesticide with the intention of committing suicide (Case 15), while all others made use of the pesticides already available with them to kill themselves. Three sample farmers were reported to have consumed poison in a drunken state (Cases 5, 21 and 28), while in one case (Case 28), both the husband

and wife committed suicide due to a quarrel over the marriage of their daughter; the daughter loved and married a person of another caste, the drunk husband used to beat his wife for extending moral and financial support to the daughter, the wife could not bear the beatings by her husband and consumed a pesticide, and the husband followed suit There were two cases (Cases 5 and 23) where bad habits such as addiction to alcohol and gambling played havoc with their lives.

In the case of 13 farmers (43 per cent), the chief reason for committing suicide could be exclusively attributed to losses in agriculture. In addition to the nine cases presented in Box 1, these include four cases where the suicide could be primarily due to the losses in agriculture, even though the domestic expenses also contributed to the indebtedness of the deceased farmers, as evident from Box 3.

Box 3

Other Cases of Sample Deceased Farmers who Died Primarily due to Losses in Agriculture

Case 11: The deceased farmer had a dry agricultural land of 7 acres at his native place. He migrated to the present village for the education of his children. He used to cultivate groundnut. He experienced crop failures at his native village and at the present place by taking the land of his co-brother on lease basis. He had performed the marriage of his daughter about a year back. He did not have an own house, but stayed in a house that is used to run a fair-purchase store by his co-brother. His debts got accumulated to about Rs.210000. The situation of the family was pathetic with one physically handicapped son aged 28 years and another son engaged as a teacher in a private institution at a nearby place, and dependent upon his co-brother for sustenance. Vexed with the financial problems, he seems to have killed himself.

Case 14: The deceased farmer grew paddy, sunflower and groundnut. When the well dried up, he went for three bore wells. In each case there was water in the bore well for three or four months and ultimately the bore wells failed to yield water. He had spent about Rs.1 lakh on bore wells. He was sanctioned Rs. 18000 for a house under the housing programme, but he spent about Rs.1 lakh on house construction out of which Rs. 20000 was due at time of his death. His debts got accumulated to Rs. 2.5 lakhs due to losses in agriculture, and under these circumstances he seems to have taken the decision to end his life.

Case 20: The deceased farmer dug two bore wells and grew paddy. He had a debt of about Rs.1.8 lakhs from the bank/ society and Rs.1.5 lakhs from the farmers. He was the eldest of three brothers, and reported to have inherited a debt of about Rs.1.8 lakhs. He performed the marriage of his sister and incurred some expenditure. He was actively involved in politics and used to spend money lavishly. He had the dealership for the ration shop. He was reported to have committed suicide mainly due to pressure from the creditors to repay the loan.

Case 24: The deceased farmer had two wives, the first staying at the village itself and the second at another village. Besides his own land, he used to cultivate 4 acres belonging to his niece by taking a crop loan on it. Groundnut was the main crop grown. He had a total debt of about Rs. 4 lakhs.

He was reported to have sold his pucca house for Rs. 1.75 lakhs and cleared dues to some extent, including Rs.90000 in the name of his niece but she did not allow him to take a fresh loan on it. He could not repay the other dues. His family members also ill-treated him. Unable to bear the humiliation from his own people, he seems to have decided to end his life.

In all other cases, actors other than losses from agriculture were largely responsible for the deceased farmers to take to the extreme step of committing suicide. Important among these factors include severe illness in the case of four farmers (13 per cent) as presented in Box 4.

Box 4

Cases of Sample Deceased Farmers who Committed Suicide Primarily due to Ill Health

Case 3: The deceased farmer was quite old and had an ailing wife. He was reported to be suffering from pain in the throat, suspected to be cancer, and he was not in a position to speak for about six months before his death and was leading a pathetic life. He was reported to have taken treatment for this disease. It was informed that he committed suicide on account of unbearable pain and poverty.

Case 4: The deceased farmer had about 2 acres of dry land on which he used to grow groundnut. He also took some 4 acres of land on lease basis about three to four years before his demise and cultivated it for two years, but he suffered losses. He had a debt of Rs.60000. He also used to maintain some 30 to 40 sheep, but sold them off before his death. He was reported to be suffering from tuberculosis. In fact, his wife had this disease and it spread to him. She used to take medicines properly and got rid of the disease to a greater extent. But, he never took proper care of his health and did not take medicines properly. Before his death, he underwent treatment for this disease for about five months at two places. He also had the habit of beedi smoking. The disease went out of his control and reached an unbearable stage. His wife informed that because of debts due to losses in agriculture as well as for the treatment of his disease and also due to intolerable suffering due to tuberculosis, he committed suicide by burning himself.

Case 8: The deceased farmer had 4 acres of land out of which two acres was irrigated and two acres dry. He belonged to a very sound and big family. The entire family was reported to have been involved in a faction in the village, due to which they suffered financial losses on account of the theft of the starters and closure of bores by the opposite group. Now, the faction feuds have subsided. The deceased farmer had inherited a debt of Rs.1 lakh. In addition, he borrowed Rs.30000 from bank and Rs.60000 from other farmers. He was reported to be a sensitive person and could not withstand the insults from the creditors and therefore he committed suicide. But, according to a villager, he was suffering from severe stomach pain for which he also took treatment. Unable to bear the pain, he might have taken the extreme step of ending his life.

Case 13: The deceased farmer had 3.31 acres of dry land and took 2 acres of irrigated land on lease basis. Because of house construction and successive crop failure, he had accumulated a debt of about Rs.170000. He was also reported to be having a serious health problem. Unable to bear the burden of debt and ill health, he seems to have taken the extreme step of ending his life.

There were seven cases of farmers (23.3 per cent) committing suicide primarily due to family disputes, out of which the death in the case of four (Cases 9, 15, 21 and 28) could also be attributed to bad habits as presented in Box 2, while the remaining three cases are presented in Box 5. It becomes clear from the Box 5 that disputes with the family members, particularly the spouse, on account of various domestic and personal issues were largely responsible for the deceased farmers to commit suicide.

Box 5

Cases of Sample Deceased Farmers who Committed Suicide Primarily due to Family Disputes

Case 1: The deceased farmer owned about 1.96 acres of dry land inherited from his father and the main crop grown was groundnut. According to two informed sources-neighbour and his own brother-he used to have frequent quarrels with his wife. He used to have disputes with his wife very frequently on various matters. She used to be crazy of steel vessels and other household articles. She also forced him to construct a good house by borrowing money from others. He undertook house construction under the Housing Programme of the govt. for which he was sanctioned Rs.18000 and he spent about Rs.15000 borrowed from other sources. The house construction was completed, but before the housewarming ceremony, he died .She was also reported to have an extra-marital affair, which was stated to be the main reason for the deceased farmer to take the extreme step of ending his life.

Case 18: The deceased farmer had a wife and two sons. The sons were aged 6 years and 3 years, the elder one being a physically handicapped person. He had about 5.25 acres of dry land given by the government to his father. Since his two brothers were staying at Hyderabad and Bangalore, he was cultivating this land. About half of this land is fallow. The only crop grown is groundnut. He was staying in a small hut. He was not keeping good health due to an accident about 10 years back which made him unable to lift heavy weights. He was also worried about his elder son's health and spent some amount towards his treatment. He had a debt of about Rs.70000, of which Rs.10000 was towards crop loan from the bank and the rest from the farmers. He committed suicide on the day when his wife's parents had come to the village and his wife went to the bus stop to see them off. It seems there was some altercation in the family on that day, which led him to take the extreme step of ending his life.

Case 22: The deceased farmer had a wife, two sons and one daughter, and resided in his own, pucca house. His eldest son was studying Bachelor of Technology in a private engineering college at Nellore, while his other children were studying at Hyderabad where his co-brother is employed. He had huge commitments towards education for his children. He grew groundnut on his dry land. He used to do business of purchasing and selling the cattle. He had a total debt of 92000. He was accustomed to the habit of consuming alcohol. According to informed sources in the village, his wife also got habituated to alcohol. As he could not withstand her behaviour, he seems to have decided to end his life.

There were six cases where pressure from creditors was intense to repay the loans taken. While four cases were already presented (Cases 2,6, 19 and 20), the other two cases where there was intense pressure to repay loans taken mainly for meeting domestic expenses (Case 12) and to do cattle business where the losses were suffered resulting in accumulated debts (Case 25), are shown in Box 6.

Box 6

Cases of Sample Deceased Farmers who Committed Suicide Primarily due to

Pressure from the Creditors

Case 12: The deceased farmer had an agricultural land of 2.13 acres, with canal irrigation facility. He used to cultivate groundnut. He had a wife, one son and one daughter. Both the husband and wife used to look after their agriculture and also work as agricultural labourers. He had a debt of Rs.80000. His land was reported to be under mortgage with a private moneylender. He was reported to have committed suicide under pressure from the creditors to repay the debt.

Case 25: The deceased farmer, besides cultivating 5 acres of land given by the govt. and one acre near the stream, was also cultivating about 10 acres on lease basis. In addition, he was also doing the business of purchase and sale of cattle. It was informed by the villagers that he had incurred heavy losses in this business and left the village for some time. He had a total debt of Rs.175000. His wife and son reported that due to leasing-in of the land, he had incurred losses. The son's marriage was another factor responsible for his accumulated debts. They also reported that one of the creditors was harsh and humiliated him several times and threatened to make him or his family members work as bonded labour if he did not repay the loan with interest. Unable to bear the losses in agriculture and cattle business and clear the accumulated debts, besides humiliation from the creditors, he was reported to have taken the extreme step of killing himself.

It follows from the above discussion that in many a case, there were multiple factors that drove the farmers towards suicide. The cases of farmers whose death could be attributed to losses in agriculture need a closer look to identify the factors responsible for such losses, besides the immediate reasons for suicide. In a number of cases, the main reason for the losses in agriculture was the digging of more and more number of bore wells to save the standing crops such as sweet orange, papaya, chillies and paddy, and failure in this venture resulted in a double loss, i.e., the loss of investment and the loss of the standing crop. There was not a single instance where the sample deceased farmers had consulted the geologist for digging the bore wells. The other reasons include lack of remunerative prices for chillies (Case 2), cheating by the traders (Case 6), use of fake seed (Case 26), and crop losses due to cultivation of land on sharecropping basis (Case 27) or lease basis (Case 29). In most of these cases, the losses got accumulated over a period of time. In addition, there were five cases where the chief reason forcing them to commit suicide was intense pressure or humiliation from the creditors comprising mostly the private sources. In one case (Case 19), the pressure was so intense that one day before the due date, the farmer committed suicide because he was unable to repay the loan. In another case (Case 6), the farmer could not stand the humiliation from one of the creditors who reportedly went to the extent of manhandling him, and resorted to the extreme step of ending his life. There was also a case (Case 20) in which lavish expenses and pressure from creditors claimed the life of an upcoming farmer, and another case (Case 11) where the farmer ended his life because the domestic burdens, besides successive crop loss, proved to be unbearable.

Relief and Rehabilitation Measures Undertaken

As per the GO Ms No. 421, the government machinery plunged into action to implement the economic relief and rehabilitation package to the family/next of kin of the deceased farmers. In the case of all but two sample deceased farmers, the relief was sanctioned to their families. The cases of two sample deceased farmers (Cases 3 and 11) were still under process. The creditors including bankers were paid cheques for amounts for which documentary evidence could be established, proportionately where the total debt exceeded Rs.50000, as one-time settlement. In a few cases, the process of one-time settlement could not be completed due to disputes (Cases 1 and 25). In the latter case, one of the creditors obtained a Court decree for auctioning the land, and the wife of the deceased farmer agreed to pay the additional amount demanded by the creditor over and above the amount for which cheque is available. In another case (Case 29), the son of the deceased farmer had to pay an additional amount of Rs.20000 from out of his own savings to settle the matter, as some of the creditors were not satisfied with the govt. offer of one-time settlement. In yet another case (Case 26), the wife of the deceased farmer promised to pay over and above the one-time settlement amount on the apprehension that if she failed to do so, she would not be able to get hand loans when needed. There were few cases where the bank managers transferred the crop loans held by the deceased farmers in the name of the son (Case 6) or refused to close the crop loan (Case 14), and the sword of debt is still hanging on the neck of the survivors.

According to the said GO, the exgratia of Rs.1 lakh per household is to be kept in the joint account of the next of kin of the deceased farmer and the concerned Mandals Revenue Officer (MRO), and utilised for future farm rehabilitation including diversification of crop or change of technology and inputs or other source as advised by the agricultural or other appropriate departments. The rehabilitation measures including the benefits provided as a measure of social cushion by the government and the utilization of the same by the family members of the sample deceased farmers are shown in Table 4. It may be noted from Table 4 that out of 28 sample households who were sanctioned the exgratia, as many as 22 households (79 per cent) had withdrawn amounts ranging from Rs.5000 to Rs.1 lakh and used it for various productive and non-productive purposes. The amount withdrawn was less than Rs.24000 in the case of 16 households (57 per cent), and was mostly used for crop production expenses and to some extent to meet the domestic expenses including medical treatment. While four households had withdrawn amounts ranging between Rs.30000 and Rs.50000 and utilised it for, besides agriculture, dairying (Case 2), business (Case 9), education (Case 22) and housing (Case 25), two households withdrew the entire amount and used it for marriage, purchase of gold and consumption expenses (Cases 26 and 27). In the latter two cases, marriage of children was performed due to a strong sentiment that it would keep the departed soul at rest if the marriage of one of the children is performed within one year of the demise of the father. There were six households which did not withdraw any amount from the joint account so far; some of them had plans to utilise it for children's education or keep it in a fixed deposit in the name of children (Cases 17, 20 and 28)), while one of them had plans to perform the marriage of daughter (Case 15). Some others (Cases 5 and 18) were yet to decide as to how to utilise the amount.

There is a provision in the GO to arrange for financial assistance under govt. schemes and extend certain other benefits such as housing, children's education and old age pensions to the family members of the deceased farmers. There were only two cases (Cases 5 and 10), where financial assistance for dairying was provided under SGSY. It was observed that in the case of three households (Cases 2, 14 and 23), the amount withdrawn from the joint account was utilised for dairying, in addition to crop investment. These households could have been helped to take to dairying under SGSY as had been done in the earlier two cases, and it would have left them with some additional cushion. There was another household (Case 23), in which one of the dependents was pursuing power-loom weaving on hire basis, and permission was sought to utilise some amount from the joint account to purchase a power-loom. But, it was reportedly denied on the ground that the amount should be utilised for agricultural purpose only, even though there is no such implication in the GO. The dependents felt that agriculture was not a viable venture and setting up of own power-loom would help them to obtain relatively more secured

Table 4
Rehabilitation Measures and other Benefits Provided and Utilization of the same by the Dependents of the Sample Deceased Farmers

Case number	*Amount with drawn form joint account (Rs.)*	*Purpose for which the amount was utilised*	*Other benefits provided as a measure of social cushion*
1	6000	Consumption	Housing*
2	38000	Agriculture and dairy	Housing
3	Nil	NA	Nil
4	6000	Agriculture and consumption	Nil
5	Nil	NA	Rs.16000 for dairying (SGSY)
6	20000	Agriculture	Nil
7	10000	Agriculture	Housing
8	10000	Agriculture	Nil
9	30000	Agriculture and business	Nil
10	20000	Agriculture	Rs.16000 for dairying (SGSY)
11	Nil	NA	Nil
12	5000	Agriculture and consumption	Nil
13	15000	Agriculture	Housing*
14	20000	Agriculture and dairy	Housing*
15	Nil	NA	Nil
16	15000	Agriculture and consumption	Nil
17	Nil	NA	Nil
18	Nil	NA	Nil
19	20000	Agriculture and education	Education
20	Nil	NA	Nil
21	10000	Agriculture and consumption	Housing*
22	30000	Agriculture and consumption	Housing*
23	10000	Agriculture and dairy	Nil
24	18000	Consumption	Nil
25	50000	Agriculture, housing and consumption	Housing
26	100000	Agriculture, consumption and marriage	Nil
27	100000	Agriculture, consumption and marriage	Nil
28	Nil	NA	Education
29	20000	Agriculture and medical treatment	Nil
30	24000	Agriculture	Nil

* Provided prior to the death of the farmer

There were only three cases where, in addition to govt. help, assistance was provided to the families of the deceased farmers by other organizations. In two cases, the Congress party provided help to the extent of Rs.22000 (Case 1) and Rs. 40000 (Case 5). In another case (Case 14), both the children of the deceased farmer were adopted by a Non Governmental Organization from Guntur district and given a scholarship of Rs.300 per head per month. There was only one case (Case 1) where the family could get an amount of Rs.5000 from the Insurance Company.

income. Three households (Cases 2,7 and 25) were sanctioned Rs.25000 per head towards pucca houses under the weaker sections housing schemes, while five others were already covered under earlier housing schemes of the government before the demise of the sample farmers. There was only one case (Case 19) where one child was admitted into the government Industrial Training Institute at the district headquarters, but without hostel accommodation. In another case (Case 28), two children were admitted into social welfare residential school as they lost both the parents. There were two cases where the sample households rejected the offer for admission of children into social welfare hostels on the ground that the children were still young (Cases 8 and 20), and in one case (Case 2) the mother is yet to take a decision. In another case (Case 15), the services of the young girl were needed for cooking as her mother did not keep good health and hence the hostel accommodation was not accepted.

CONCLUDING REMARKS

Based on the findings of the study, it may be concluded that the farmers' suicides in Anantapur district during the last five years could not be exclusively attributed to indebtedness on account of losses in agriculture, as their debts were also due to their inability to repay the loans made for fulfilling their life cycle needs such as house construction and marriage and to meet domestic expenses including medical treatment. It cannot be denied, however, that they had no source other than the anticipated income from agriculture to repay the loans made for these purposes, and they could not repay their dues mainly because of the crop failure during successive seasons that landed them into debt trap. It needs to be admitted that the extent of indebtedness is not truly reflected in the official records because in certain cases the legal heirs had already cleared some debts before the govt. hep reached them.

Thus, it becomes clear that indebtedness, wholly or partly attributable to losses in agriculture, alone cannot explain the suicides. Parthasarathy and Shameem (1998) also observed that that though mounting indebtedness is the main reason for the farmers' economic distress, it does not entirely explain the suicides since the social situation in which an individual gets alienated from the family and the society also needs to be taken into account. A close look at the case studies revealed that there were multiple factors at work that drove the farmers towards suicide. The chief reasons for farmers' suicides include, besides losses in agriculture, family disputes, severe illness causing unbearable pain, bad habits such as addiction to alcohol and gambling, problems related to love affair / extra-marital affair, unplanned way of life and loss in business. Even in the case of those farmers whose death could be wholly or partly attributed to agriculture-related indebtedness, the immediate causes that drove them towards suicide were intense pressure from the creditors to repay their dues and humiliation caused to them, besides their inability to clear off the debts apparently on account of domestic burdens and to some extent unproductive expenses. The main reasons for losses in agriculture include the failure of bore wells and consequently the loss of standing crop, successive crop failure, use of fake seeds, and lack of remunerative prices for agricultural produce, which got accumulated over a period of time and landed the farmers in debt. Thus, it is clear that in addition to the crop loss and indebtedness there were a number of social issues that were responsible for the suicide of farmers. The study of Mohanty and Shroff (2004) also came to a similar conclusion that though the losses in agriculture and indebtedness appeared to have taken the lives of a number of farmers, the roots of such deaths could be traced to the social issues as well.

Regarding the relief and rehabilitation measures by the government, it may be concluded that these measures provided immediate relief to the families of the deceased farmers left in severe distress. In most cases, the one-time settlement of debts by paying cheques directly to the creditors relieved them from the clutches of the creditors, even though a few of them faced problems from the bankers and private moneylenders in this regard. There was no effective linkage with the other government schemes under which the family members could be extended financial assistance and help as a measure of social cushion; the low coverage under different schemes stands testimony to this fact. The genuine needs of the household should be taken into account while planning the rehabilitation schemes and non-agricultural activities should be encouraged wherever they are found feasible and viable.

The mandals team responsible for rehabilitating the families of the deceased farmers, comprising the Mandals Revenue Officer, Mandals Agricultural Officer and other officials, has not been put in place and the entire responsibility seems to lie with the MRO, who looks over-burdened with several tasks and unable to concentrate on the problems faced and rehabilitation measures suitable to the dependents. It may be better to entrust this responsibility to the Project Director of Indira Kranthi Patham (erstwhile Velugu), a World Bank aided District Poverty Initiatives Project (DPIP), at the district level and its Assistant Project Officers and Community Coordinators at the grassroots level. Alternatively, this responsibility could also be entrusted to the local self-government institutions, viz., Panchayati Raj (PR) set-up comprising the people's representatives at all levels and manned by the Chief Executive Officer of Zilla Parishad at the district level and the Mandals Development Officers and the Village Secretaries at the lower levels. This is because the officials of the Indira Kranthi Patham or Panchayati Raj are relatively well versed with the formulation and execution of economically viable schemes for the poor when compared to the staff of the revenue department. In fact, the largest anti-poverty programme namely, Swarnajayanti Gram Swarojgar

Yojana (SGSY) as well as the National Old Age Pension Scheme are being implemented through the PR. As such, it becomes relatively easy for the functionaries of the PR to identify suitable schemes under SGSY for the family members of the deceased farmers under which they could be assisted, if necessary by relaxing the eligibility conditions, in accordance with the provisions of the GO. It would also be relatively easy for these functionaries to monitor the implementation of the rehabilitation schemes as it forms a part of their routine job. The lapses such as allowing the families to withdraw the entire amount within a period of less than one year, mostly for unproductive purposes, would prove to be costly and may defeat the very purpose of the GO. The Commission of Inquiry into Farmers' Suicides in Andhra Pradesh also found that in certain cases the entire amount, which ought to have been spent over a period of three or four years till the family is taken out of distress, was withdrawn in a few months[6]. As such, care needs to be taken to ensure that the amount is used only for productive purposes and to cover bare minimum consumption needs.

The fact that over one-fourth of the sample deceased farmers committed suicide after the formation of the present government in the state serves as a pointer to the fact that the help line established at the district level could not prove to be effective in preventing the farmers from committing suicide, and calls for comprehensive measures to prevent such cases in future. There should be a careful blend of both short-term and long-term measures in order to ensure the sustainable development of agriculture, especially in drought prone regions like Anantapur, so that more number of farmers would not resort to suicide in future. The short-term measures include the provision of adequate wage employment opportunities in rural areas and diversification of agriculture as indicated by a shift towards vegetables, floriculture and fodder crops, and promotion of supplementary sources of income such as dairying, sheep rearing and poultry. The long-term measures include the removal of bottlenecks in respect of input supply including credit, marketing, remunerative prices for agricultural produce, and crop insurance. Provision of adequate and timely institutional credit and assured market, and ensuring remunerative prices for the farm produce in respect of all important crops, besides coverage of all crops under crop insurance would go a long way to prevent the farmers from falling into the clutches of indebtedness. The National Commission on Farmers headed by Dr. Swaminathan rightly called for a huge infusion of credit into agriculture and a 'Centre-State Contributory Price Stabilization Fund' and for linking minimum support price to the wholesale price index. It also called for protective measures such as a hike in import duties to withstand the dumping of heavily subsidised agricultural products of the United States and the European Union in the Indian market, and prevent distress sales by our farmers[7]. The government has to initiate swift measures from time to time to protect our agriculture and prevent many more farmers from committing suicide. The unit of crop insurance should be changed to that of a village instead of a mandals. It is gratifying to note that the insurance companies have agreed to do so during the current season. Besides, the low coverage of farmers under the insurance schemes suggests the need to organise them into Rytumitra groups and cover them under group life insurance schemes, which were already put in place to cover the self-help group members.

NOTES

1. [1]While the studies of Shiva and Jafri (1998), Prasad (1999), and Deshpande (2002) attributed farmers' suicides to factors like crop failure, indebtedness, etc., essentially in the case of commercial crops, other studies conducted by Assadi (1998), Vasavi (1999) and Sarma (2004) highlighted the failure of the state for these tragedies. Mohanty (2001) focused on the interaction between historical and socio-economic factors to understand the reasons for farmers' suicides, while the study of Mohanty and Shroff (2004) aimed to compare the socio-economic situation of the deceased farmers with that of the farmers of a similar background to ascertain the specific factors forcing the farmers to commit suicide. Thus, the studies on farmers' suicides were limited and mostly confined to Andhra Pradesh, Karnataka and Maharashtra,

and revealed divergent views. Thus, there is a need for more number of micro-level studies to understand the dynamics involved in the issue in a right perspective.

2. The district experienced deficient rainfall when compared to the normal rainfall consecutively during the last three years (290.2 mm. in 2002-03, 523.4 mm. in 2003-04 and 432.1 mm. in 2004-05). However, the actual rainfall was higher than the normal rainfall of 552 mm. during 2000-01 (614.3 mm.) and 2001-02 (684.5 mm.). The loss of groundnut crop was experienced in most of the mandals continuously for four years from 2000-01 to 2003-04, despite good rainfall in the first two years because the rainfall pattern in those years was not suitable for the growth of groundnut crop.

3. The normal rainfall ranged between a high of 703 mm. in Bukkapatnam mandal and a low of 339 mm. in Atmakur mandal during 2000-01. Out of 63 mandals, the actual rainfall was deficient when compared to normal rainfall in 16 mandals during 2000-01, 6 mandals during 2001-02, 62 mandals during 2002-03, 32 mandals during 2003-04 and 56 mandals during 2004-05. In spite of deficient rainfall during 2004-05, farmers received fairly good crop of groundnut in many mandals because its spread was suitable for the growth of groundnut crop.

4. For instance, a publication by the Human Rights Forum gives the list of 490 farmers who committed suicide between 2000 and April 2005, including the date of committing suicide, village and mode of committing suicide. For details, see *Arugalam Karuvu: A report on Agrarian Crisis in Anantapur District* (Telugu Booklet), Human Rights Forum, Hyerabad, n.d.

5. Justice Rama Chenna Reddy, heading the Commission of Inquiry into Farmers' Suicides in Andhra Pradesh, revealed at a press conference at the end of his assignment that out of 2861 cases reported during the TDP regime from 1999 only 1464 cases were genuine and out of 1715 cases reported during 14 months of the Congress government only 1100 cases were genuine. Thus, the proportion of non-genuine cases worked out to 48.8 per cent during the TDP regime and 35.9 per cent during the Congress regime. (For details, see Ryots suicide: Panel completes Probe, *The Hindu*, October 9, 2005, p.2)

6. The Commission of Inquiry into Farmers' Suicides in Andhra Pradesh found that Rs.1 lakh to be paid to the family of the deceased farmer over a period of three or four years to develop

agriculture, was paid in a short time of two to six months in some cases in some districts. (For details, see Dead Farmers show up at Inquiry, *The Hindu*, September 30, 2005: p. 5.)

7. For details, see Sainath, P. Vidarbha: Awaiting a Deadly Harvest, *The Hindu*, October 28, 2005: p. 11.

REFERENCES

Assadi, Muzaffar (1998), Farmers' Suicides: Signs of Distress in Rural Economy. *Economic and Political Weekly*, 33(14): 747-748.

Deshpande, R. S. (1998), Land Reforms and Agrarian Structure in Maharashtra. *Journal of Indian School of Political Economy*, 10 (1): 1-24.

Government of Andhra Pradesh (2001), *Statistical Abstract of Andhra Pradesh 2000*. Directorate of Economics and Statistics, Government of Andhra Pradesh, Hyderabad.

Human Rights Forum (2005), *Arugalam Karuvu: A Report on Agrarian Crisis in Anantapur District*. Telugu Booklet, Hyderabad.

Mohanty, B. B. (2001), Suicides of Farmers in Maharashtra: A Socio-Economic Analysis. *Review of Development and Change*, 6 (2): 146-189.

Mohanty, B. B. and Sangeeta Shroff (2004), Farmers' Suicides in Maharashtra. *Economic and Political Weekly*, 39 (52): 5599-5606.

Parthasarathy, G. and Shameem (1998), Suicides of Cotton Farmers in Andhra Pradesh: An Exploratory Study. *Economic and Political Weekly*, 33 (13): 720-726.

Prasad, C. Shambu (1999), Suicide Deaths and Quality of Indian Cotton: Perspectives from History of Technology and Khadi Movement. *Economic and Political Weekly*, 34 (5): PE 12-PE 21.

Sainath, P. (2005), Vidarbha: Awaiting a Deadly Harvest. *The Hindu*, October 28:11.

Sarma, E. A. S. (2004), Is Rural Econom y Breaking Down? Farmers' Suicides in Andhra Pradesh. *Economic and Political Weekly*, 39 (28): 3087-3090.

Shiva, Vandana and A. H. Jafri (1998), *Seeds of Suicide: The Ecological and Human Costs of Globalization of Agriculture*. Research Foundation for Science, Technology and Ecology, New Delhi.

Vasavi, A. R. (1999), Agrarian Distress in Bidar: Market, State and Suicides. *Economic and Political Weekly*, 34 (32): 2263-2268.

6

LAND RIGHTS OF WOMEN IN ACHIEVING SUSTAINABLE LIVELIHOODS

ROSALUD DE LA ROSA & ALEXANDRA AQUINO-FIKE

INTRODUCTION

More than half of the world's population live in rural areas and have not yet benefited from the impacts of globalization. Women represent the majority of the world's rural poor of up to 70 per cent, especially where migration, marital instability, male mortality and single parenthood have left them as heads of households. Women own only about one percent of all land, while accounting for a large share in small-scale food production. Women farmers are largely engaged in subsistence agriculture and thus their labour is often not considered as productive output in agriculture sector. In Africa, they account for 80 to 90 per cent of the labour in subsistence production, and over 70 per cent in cash-crop production. Studies carried out by FAO accomplished that only about five percent of services provided by agricultural extension workers reached women farmers, although they constituted the majority of food producers in many developing countries. Studies revealed that the majority of those living in absolute poverty were women (FAO 2000). Beginning with the 1979 FAO World Conference on Agrarian Reform and Rural Development (WCARRD) and continuing with the United Nations conferences of the 1990s, governments have made significant commitments on land access to reduce rural poverty. In recent years, the United Nations organizes follow up ten-year review conferences (also known as +10s) and the *Millennium Summit Review* of the *Millennium Development Goals (MDGs)* to revitalize these commitments. The follow-up processes to these summits, as well as the forthcoming FAO International Conference on Agrarian Reform and Rural Development (ICARRD) in March 2006; present a window of opportunity for international agencies and civil society organizations to assess progress of governments' commitments. However, unless greater thought is given to strengthening the reporting mechanisms of these conventions and national data collection programmes in general, progress on revitalizing these commitments will be feeble.

Legally binding instruments like the Convention on the Elimination of All Forms of Discrimination Against Women (CEDAW) and International Covenant on Economic, Social and Cultural Rights (ICESCR) are failing to hit the mark due to lack of proper tools to measure progress and a common framework on agreed indicators. The effectiveness of these relevant global commitments in inducing positive changes to women and men remains questionable to many stakeholders. Many international agreements or conventions have voluntary reporting structures. This kind of reporting structure presents a major challenge in monitoring progress made in the implementation of conventions. One example is CEDAW which despite having been ratified by over 175 countries has a significant number of countries who have either not fulfilled their reporting requirements or have not yet presented their initial report to the Committee of CEDAW (FAO, IFAD and ILC 2004).

One reason that so many countries fail to report on women and land access is that data collection puts a huge burden on national governments. It requires a significant investment of financial and human resources, especially capacity building of the technical capabilities of the national collection agencies. Many agencies require technical assistance and training to conduct national censuses, but also to conduct sample surveys of population relevant to the needs of sector policy reforms.

There is a role for international organizations that compile and analyze this data, to advise governments on how to collect data. Currently, there is a bewildering amount of statistics and reporting formats, depending on the agency that requires it. In recent years, much of the discourse among policy makers at the global levels has focused on the need to increase and improve gender-disaggregated data and to develop measurable indicators. While attempts have been made at the global level to initiate a process for developing a common framework on indicators, a prerequisite is to ensure that such the capabilities and interest exists at the national level (ILC 2005).

Before prescribing new data and reporting formats, it would be prudent to assess to what extent existing data might serve the unquestionable need for gender sensitive indicators of rural development. Given the tremendous amount of available statistics and data that can have a potential to be used as source of developing indicators, the paper seeks to a review of existing data and assessed their suitability for inclusion of a list of data that can used as source of indicators in measuring progress of the status of rural women.

ACCESS TO LAND AS A BASIC VARIABLE

An essential prerequisite for rural development projects is the compilation and analysis of socio-economic and agricultural data, as well as environmental data. Evidence-based analysis and statistical data particularly on agriculture and natural resources are inadequate. This is one of the major criticisms among women advocates in the rural development arena. These advocates often find that the institutions responsible for agriculture and natural resource management are generally 'gender blind' and professionally male-dominated throughout most of the developing world, especially in Africa and South Asia. Data is the key to catalyzing and monitoring progress, as well as supporting country-level planning and local accountability (Mikkelsen 2005).

Rural development policies and programmes cannot be designed and implemented unless a clear understanding of the target community's situation is first obtained. A community can be understood on various levels and from various perspectives (e.g. micro, macro, economic, educational, political, etc.) thus, an in-depth understanding of the local and national context is fundamental. Gender is one area that continues to be given less attention. Despite the vast amount of information and data available on rural development and agriculture, gender-sensitive data is still insufficient in the area of women's access, use, and control of land and land-related resources. FAO recently noted that data on rural producers in general and women in particular, are still regarded as being of only marginal relevance to policy-making. This may be a result of policies in agricultural development that are often narrowly aimed at product growth, overlooking labour welfare aspects of development (FAO 1999a).

Furthermore, as FAO recognizes, the collection of gender-sensitive data involves much more than simple disaggregation of data by sex. Gender-sensitive data ideally would involve both quantitative as well as qualitative indicators to collect data that reflects the different yet related situations and roles of men and women, such as, how each access household resources and how they specifically contribute to the agrarian economy. One resource, which is of fundamental importance to the agrarian economy, and to rural development, in general, is land. Yet, not enough information is available on women and land, specifically data on women's ownership, access to and control of land and land-related resources (e.g. secure access to safe water, agricultural credit, or extension services).

Access to land can refer to ownership, lease rights, or customary user rights (right of way, right to use land for certain productive purposes, but not right to transfer land). Access to land can also refer to access to various other resources, essential for making the land viable (e.g. water, credit, etc.). In short, land rights are a bundle of rights and it is difficult for one indicator or even a couple of indicators to provide a full picture of how women interact with land resources. Also, cultural definitions and perspectives of land rights must be addressed, further complicating the concept of land access and land rights. What one culture calls ownership, another culture may not. This relates to the complexity of *de jure* and *de facto* rights and uses of land. In some cultures, a woman may not seem to officially be the owner of the land because only her partner's name is on the title, yet she may or may not be guaranteed by law or even by community tradition to equal control and access to the land–thus her *de facto* rights may differ from her *de jure* rights.

Understanding rural women's access to and capacity to utilize productive resources like land is of fundamental importance in today's world as women play a major role in food production and food security in developing countries (FAO 2002). Land is a critical resource in these activities and in the face of sudden socio-economic changes like a partner's death or male migration; a woman's control over the resource determines how the household will respond (Giovarelli and Lastarria *et al.* 2005).

An overview of available data from the major international development agencies and the reporting mechanisms of one international agreement, the Convention on the Elimination of all forms of Discrimination against Women (CEDAW), and identified existing indicators on the issue of rural women's access to land ahs been focused. Yet it is important to stress that even the definition of 'access to land' has diverse definitions and meanings. For some, land access does not necessarily mean individual ownership of land; it can imply another form of secure, protected and sustainable access and control of land and related resources, such as a leasing arrangement or communal ownership. Increasing debate among legal scholars, economists and policy-makers on the important issue of common property resources and on the concept of the 'bundle of rights' has resulted in some scholars arguing for less emphasis on private property. Some scholars propose defining finer gradations of ownership and strengthening the right and ability to participate in collective decisions as central to women's land rights (Schlager and Ostrom 1992). Access to land is also bound up with access to access to water, access to financial services (such as micro credit loans), access to extension services, etc. We have attempted to look as broadly as possible to what access to and control of land resources might implicate, thus not restraining ourselves to looking at indicators demonstrating only legal title to land or property.

GLOBAL LEVEL INDICATORS

The majority of the statistics available at the global level are clustered around what United Nations Development Fund for Women (UNIFEM) calls the UN indicator framework for gender, education (measured by the ration of girls' enrolment ratio to boys' enrolment ratio in secondary education), political participation (measured by women's share of parliamentary representation), and economic participation in the market economy (measured by women's share of paid employment in industry and services, i.e. no-agricultural activities) (UNIFEM 2000). The focus of this framework is largely on urban women, not rural women, thus from the beginning of our research it has been challenging to find indicators on rural women and their access to land and related resources. Oftentimes one can find indicators within the vast list of indicators available within the UN System that look at the rural population or women in the agricultural sector. But it is rare to find indicators focused specifically on rural women.

One of the major sources of global level data and indicators is the United Nation System. In many sectors the United Nations is the principal institutional system, which tracks changes from a broader, international perspective. Within the United Nations, the main organizations which look at gender, population and agriculture are the United Nations Statistical Division (UNSD), the Food and Agriculture Organization (FAO), the United Nations Development Programme (UNDP),

United Nations Human Settlement Programme (UN-Habitat), the United Nations Children's Fund (UNICEF) and the World Health Organization (WHO). For the purposes of our study, the major organizations, which compile data relevant to rural women, are the UNSD and the FAO; UNSD collects data from member countries' population censuses, while FAO collects data from member countries' agricultural censuses.

In this study the global level data and indicators has been organized under two categories namely commercial agriculture and subsistence agriculture (Table 1). This reflects the two dominant approaches by development agencies towards rural, agriculture-dependent communities - a commercial agriculture approach, and a subsistence-farming approach. The first approach focuses on increasing agricultural productivity and exports, thus, economic growth and labour activity indicators are important. Under the second approach agriculture is viewed as a subsistence activity, not a commercial, export activity, thus social and demographic indicators are more important. These two approaches reflect different cultural and economic realities and values; in some developing countries, agriculture has converted into a large, export-producing, industry; in other developing countries, agriculture remains a small economic activity - people engage in agriculture only to the extent necessary to feed their families. It is important to note that while we have divided the sources of data and indicators into these two categories for purposes of analysis, they are not mutually exclusive. In fact, in order to best understand women's access to and control over land resources; one must look at the three dimensions of sustainable development - economic, social and natural resources/environment indicators. The FAO, which in the past tended to focus only on the economic agricultural data, is now recognizing the importance of linking agricultural and population censuses. This analytical shift will be seen more visibly in the upcoming 2010 round of the World Census of Agriculture (WCA) Programme, whereby the FAO assists countries in conducting their agricultural censuses.

Table 1
Global Level Indicators

Commercial data and indicators– by organization	Subsistence data and indicators – by organization
UN Statistical Division[1] Under the Demographic and Social Statistics – Statistics on Women and Men: 1. Adult economic activity rate (%) (by sex)[2] 2. Women's share fo the adult labour force (%) Under the Women's Statistics and Indicators Database: 1. Estimated and projected economic activity rate by sex and age group 2. Total, economically active and not economically active population by sex, for total, urban and rural 3. Female economically active population by marital status and age group 4. Economically active population by sex, status in employment and major industry group 5. Women's wages in agriculture, in non-agricultural activities and in manufacturing, as percentage of men's wages	Under the Demographic and Social Statistics – Social Indicators Database: 1. Estimated percentage of population with access to improved drinking water sources 2000 (for urban and rural arear)[3] – this indicator is important for understading women's access to water, which is directly related to their access to land.
UNDP[4] 1. Gender Empowerment Measure (GEM) – A composite index measuring gender inequality in three basic dimensions of empowerment: economic participation and decision-making, political participation and decision-making and power over economic resources. 2. Gender-related Development Index a. Listed under the GDI is the indicator Estimated Earned Income, which provides data by sex.	1. Gender Empowerment Measure (GEM) 2. Gender-related Development Index (GDI)

Contd...

3. Gender Inequality in Economic Activity Indicators–UNDP also provides indicators on women's participation in the economy, specifically:
a. Female Economic Activity Rate
b. Female Employment by Economic Activity (of which agriculture is one of the main sectors examined).
c. Contributing Family Workers - both female and male 4. Gender, Work,
4. Gender, Work, Burden and Time Allocation Indicators - for selected developing and OECD countries, UNDP provides data on women's workloads compared to men's workloads.
a. Burden of work
b. Total Work Time (minutes per day) by sex
c. Female Work Time as percentage of Male Work Time
d. Time Allocation
i. Time spent on market activities and non-market activities by sex

FAO[5]

Under FAOSTAT general statistics list:
1. Total Economically Active Population or Labour Force by Sex
2. Economically Active Population (or Labour Force) in Agriculture by Sex

World Census of Agriculture (WCA) - Recommended Census Items[6]: 1. Holding (Category 1) - FAO defines this as the economic unit of agricultural production under single management and comprises all the livestock and all the land used (wholly or in part) for agricultural purposes, without regard to title, legal form or size.

2. Land (Category 5) - The WCA Programme proposes that census questions on land be divided into two subcategories: one for items that concern the entire holding and one for items that relate to each parcel of that holding. There is an

WCA Recommended Censur Items:1. Holder (Category 1 and 2)–FAO recommends to member countries that they collect both legal and demographic information on agricultural holders. FAO defines a holder as the "civil or judicial person who makes major decisions regarding resource use and exercises management control over the agricultural holding operation. The holder has

Contd...

extensive list of suggested census items for land tenure including holdings or parcels, a. without land b. operated or held in owner like possession c. rented from others (total) i. for an agreed amount of money and/or produce ii. for a share of produce iii. in exchange for services iv. under other rental arrangements a. operated on a squatter basis b. operated under tribal or other traditional communal forms of tenure c. operated under other tenure forms	technical and economic responsibility for the holding and may undertake all responsibilities directly, or delegate responsibilities related to day to day work management to a hired manager." FAO specifically emphasizes the importance of collecting the sex of the holder and the household members. 2. Head of Household (Category 5) – FAO defines the head of the household as, 'the person (male or female) in the household acknowledged as head by the other members. The head has primary authority and responsibility for household affairs.' The head of the household is an important census item for understanding the rural women's responsibilities, particularly as they relate to land-based activities.
UN Habitat[7] 1. Secure Tenure a. UN-Habitat identifies secure tenure as one of the 20 Key Indicators of the Habitat Agenda. Secure tenure is identified by the existence legal rights relating to eviction. WHO, UNICEF	1 . Secure Tenure 2. Access to safe water by the proportion of the population with sustainable access to an improved water source. Proportion of population with sustainable access to an improved water source

EVALUATION

After studying the available global indicators on rural women's access to land, several common challenges to collecting data and developing indicators on the subject has been identified. Analysis of these challenges has been divided into the following main points:

Insufficient Disaggregation of Data by Sex

A significant amount of the economic and subsistence or population focused data continues to be collected without recording the sex of the relevant persons. It is of foremost importance that governments disaggregate data by sex - in order for this to occur, there must exist the political will and the relevant professionals must receive technical training to understand how to collect gender sensitive data and how to disaggregate data by sex. Furthermore, international organizations must continue to support disaggregation of data by sex. For example, the access to water indicators as developed by WHO and UNICEF are not disaggregated by sex. According to the Organizations, data on water and sanitation is collected at the household level and thus gender specific data cannot be calculated. The organizations argue that information on who bears the main responsibility for water collection and long it takes can be ascertained (WHO, UNICEF 2004). UN Habitat access to water indicator are also not disaggregated by sex. In its *Urban Indicators Toolkit*, 2004 the UN Habitat glosses over the need for collecting gender specific data by stating that this water access indicator 'already addresses gender, since, when water is not available, it is usually women and girls who will carry the daily burden of fetching water', and that results can be specified through disaggregation by sex of the household head (UN Habitat 1998). Clearly, collecting data on land access, including access to water is extremely difficult, but efforts must be made to disaggregate all data collected by sex.

Information often not Broken down by Rural/Urban Zones

Along with the lack of gender disaggregation data, a common issue we found was that many indicators did not call for data to be disaggregated by urban and rural zones. For example, most of the information compiled by UN agencies on economic activity rates or estimated earned income (see UNSD, UNDP indicators) do not divide the data by rural and urban areas. Some organizations clearly looked at only urban or peri-urban areas (e.g. UN Habitat), and some organizations focus on rural zones (e.g. FAO), but it would be useful for the organizations to coordinate their data sources to allow for a breakdown of data by geographic zone. In order to better understand the role of rural women in the agricultural sector, in particular their control of land assets as related to household income and their participation in agricultural production, then data must be disaggregated into rural versus urban zones.

Limitation of Commercial Indicators

Commercial or economic indicators, such as adult economic activity rate by sex, are essential to any research on the topic of women's access to land because they provide an approximate picture of the percentage of women in the paid labour force. However, these kinds of indicators are very limited because in many developing countries the majority of women do not work in the paid labour sector, rather in unpaid activities.

Indicators not Sufficiently Defined at Smaller Units

It is important to define census data items to include smaller, sub-category and more specific levels of data. Data and indicators, which call for broad economic levels, tend to exclude rural women. Examples of how census items can be too broad are given below within the context of the FAO's recommended census items.

(a) The Holding census item as proposed in the FAO and WCA: Women generally have rights and responsibilities relating to natural resources at levels lower than the holding (e.g. the agricultural plot level, etc.). Agricultural censuses tend not to collect the sex of the persons responsible for various agricultural activities below the holding level, resulting in a serious underestimation of the contribution of adult women to agricultural production. Furthermore, in some regions (for example Africa) a one-to-one correspondence is generally assumed between a household and a holding. This can exacerbate the underestimating of (sub) holdings belonging to one household, usually managed by women farmers within a male-headed agricultural holding (Templeman 2005).

- In response, FAO is recommending the use of the sub-holder concept for the upcoming WCA 2010 Round (which will begin in 2006) (FAO 1999a).

(b) Holder item: FAO itself recognizes that from a gender perspective, the term "holder" is not very appropriate because it generally refers to just one male individual. In spite of FAO's definition of a holder which states that more than one person may be responsible for a holding (which would allow for both men and women to be included), generally only one person is included, and in many cultures this means that only the man is recognized 'when only one person is considered, that person is unlikely to be a woman' (FAO 1999a).

- FAO experience in Africa has shown that by refining the indicator to include smaller levels of management of agricultural resources, such as the sub-holder, a fuller picture of women's role in agriculture is revealed.

(c) Head of household item: According to the FAO, there is a tendency to only report a man, usually the eldest male, as the head of the household and the holder, even when he is not the person who makes the actual on-farm decisions (FAO 1999a). Diana Templeman of the FAO Regional Office for Africa reports that socio-cultural perceptions may well have contributed to the low figures of female-headed households in: Guinea (2 percent), Tunisia (6.7 percent) and Benin and Burkina Faso (10 percent each) (Templeman 2005).

(d) Land items: While the more detailed land tenure items are indeed useful for a fuller understanding of how land is used, operated and what are the existing legal relationships to the land, this information will not assist researchers and policy makers understand women's relationships to land until a more appropriate definition of holder is developed – which corresponds directly to this section.

Diverse Cultural Perceptions Limit Gender Reporting

Another common challenge we identified in the data collection process is the existence of different levels or realities of women's roles and rights. On one level a woman may have *de jure* rights to own land yet at another level, at the community or household level, her actual or *de facto* rights to own, and perhaps more importantly, control the land resources may be completely different. For example, in some cultures, a woman may not seem to officially be the owner of the land because only her partner's name is on the title, yet if one looks closely at her role and responsibilities, she is in fact the manager of the land, or a section of the land, and related resources. Furthermore, FAO has faced difficulties in collecting data on female heads of households because of cultural perceptions of what defines a head of household.

In order to collect data on women with regards to land and related resources, governments and international organizations must develop innovative ways to approach the organization of household labour. As mentioned above, one way to do this is to present census questions which address specific tasks and not only present a broad question such as 'who is the head of the household' which may trigger debates and reactions relating to male/female power relations. FAO has found that by specifying the indicator or census item at lower household levels, they are able to harvest greater data on women's roles and contributions to agricultural productivity (see Table 2, introduction of sub-holder concept to a set of data in Burkina Faso).

Table 2
Introduction of the Sub-holder Concept to Data on Distribution of Areas Cultivated by Crop in Burkina Faso

Crop	*Head of household /sex (collective cultivation)*		*Plot manager /sex (individual cultivation) %*		*Both*	
	Male	*Female*	*Male*	*Female*	*Male*	*Female*
Millet	97	3	45	55	87	13
Maize	99	1	90	10	89	2
Rice	98	2	65	35	85	15
Groundnuts	97	3	32	68	54	46
Vouandzuo	96	4	20	80	50	50
White sorghum	98	2	58	42	90	10
Red sorghum	97	3	55	45	91	9
Sub total	98	2	48	52	86	14

Source: Tempelman and Keita [2005].

It should be noted that assessing indicators of a particular single functioning (for example, only economic equity function) might give the false impression of equality (if inequality is present in un-assessed functioning). For example, some countries may show a balanced female male ratio but have large gender gaps in enrolment rates. On the other hand, the current trend to compress multiple elements of a functioning vector into composite indices raises many other issues. Value judgments have to be made about the components to be included (based on the intended use of the index) and excluded, and the weights to be allotted. Such indicators, also known as composite indicators, that are constructed with specific purposes in mind can be useful and have proven to be helpful for preliminary comparisons in global analyses. Currently available composite indices, for example the Gender-related Development Index (GDI), may need to be adapted if they are to be used for comparing gender gaps among or within developing countries. Indicators used should further take into account the nature of the population, for example, the use of age-specific disaggregated female male ratios; adult literacy component, etc. are other appropriate considerations. Furthermore, the income component of the GDI, if standardized for skills and supplemented by a 'drudgery' indicator, could provide gender-sensitive information superior to that provided by the functioning components.

CONVENTION REPORTING MECHANISM

The reporting mechanisms of international conventions also can provide a different perspective on what kinds of information (in particular statistical information) governments are reporting. At present, the only international agreement that addresses rural women and land access is the Convention on the Elimination of all forms of Discrimination against Women (CEDAW). Article 14 of the Convention is the in fact the only international legal article devoted to rural women exclusively. Article 14 provides that State parties shall ensure that rural women have the right to have access to agricultural credit and loans, marketing facilities, appropriate technology and equal treatment in land and agrarian reform as well as in land resettlement schemes[8]. While Article 14 does not explicitly guarantee rural women the right to land, it does provide them with equal access to land programmes and just as importantly, equal access to the financial and technological resources necessary to acquire and invest in land.

Once a country has ratified or acceded to the convention, it must within one year submit an initial report on the legislative, judicial, administrative or other measures it has adopted to implement the convention. Afterwards, it must submit a periodic report at least every four years. The reporting guidelines issued by the Committee on the Elimination of Discrimination against Women are very general; they require reporting on legislative, judicial, administrative progress on all the articles[9]. The general recommendation that provides more detailed advice on statistical reporting only recommends that countries make every effort to ensure that national statistical services responsible for planning national censuses and other social and economic surveys formulate their questionnaires in such a way that data can be disaggregated according to gender, with regard to both absolute numbers and percentages, so that interested users can easily obtain information on the situation of women in the particular sector in which they are interested[10] (Committee on the Elimination of Discrimination against Women 1989). While it is important to formally make such a recommendation to State parties, the level of statistical information desired is left unclear.

The Committee does not provide any indicators or baselines for measuring progress on each article. This is likely due to the Committee's effort to encourage governments to submit reports (there may be a fear that the more technical requirements they insert into the guidelines, the less willing governments will be to undertake and submit reports). However, the result is a diverse range of information being reported, with some countries submitting general statistics such as the percentage of the rural population that is female, the economically active female proportion, or the distribution of women employed (Algeria 2003 report, Nicaragua 1999 report), other countries submit more technical statistics such as the percentage of beneficiaries of national land distribution programs or credit programs that are female (Brazil 2002 report); and lastly, some countries do not submit statistics at all and only explain their policies and programmes (South Africa 1998 report).

VALUABLE INDICATORS

After analyzing the existing global level indicators a list considering being useful or valuable indicators on women and land access has been formed (Table 3). While the list is not exhaustive, the following indicators if disaggregated by gender and by urban/rural zone, and if specified appropriately at lower community and household levels, could provide key pieces of information relating to rural women's access to land.

Table 3
Valuable Indicators

a. Economically active population (or labour force) in agriculture by Sex
b. Estimated percentage of population with sustainable access to an improved water source
c. Work and time allocation:
   i. Total work time (minutes per day) by sex
   ii. Female work time as percentage of male work time
   iii. Time spent on market activities and non-market activities by sex
d. Holding, holder
e. Head of household
f. Land tenure (for both holding and parcels)
   iv. Without land
   v. Operated or held in owner like possession
   vi. Rented from others
1. for an agreed amount of money and/or produce
2. for a share of produce
3. in exchange for services
4. under rental arrangements
   vii. Operated on a squatter basis
   viii. Operated under tribal or other traditional communal forms of tenure
   ix. Operated under other tenure forms
g. Existence of laws, policies and institutions to protect equal rights for women and men
h. Percentage of male and female access to and use of credit, markets, financial services
i. Percentage of male and female ownership of businesses (in particular micro-businesses) and capital

A MULTIDISCIPLINARY FRAMEWORK

The valuable indicators identified must be justified by an analytical framework - a set of commonly agreed upon principles with regards to research and policies on women's land access. There is no need for one single framework, as frameworks may and in fact should vary from country to country. Whatever the setting, it is necessary to engage diverse stakeholders from a range of disciplines, i.e., economics, demography, anthropology, sociology, environment, gender dynamics, etc., to ensure that the analytical framework and the data indicators and reporting standards are implemented. A national participatory process will ensure that the indicators developed or refined will secure sufficient buy-in and support to actually be incorporated into data collection programmes. Also, expertise from such cross-disciplinary perspectives will support the linkage of gender policies with environmental and economic policies.

The need to engage such multi-disciplinary of stakeholders in developing a common framework at the national and global levels is also justified by the fact that the land agenda cuts across the poverty reduction agenda. However, the fact that the land agenda does not enjoy a 'depository' mechanism likes desertification and climate with already existing conventions with involvement of multidisciplinary experts. There is much to learn from many interesting examples like the Clean Development Mechanism (CDM) of the Kyoto Protocol of the Convention of Climate Change that have gone through such global and national processes since 1997. At the global level, the starting point for a framework on women and land access should be the CEDAW, yet there may be other useful entry points within related conventions like biodiversity, climate change and desertification.

ConcluDING REMARKS

Our assessment confirms that there is significant gap on reporting and data on rural women's access to land. As one expert put it, gender inequality in rights to land is one of the most inadequately recognized enormities of gender disparity and figure in few statistical systems. Not unexpectedly, we did not find any one single indicator on women's access to land. This is not to say that the information, at least approximate information, is not out there ready to use and improve development work. It is not entirely surprising that there is no indicator on women's access to land because of the difficulty in defining the concept of 'access to land' or even 'land ownership'. In spite of the diverse cultural and legal realities, which have made it difficult to develop an accurate indicator on rural wornan's access to land, the most important lesson we have learned is that there is a wealth of information available already that if properly analyzed could provide an approximate picture of rural women's land access. By bringing together the diverse perspectives, expertise and knowledge of these global institutions, government technical agencies, and civil society stakeholders, the pockets of information available on rural women and land resources can be better refined and analyzed to create a broad map or picture of rural women's access to, control of, use of, land and related resources like water, extension services, credit, etc. The information available is like a puzzle; it needs to be put together carefully and include the participation of rural community stakeholders, the end target group of rural policies and programmes. The challenge is not so much in developing new indicators as refining the indicators are already in existence and pushing governments to report gender sensitive data. The challenge lies in developing a mechanism or a framework whereby organizations like the FAO UNSD, UNDP, UNIFEM, UN Habitat as well as others such as the World Bank that bears a significant amount of data, in collaboration with relevant government ministries, statistical agencies and civil society organizations. Together, they can pull together their knowledge on various aspects of rural women and land and analyze the situation of rural women in relation to land ownership, access, use, etc. It is found that in order to more effectively collect data on rural women's access to land, we do not need to develop new indicators, but rather create a mechanism to compile and analyze the existing data and provide incentives to use them. Greater understanding of rural women's resources and capacities with regards to land will allow for development agencies and governments to refocus their policies and programmes and provide the tools for civil society organizations to lobby these actors for accountable and effective policies and programmes. The task ahead requires exhaustive resources but if not given priority it can be even more costly in terms of undesirable outcomes for the lives of rural poor.

NOTES

1. UNSD collects and collates data from population and housing censuses, and social and demographic surveys conducted by national governments and international organizations within the UN system. Other sources of data include administrative records, such as civil registration, population registers, etc.
2. Found under the category 'indicators on income and economic activity'. The statistical information available here was compiled by the International Labour Organization from population census and labour force sample survey data collected by national statistical services.
3. Found under the category 'indicators on water supply and sanitation'. This data was compiled by UNICEF-WHO in coordination with national statistical services.
4. UNDP links and coordinates global and national efforts to reach the Millennium goals. As part of this obligation, it compiles data already collected by governments, other UN agencies, in particular the FAO, UNICEF, ILO, WHO, etc., and analyzes the data under its own criteria or frameworks, for example the Human Development Index, which has three main groupings of indicators: a long and healthy life (measured by life expectancy from birth), knowledge (adult literacy rate), and decent standard of living (measured by GDP per capita in purchasing power parity US Dollars). It is important to note the GEM, GDI and the HDI are composite indexes, created by mixing the raw data collected by governments and some of the above-mentioned organizations.
5. The primary sources of data for FAO's Statistical Division (FAOSTAT) are periodic agricultural censuses and yearly surveys of agricultural production conducted by its member countries. It also compiles the demographic and labour data disseminated by

the UN Statistics Division and the International Labour Organization (ILO) to create a range of databases.

6. As part of its technical assistance to member countries, FAO's WCA programme assists governments to carry out an agricultural census every decade. The WCA provides countries with recommendations for basic census concepts, definitions and methodologies, including cross-tabulation of census variables, which is fundamental for understanding the agricultural sector from a gender perspective. The last WCA Programme was launched in 2000 and proposed various census items related to rural women and land use/access. The WCA 2010 round is already in its preparatory phase.
7. UN Habitat collects, collates and analyzes data on human settlement trends from national and local level government offices in both urban and rural zones.
8. Article 14 CEDAW, 1981.
9. Compilation of Guidelines on the Form and Content of Reports to be Submitted by State Parties to the International Human Rights Treaties, HRI/GEN/2Rev.1/Add. 2, 2003.
10. General Recommendation No. 9 made by the CEDAW (Eight Session, 1989).

REFERENCES

Committee on the Elimination of Discrimination against Women (1989), *General Recommendation No. 9, Eighth Session*. United Nations, New York.

Committee on the Elimination of Discrimination against Women (1998), *Consideration of Reports Submitted by State Parties under Article 18 of the Convention on the Elimination of All Forms of Discrimination Against Women, Initial Reports of State Parties, South Africa*. United Nations, New York.

Committee on the Elimination of Discrimination Against Women (1999), *Consideration of Reports Submitted by State Parties under Article 18 of the Convention on the Elimination of All Forms of Discrimination Against Women, Fifth Periodic Reports of State Parties, Nicaragua*. United Nations, New York.

Committee on the Elimination of Discrimination against Women (2002), *Consideration of Reports Submitted by State Parties under Article 18 of the Convention on the Elimination of All Forms of*

Discrimination Against Women, Combined Initial, Second, Third, Fourth and Fifth Periodic Reports of State Parties, Brazil. United Nations, New York.

Committee on the Elimination of Discrimination against Women (2003), *Consideration of Reports Submitted by State Parties under Article 18 of the Convention on the Elimination of All Forms of Discrimination Against Women, Second Periodic Reports of State Parties, Algeria*. United Nations, New York.

FAO (1995), *Programme for the World Census of Agriculture*. Rome.

FAO (1999a), *Filling the Data Gap: Gender-Sensitive Statistics for Agricultural Development*. Rome.

FAO (1999b), *Agricultural Censuses and Gender Considerations: Concepts and Methodology*. Rome.

FAO (2000), *Gender and Food Security: The Role of Information Strategy for Action*. Rome.

FAO (2002), *Gender and Access to Land*. Land Tenure Studies, Rome.

FAO, IFAD and ILC (2004), *Rural Women's Access to Land and Property in Selected Countries: Progress Towards Achieving the Aims of the CEDAW*. Rome.

Giovarelli, R. and Lastarria, S. *et al.* (2005), *Gender Issues and Best Practices in Land Administration Projects: A Synthesis Report*. World Bank, Washington DC.

Guyer, J. (1986), Intra-household Processes and Farming Systems Research: Perspectives from Anthropology. In: Moock, J. L. (ed.). *Understanding Africa's Rural Households and Farming Systems*. Westview Press, Boulder.

International Land Coalition (ILC) (2005), *Indicators of Secure Access to Resources*. Paper Presented at the UN Commission on Sustainable Development (CSD-13), New York.

Mikkelsen, L. (2005), *Gender Equality and Empowerment: A Statistical Profile of the ESCAP Region*. United Nations Economic and Social Commission for Asia and the Pacific, Bangkok.

Schlager, E. and Ostrom, E. (1992), Property-Rights Regimes and Natural Resources: A Conceptual Analysis. *Land Economics*, 68 (3): 249-262.

Tempelman, D. and Keita, N. (2005), *Gender Concerns in Agricultural Census in Africa*. S. D Dimensions, Food and Agriculture Organization of the United Nations, Rome.

United Nations (2003), *Compilation of Guidelines on the Form and Content of Reports to be Submitted by State Parties to the International Human Rights Treaties*. HRI/GEN/2 Rev. 1/Add. 2, United Nations, New York.

UN Habitat (1998), *Urban Indicators Tool Kit*. United Nations Human Settlement Programme. Nairobi.

UNIFEM (2000), *Progress of the World's Women*. New York.

WHO and UNICEF (2004), Meeting *the MDG Drinking Water & Sanitation Target: A Midterm Assessment of Progress*. Geneva.

7

COOKING WITH BIOFUEL AND WOMEN HEALTH

SIDDHARTHA SARKAR

INTRODUCTION

The concentration of indoor air pollutants coming out from combustion of biofuels such as wood, agriculture crops and dung cake used by rural households in developing countries cause severe health problems especially to women and children below five years. It has been estimated that approximately half the global population and up to 90 percent of rural households in developing countries still rely on biomass fuels (World Resource Institute 1999) and about 75 per cent of Indian households use biofuels for cooking purposes. Typically cooked indoors in open fires or poorly functioning stoves, which leads to levels of air pollution that are among the highest ever measured. Therefore indoor air pollution with biofuels is an issue that requires to be addressed through gender, energy, environment and health policy. Some of highest concentrations of pollutants come about due to the use of biofuels for cooking in rural indoor environment (Sarkar 2004 a). In developed countries transformation has without exception been come with by a shift from biofuel to petroleum products (kerosene, LPG) and electricity.

In developing countries even where cleaner more sophisticated fuels are available, households often continue to use biomass (Smith 1987). Although the portion of global energy derived from biofuel has fallen substantially which is evidence that biofuel use is increasing among the poor. Poverty is one of the main hurdles to the adoption of cleaner fuels and slow pace of development in many countries implies that biofuels will continue to be used by the poor for many years. Despite the magnitude of the problem of indoor air pollution, the health impact of this environmental exposure has been relatively neglected by research and policy makers.

Biofuels, being an important traditional source of energy, has developed a burly context. It has been showed that nearly 2 million people across the world struggle to meet their basic needs affordable and adequate energy services. In sixteen countries in South and South East Asia over 2 billion people rely on biofuel for cooking, space heating and agro-processing (United Nations 2000). Its crucial importance to sustaining social life, food and nutrition and production activities has supported various national governments to focus heavily on the production and management of biofuel resources. Biofuel refers to any plants or animal based material deliberately burned by human beings. Wood is the most common biofuel, but use of animal dung and crop residues is also wide spread (De Koning *et al.* 1985). Some countries, including China and South Africa also use coal extensively for domestic needs. The types of fuels used typically amplify in cleanliness, convenience, efficiency and cost as people move up what has been termed the energy ladder (Figure1). Animal dung is on the lowest rung of the ladder progressing to crop residues, wood, charcoal, kerosene, gas, and finally electricity. People generally move up the ladder as socio-economic conditions improve. Other sources of indoor air pollution in developing countries include smoke entering the home from nearby houses (Smith *et al.1994*), burning of forests, agricultural land and household waste, the use of kerosene lamps (McCracken and Smith 1998), and industrial and vehicle pollution. Environmental tobacco smoke is another source of indoor air pollution exposures, which can be expected to increase in importance in developing countries. It is important also to recognize that the open hearth and resulting smoke often have considerable cultural and practical value in the home, including control of insects lighting, drying food, fuel and housing materials and for flavouring foods (Smith 1987). The need to encompass biofuel for food and nutritional security has recently been reorganized and the provision of this essential need from production sources to consumption units, mostly households and the process of converting raw biomass into consumable energy are related to overall development.

Figure 1: The Energy Ladder

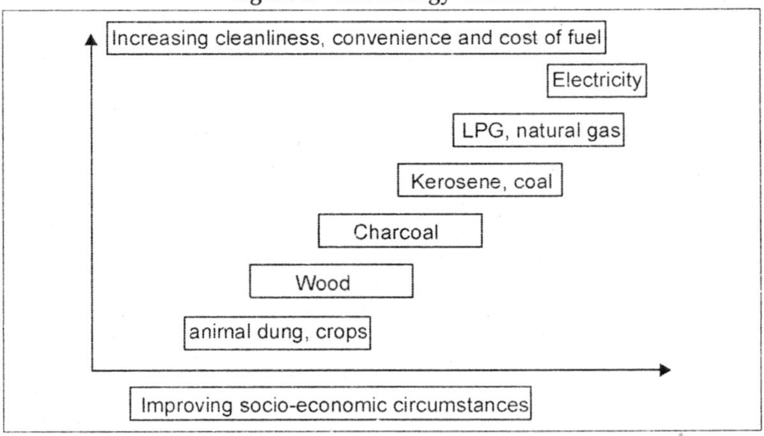

Source: Smith *et al.* [1994]

The implications of this process for the physical and psychological well being of the population or the total well being of those who are engaged in this development paradigm are central to sustainability. Their access to production sources, authority over production, modes of transportation and technology and also a nutritionally adequate diet to bear their daily workload are crucial aspects. From these perspectives what is fundamental is the social domain within which a clear distinction between men's and women's responsibilities, work, social power and authority over resources and technology has been traditionally established. Their biological differences have been instrumental in the gender differentiation of their responsibilities in the biomass cycle. On this basis, the labour performed by women in the promotion of subsistence and well-being has been separated from the work performed by men for cash and income. Similarly mostly in economically backward areas and communities, health repercussions are separated from energy systems and also from the benefits of using biomass as matters pertaining to women's ecology. Biofuel is composed of various portions of plants, including woody stems, barks, roots, twigs, and leaves, which can be burned in raw form to generate energy and it is used primarily by two sectors, wood energy based industries and the household sector, where it is used as a primary source of cooking energy. In South Asia the share of biofuel in the total energy consumption remains high, except in India (Table 1). These countries namely, Bangladesh, India, Pakistan, Nepal and Sri Lanka rely heavily on non-forest sources or on agricultural and other lands for fuel wood. Non-forest sources provide 75 per cent of the fuel wood requirement in Sri Lanka. This indicates the importance of users' access to production sources or the mechanisms through which users get access to resources. The renewable nature of biofuel, its ability to meet the local needs, and the possibility of getting it freely from various sources for direct day to day domestic consumption are the practical advantages that work to preserve the strong links between the household sector and biomass production sources. The implications of using biofuel energy for the society and the economy, particularly of economically less advanced countries, communities and families, are important policy considerations. However, the biofuel energy scenario is marked by features of concern common to many developing countries (Wickramasinghe 2003).

- The first is that biofuel still remains a dirty, messy, unhealthy fuel. Its use is very time consuming and undervalued and dominated by women, and it is used by a majority in developing countries.

- The second is that the unmeasured human costs in terms of human energy, time, discomfort, and personal health are paid mostly by the providers of this basic need from the multiple sources of supply to the household units of consumption.
- The third is that the contributions made by women to sustain biomass energy systems are reckoned solely in the domestic domain, especially as a matter pertaining to domestic cooking, rather than as contributions towards maintaining human capital and quality of life.
- The fourth is related to the underreported realities of psychological trauma and the physical exhaustion of those whose lives are trapped in the biofuel cycle.
- The fifth is that the health risks of procuring and transporting biofuel are on the increase because of many changes in the supply domain, including resource tenure, deforestation, degradation, market demand and competition for better quality wood and the burden of poverty and malnutrition experienced by women in particular.

Table 1
Fuel Wood Consumption in Some South Asian Countries

Country	*Total fuel wood consumption (Mt)*	*Share of (%) forest wood (%)*	*Share of non forest wood (%)*	*Share of biofuel in total energy consumption (%)*
Bangladesh	5.5	13	87	71
India	94.5	26-53	43-74	33
Nepal	11.3	66	34	92
Pakistan	29.0	10	90	46
Sri Lanka	9.1	25	75	55

Source: Bhattarai [1996]

In the developing economies a substantial share of employment is indeed in informal category and women in all age groups depend on the informal sector more heavily than men. Women are over represented in this sector in the sense that their share in the sector is higher than their share in total labour force. Most women tend to be own account workers and only a few are heads of micro enterprises. Relatively lower level of education among women, compared to men, seems to explain, in part, this gender differential in informal employment. Discrimination in the labour market also explains in part the disproportionate concentration as it limits women's access to formal and wage employment. Women also face additional constraints because of their homemaking and childcare responsibilities, which limits their participation in formal employment. Even within the informal sector more women than men seem to be in poor quality employment. In Latin America more women seem to be in the unpaid categories than men. In Africa the proportion of unpaid workers working in family owned enterprises among women appears to be relatively high compared to other regions. The causes for participation in the informal sector can be economic and non-economic. Economic reasons are related to unemployment and an inflexible formal labour market, a declining real price of capital and the high cost of formal production. Besides, non-economic causes are concerned with a greater flexibility and satisfaction in work, a complete use of workers professional qualifications and increased leisure time. There are two groups of factors, which determine the decision to become active in the informal sector, more specifically, the structural as well as opportunity factors. The structural factors consist of financial pressure, socio-psychological pressure and institutional constraints. The opportunity factors consist of individual background, skills, education, living condition or non-individual components, environment, values, standards etc. (Sarkar 2004 b). Unlike modern fuels, the supply of biofuels such as wood and charcoal are still largely uncontrolled and based in the informal sector. Rural populations generally supply themselves from surrounding forests and from trees in the landscape, in most cases in quantities that do not exceed sustainability limits. The supply of biomass fuel for the cities is also uncontrolled and in most cases, biomass production is unsustainable. Wood is felled in state-owned forests by dealers, but the cost of replacing the trees is not paid, with the result that forests are deteriorating rapidly around major cities. Past efforts to relieve the resulting firewood shortage by encouraging farmers to grow trees have largely failed because the costs of this far exceed the short term costs of gathering fuel from existing forests (French 1986). However new efforts to empower local communities to manage the forests in their areas in a sustainable way for the production, among other things, of biomass fuels are encouraging, particularly as this could provide income sources for the poor within the community. In most developing countries the majority of informal sector enterprises are owned and operated by women, with women making up the largest proportion of the work force. Despite this, the contribution of women entrepreneurs to national economies is not explicit in national statistics, leading to the development of policies that do not deal with the specific barriers faced by women linked to their gender-defined roles. Their enterprises tend to be concentrated in a relatively narrow range of activities such as knitting, dressmaking, crocheting, cane work and retail trading. These activities tend to have disproportionately low rates of return compared to the activities undertaken by men. However despite the low financial returns, women's enterprises provide important sources of household income, even in male-headed households. Women headed enterprises are frequently located in the home and these cottage industries tend to be overlooked by agencies because they are in the informal sector, which is diffuse and difficult to reach. When women are forced to close their enterprises, it is often for non-business reasons and linked to factors associated with working from home. The low rates of return prevent inward investment, hindering innovation and expansion, which are regarded as key factors in enterprise sustainability (Grosh and Somolekae 1996). There is little research to explain what forces drive these startups and shutdowns, and how gender influences these processes. Women's access to resources (such as credit, land and education, which are recognized as key factors in micro enterprise development) is significantly less than that of men.

Generally, research in small and medium-scale enterprise sustainability indicates that a lack of working capital is one of the two most common causes of enterprise failure (Grosh and Somolekae 1996). Women's access to decision-making within the household and community is also restricted, reducing their ability to influence processes and resource allocation. Given the disproportionate number of poor women in rural areas, research which takes into account gender aspects of the transformation of structures and processes could make a significant contribution to the development of gender equitable sustainable livelihoods. The role of energy in the sustainability of women's enterprises is also not well understood. In food processing enterprises it has been estimated that energy costs are 20 to 25 per cent of the total inputs, which would suggest that technological interventions could increase the scale and profitability of these businesses. Figure 2 gives some examples of how energy can act as an opportunity or a constraint on women's productive activities. The types of enterprises that women are traditionally involved in are energy intensive and rely on biomass fuels. Even in rural areas, women may have to buy fuel wood to run enterprises such as beer making (McCall 2001). An important issue is what sort of mechanisms can assist women in gaining access to improved energy services. Grain mills, which are very popular with women, since they improve product quality as well as reducing women's labour, are typically only provided by the private sector, and are still absent in many rural locations. A much more systematic approach is needed, possibly with some form of incentive to encourage the spread of mills to areas not yet served. A general rule that can be learnt from attempts to introduce technology for women is that if it does not reduce the labour in household tasks then, no matter how beneficial the technology, it is likely to have low acceptance. There are positive examples of women taking up energy technologies that have contributed to increasing their incomes. It is found that women's groups in Ghana use LPG for fish preservation, giving them a better quality product than when using wood, and enabling them to reach export standards, considerably improving their income (Mensah 2001). Women may in fact be best entrants to become energy entrepreneurs. It has indicated that improved stove programmes in India run by women tend to be rather successful because they are able to more easily approach their clients (Sarin 1984). However energy entrepreneurship could extend beyond stoves to include energy services, for example the supply of and even the repair of, modern energy appliances such as solar panels. There is an enormous need for agents in rural areas who can distribute such equipment on a viable basis, notwithstanding with some support in the short term. Women who live in rural areas know and understand local circumstances and needs and may have a much clearer idea about the energy services that rural people desire. In addition a woman may be able to sell more effectively to other women, since access to female clients is not hindered by social constraints. This may in fact be the best route to greater women's participation in household energy choice.

Figure 2: Energy in Livelihood Strategies: Improving Position of Women

Energy availability that creates opportunities (increased income/more sustainable use of natural resources)

- Community level sustainable management of forests can provide income through organized firewood production and sale.
- Energy entrepreneurship as a secondary activity for community service and income generation.
- Improved technologies for charcoal production can boost sustainability and incomes.
- Availability of mechanical and process heat technologies can be a stimulus to the start up of various small-scale enterprises (sawing, food processing etc.).

Energy scarcity as a constraint (which if removed, can bolster other activities, reduce vulnerability, improve food security, increase well being)

- Lack of transport for moving harvest products to storage and to market may be a disincentive to produce (increases vulnerability, and reduces food security).
- Poor cooking technology results in unnecessary ill health for women and children reducing their productivity (and threatening well being).
- Lack of cheap, easily available, fuel forces women to spend large amounts of time gathering fuel, and restricts the boiling of water and in some cases the adequate cooking of food resulting in ill health (threatens well being, increases vulnerability) as well as limiting time available for other enterprises.

REVIEW OF LITERATURE

Air pollution has been consistently linked with substantial burden of ill health in developed and developing countries (Bruce et al. 2000; Schwartz 1994; Smith et al. 2000). The bulk of indoor air pollution research and control has focused on sources of concern in developed countries based on solid fuel and tobacco combustion (Smith and Mehta 2003). Exposures to indoor air pollution are of importance cause of morbidity and mortality in developed countries (World Health Organization 1997, 2002) as well as developing countries (Florig 1997; Saksena and Dayal 1997; World Bank 1997; World Health Organization 1997). However the most important indoor air pollutants are the combustion products of unprocessed solid biomass used by the vulnerable section urban and rural people in developing countries for cooking and heating purpose. Exposure to biomass smoke enhances the risk of acute respiratory infection among women and children below five years. A study in Gambia focuses that infants who were exposed to smoke by being carried on their mother's backs during cooking were nearly three times more likely to develop significant cases of acute respiratory infection. A study in Colombia expresses that women cooking over open fires had almost four times more chronic lung disease compared to those cooking in other manner (Parikh 1996). A study in Tanzania finds that children younger than five years who died of acute respiratory infection were almost three times more likely to be sleeping in a room with an open cook stove than healthy children in same age group. Studies in India, Nepal and Papua New Guinea show that non-smoking women who have cooked on biomass stoves for many years exhibit a higher prevalence of chronic lung disease. In Mexico, women exposed to wood smoke for many years faced 75 times more risk of acquiring chronic lung disease, about the level of risk that heavy cigarette smokers face than women not exposed to wood smoke. A recent study in Colombia discloses that women exposed to smoke during cooking were three times more likely to suffer from chronic lung diseases. A study in Japan delves into high rates of cancer among women who had previously used wood as fuel. The risk of lung cancer is high in Chinese women exposed to coal smoke in homes. Likewise a study in Africa encompasses that cooking with wood greatly increased the risk of stillbirth. Considerable amount of carbon monoxide have been detected in the bloodstream of women cooking with biomass in India and Guatemala (World Bank 2000). It has been estimated that about half a million women and child die each year from air pollution in India. Compared to other countries India has among the largest burden of disease due to the use of dirty household fuels and 28 per cent of all death due to indoor air pollution in developing countries occurs in India (Smith 2000a). It is estimated that use of open fires with biofuels exposes nearly 2 billion people in the world to enhanced concentrations of particulate matter and gases, up to 10-20 times higher than health-based guideline values available for typical urban outdoor concentrations (Barnes et al. 1994; Reddy et al. 1996; World Health Organization 1999). Assessments of the burden of disease attributable to use of biofuels use in India have put the figure at 3-5 percent of the national burden of disease (Smith 2000b; Smith and Mehta 2003). Some of the earliest human evidence linking indoor air pollution from biomass combustion with respiratory health came from studies carried out in Nepal and India (Pandey 1984a; Ramakrishna et al. 1989; Smith *et al.* 1983). Since then, there has been a steady stream of studies, especially on women who cook with these fuels and young children (Bruce *et al.* 2000; Smith et al. 2000). Associations between exposure to indoor air pollution and increased incidence of chronic bronchitis in women and acute respiratory infections in children have been documented (Armstrong and Campbell 1991; Bruce *et al.* 1998; Ezzati and Kammen 2001; Robin *et al.* 1996). Many recent studies have also been conducted in rural Indian villages (Awasthi *et al.* 1996; Behera *et al.* 1991; Mishra and Retherford 1997; Smith 1993; Smith 1996). A recent study has also characterized the exposure response relationship between biomass smoke exposure and acute respiratory infection in children of rural Kenyan households (Ezzati *et al.* 2000a). The incidence of chronic obstructive pulmonary disease in non-smoking women using biomass for cooking has also been shown to be dependent on the number of years cooking with biofuels and often to be comparable to that of men who usually have high smoking rates. Based on this evidence, it has been estimated that the indoor air pollution contributes to 3-5 per cent other causes as well, it is difficult, lengthy, and of the national burden of disease in India (Smith 2000b).

Exposure to indoor air pollution, especially to particulate matter, from the combustion of biofuels has been implicated as a causal agent of respiratory diseases in developing countries (Chen *et al.* 1990; Ellegard 1996; Pandey 1984b). This association, coupled with the fact that globally more than 2 billion people rely on biomass as the primary source of domestic energy, has put preventive measures to reduce exposure to indoor air pollution high on the agenda of international development and public health organizations (Ezzati *et al.* 2000b; World Bank 1993). The evaluation of the benefits and effectiveness of measures that aim to reduce these negative health impacts, such as design and dissemination of improved stoves and fuels, requires knowledge of the exposure response relationship between indoor particulate matter from biomass combustion and acute respiratory infections. There is little information on the shape of the exposure response relationship at concentrations of hundreds to thousands of micrograms per cubic meter that are commonly observed in indoor environments in developing countries (Ezzati *et al.* 2000b).

The epidemiological studies have provided some evidence of an association between cataract or blindness and exposure to indoor smoke from household use of solid biofuels fuels such as animal dung, wood and crop residues (Mishra *et al.* 1999; Zodpey and Ughade 1999). However, these studies have had limitations that have precluded establishment of a definitive causal relationship. The study of Zodpey and Ughade (1999) found an association between cataract and cheaper cooking fuels such as coal, cow dung and wood presented limited data on potential confounding factors, other than age and socioeconomic status. The other study, with a cross sectional design, used data from the 1992-93 Indian National Family Health Survey which found an association between biomass fuel use and partial and complete blindness after adjustment for a number of potentially confounding factors (Mishra *et al.* 1999). Use of biofuels causes a number of respiratory problems, which include acute respiratory infections in children, chronic obstructive lung disease in nonsmokers (Samet *et al.* 1987). It has also been implicated as a risk factor for lung cancer in women (Gao 1996; Wu and Du 1996).

OBJECTIVE AND METHODOLOGY

Rural women have often been ignored in policies to enhanced access of the poor to more efficient and convenient forms of energy in developing countries including India. Rural development programmes have therefore had limited success in alleviating air pollution, including the drudgery of fuel wood collection and biomass based cooking that cause danger to the health of rural women and children. The challenge has to be addressed in a broader perspective including social and behavioural aspect. A community cooking with biofuels can be exposed to several health diseases and to alleviate such problem gender participation promotion may be an appropriate solution. The highest concentration of indoor air pollutants emerges from burning of biofuels such as wood, agriculture crops and dung cake, which are widely used by rural households in rural North Bengal, India. Compared to the thousand of studies outdoor air pollution in developed country urban settings, only a handful of studies nearly a few dozen have been carried out in biomass using households in developing countries, most of which are rural settings. The different characteristics of fuel uses such as major fuel used for cooking time and effort involved in getting that particular fuel and availability of other type of fuels in the area, cooking practices, exposure to indoor pollution, health impact along with socio-economic conditions of households in rural villages especially women in rural North Bengal can be comprehended from the study. The pollutants released due to use of biofuels for cooking need to pay more attention to the mass rural women living daily with exposure to indoor air pollutants and to curb indoor air pollutants exposure to acceptable level access of clean fuels is required for the better health of rural women. Policies for rural areas that encourage the uptake of efficient use of biomass fuels can effectively address the problem of indoor air pollution and physical drudgery of women. But women must involve in the planning of these policies and interventions to ensure their successful implementation and sustainability. Energy policies and projects by themselves will not change the plight of women in the society, but these can be used as entry point for reducing a preventable burden of death and illness among women and promoting greater fairness in the allocation of opportunities and resources between men and women.

The present study on indoor air pollution and women health in the informal sector of rural North Bengal is purely based on primary data using survey research technique. There is a definite need for better and comprehensive household energy survey in rural areas in developing countries with a view to better understanding the current and changing pattern of fuel use over time and to ensure women participation in planning and execution of programmes targeting indoor air pollution and build up their awareness towards health, environment and energy issues. The study strongly purports to seek interdisciplinary relevance with issue relating to gender studies, health economics, energy and environment perspective. The different characteristics of fuel uses such as major fuel used for cooking time and effort involved in getting that particular fuel and availability of other type of fuels in the study area, cooking practices, exposure to indoor air pollution, health impact along with socio-economic conditions of households in rural villages of North Bengal especially women engaged in informal activities and children below five years of age can be comprehended from the study. However the major objective of the study includes the following:

- Socio-economic status of the households
- Fuel use pattern and cooking practices of the households

- Reasons for not using clean fuel and willingness to pay for it
- Association among combustion of biofuels, air pollution and women health

The selection of villages from rural North Bengal for the purpose of extensive survey was carried out using multistage sampling method. At primary stage stratification of the regions was done on the basis of socio-cultural districts. At the second stage selection of one district per socio-cultural districts was done based on the population median class. At the third stage allocation of households to each district based on the universe of rural households was undertaken. Then stratification of each selected district was done by village population size. The villages were categorized into four different strata on the basis of population. In stratum I villages with population less than 1500 were included; stratum II had villages with population 1500-3500, whereas in stratum III villages with population between 3500-5500 were included. In stratum IV villages with population more than 5500 were considered. Stratum IV was excluded from the sample because these villages resemble semi urban areas. The selection of the villages from each stratum was done using population proportion sampling and selection of households within the selected villages was performed based on systematic random sampling. The survey was carried out at household level including individual responses for health status, village level as well as local health care facility. Village level and health centre surveys were performed for the sake of validation of data acquired at household and individual level. At the household level a multi pronged approach was used while collecting different types of information. Data were collected through face-to-face interview of the chief cook of the house along with any helping hands and health status was assessed with the help of qualified medical practitioners. Various socio-economic information and other details as well as individual self-reported data were gathered through structure questionnaire survey. The information collected for the study comprise of socio-economic characteristics, fuel consumption pattern, cooking behaviour along with health profile.

The survey was conducted in rural villages of Cooch Behar, Darjeeling, Jalpaiguri, and Malda districts covering 2,580 individuals, of which 967 women, 1,082 men, 255 girls and 276 boys below 14 years in 740 households in 20 villages. The sample respondents were selected using stratified random sampling techniques from the surveyed villages. The village level information was collected from the head of village panchayat whereas health centre level information was gathered from administrative officer or chief doctor. The data at household level were congregated to get a comprehensive picture of socio-economic conditions, energy use pattern, cooking behaviour, willingness to pay to curb indoor air pollution and health considerations.

FINDINGS

In rural North Bengal most of the people are engaged in the informal sector, of which women are generally employed in domestic services, *beedi* making, agriculture and allied activities, construction work, brick making and rural artisans. It is observed that most of the surveyed villages are linked with road network and have some mode of transportation. In the selected villages 13 villages have *pucca* road within a kilometre distance and other 2 villages have pucca road within 2 kilometres distance and 5 villages have pucca road beyond 2 kilometres but less than 4 kilometres distance. Only 2 villages have railway station within a distance of 3 to 6 kilometres and people in rest of the 18 villages face difficulties to avail railway transportation because of locating station at long distance. Most of the villages (60 per cent) have a town within a distance of 2 to 5 kilometres. As the majority of the surveyed villages are close to pucca roads, the main mode of transportation is bus. Add to there is other modes of transportation such as van rickshaw and bicycle. Almost all villages have at least a primary school and 7 villages have secondary school also. 16 villages have primary health centres with an average distance of 2 to 4 kilometres.

Economic compulsion is the main reasons of the women behind taking the job as informal workers (98 per cent). However there is a tiny percentage (2 per cent) of the workers mostly the wives from middle class families, who entered the informal job market for passing out idle time. Besides child labourers entered the workforce for meeting their own educational expenses. 16.96 per cent of women workers reported that they have chosen the job for supporting their family and 29.68 per cent of the workers serve for independent income. It is also reported that most of the adult male members of the households are agriculture workers (62.01 per cent). Others engage as casual labour (5.53 per cent), rickshaw puller (9.89 per cent), petty trader (7.76 per cent), wholesale trader (3.79 percent) and government employee (1.02 per cent). It is found that 10 percent among them do not work at all.

The women do simultaneously their own household task. They combine wage work with their domestic responsibilities. Table 2 discloses the level of participation in own household task as reported by female members of the households.

Table 2
Level of Participation in Own Household Task

Household task	*Self*	*Husband/Other members*	*Jointly*
Washing clothes and utensils	1043 (85.35)	57 (4.67)	122 (9.98)
Water collection	1117 (91.41)	32 (2.62)	73 (5.97)
Fuel collection	937 (76.68)	187 (15.30)	98 (8.02)
Food preparation	1222 (100.00)	0 (0)	0 (0)
Maintenance of house	482 (39.44)	527 (43.13)	213 (17.43)
Childcare	1098 (89.85)	83 (6.79)	41 (3.36)

Note: Figures in the parentheses are percentages and female members include girl children

Therefore women including girl children have nearly full responsibilities in activities such as washing clothes and utensils, water collection, fuel collections, food preparation and childcare activities. Apart from the large bulk of sundry task often some workers are to assist their counterparts in agriculture activities. In addition girl children are to help their mother in sundry household task especially water collection, fuel collection and food preparation.

The survey shows that 52.3 per cent of the households have annual income less than Rs. 25,000 while 35.54 per cent of the households have annual income above Rs.25,000 but below Rs. 50,000. only 7.16 per cent of the households have income more than Rs. 50,000 but below Rs. 75,000.The different types of durables owned by the households reveal the purchasing power/economic status of the households. The survey discloses that majority of the households are unable to buy anything additional for the family. It is also found that female members of the households working for more than ten years failed to save sufficient amount of money to buy durables.

It is found that almost all (94.46 per cent) of surveyed households in rural villages North Bengal use biofuels for cooking. Among biofuels using households, 78.25 per cent use fuel wood. Dung cake and crop residue are used in 73.4 per cent and 35.48 per cent of households respectively. The average consumption of fuel wood is about 5.4 kgs per households, supplemented by other biofuel sources. Kerosene is mostly used for lighting and its use for cooking is restricted to only 5.68 per cent of the households. Only 14 households make use of LPG and use of electricity and biogas for cooking is almost trivial. The study reveals that most of the households cook (87.03 per cent) twice meals a day. 5.41 per cent of the households cook once. Remaining 7.57 per cent of the households cook thrice a day. The average time spent for cooking a day is about 4 hours along with other associate sundry household task.

Willingness to pay of the participants estimates the probable demand for kerosene. The kerosene supplied through public distribution system is mostly limited to quota. The study shows that most of the villages do not get kerosene through rationing system and 3 villages reported to have an irregular supply of kerosene. The use of clean fuel is higher among higher income group. Only 48.24 per cent of the households are drawing kerosene as per quota from ration shop. About 53.78 per cent of the households are to buy an average quantity of 8 litres kerosene per month for lighting and cooking from open market. The survey reveals that at the ration price almost all sampled households (99.05 per cent) are willing to purchase an additional quantity of kerosene. 62.03 per cent of the households are ready to switch over to clean fuel if made available. The results of the survey show that only 6.35 per cent of the households are willing to spend some money to improved air quality in the kitchen. There is a higher willingness to pay for ventilation in houses than for improved stoves.

Table 3
Reasons for not Using Clean Fuels

Reasons	*Percentage agree*
Lack of availability	83.67
Costly	69.78
Not willing to switch over	17.91
Anxious of using	23.93
Taste of food changes	78.52
Not persuaded of the advantages	8.31
Wood smoke repels for insects	1.58
Wood smoke enhances the longevity of thatched roof	3.3
Base: household not using kerosene for cooking	698

The households not using kerosene for cooking are asked for the reasons for not using clean fuels. 83.67 per cent of the households reported non-availability as the reason for not using it, while 69.78 per cent do not use clean fuels because of non-affordability. 17.91 per cent are not interested to switch over to clean fuel and a tiny percentage of households agree with other reasons (Table 3).

The air pollution has been consistently associated with substantial burdens of ill health in developed and developing countries. The study of selected villages reveals that women and children are badly affected by pollution. It is found that most of the diseases are indoor air such as bronchitis, tuberculosis, asthma, eye disease, adverse pregnancy outcomes, skin infection, joint pain, other respiratory diseases etc. Also general muscular weakness, phlegm and cough among children have been noticed in the villages. A majority of complaints are about problems regarding bronchitis and tuberculosis. The women suffering from respiratory diseases are 46.4 per cent. Asthma was reported by 10.1 per cent whereas 4.8 per cent reported bronchitis. The reporting of symptoms and diseases were kept into account on the basis of respondent's memory recall for all the members of the households. Incidence of asthmatic symptoms noticed to be higher among women who cook inside compared to those who cook open air. On the basis of self reported symptomatic cases of respiratory diseases cough, breathlessness, wheezing are found to be significantly higher among those living *kachcha* houses and using biofuels for cooking compared to those living *pucca* houses and using clean fuels for cooking.

CONCLUDING REMARKS

Indoor air pollution comes out to be a major environmental and public health hazard for large numbers of the world's poorest, most disadvantaged people. The existing studies on indoor air pollution in developing countries, while providing important evidence of associations with a range of serious and common health problems, suffer from a number of methodological limitations. There is also a strong case for carrying out a limited number of intervention studies, particularly for the most common and serious health outcomes from indoor air pollution due to burning of biofuels. Such studies may adopt a randomized controlled trial design, which will provide the most powerful evidence and remove the problem of confounding, or be based on natural experiments if appropriate settings are found. Case-control or cohort studies may also serve this purpose if suitable areas can be identified where a good range of exposure levels are distributed fairly evenly and confounding factors are not too strongly associated with exposure. The stress that future studies should shell out more attention to exposure assessment implies a need to further develop practical and valid methods for measuring the exposure levels and patterns particularly for women and children. However the following policy and strategy recommendations have been made.

- A general improvement in the health status especially that of women and children, is a critical input for economic growth and poverty reduction, thus addressing the health impacts of household energy and indoor air pollution should be an integral part of poverty reduction efforts.
- Improved biomass stoves and cleaner biomass based fuels will continue to be an option for reducing exposure for a large majority of the rural poor in developing countries. Facilitating behavioural changes in women, children and other household members is another way of reducing exposure and alleviating the associated health impacts. Improving the status of women can be an effective method of promoting markets for better stoves and other household energy use services.
- The government should ensure sustained upshot market mechanisms for distribution of improved stoves and commercial fuels. Programmes that propagate improved biomass stoves with higher efficiency and lower emissions commercially, with proper certification and quality control by government agencies, have greater financial sustainability, respond better to user demand and produce more durable stoves. Therefore, government interventions should be re-oriented towards creating a effective regulatory framework and incentive structure that works with the market.
- One of the most important elements of a strategy to mitigate indoor air pollution is to bring about a behavioural change, including a greater demand for cleaner cooking. This will require raising awareness amongst rural households about the health impacts of traditional household energy use and providing

specific information on the range and effectiveness of mitigation options.

- Among the rural poor, at the household level the decision making regarding fuel use patterns largely depend on men, while girls and women continue to put up with the burden of collecting fuel wood and use it for cooking, thus exposing themselves to highest levels of indoor air pollution. It is therefore important to ensure mechanisms that allow both women and men to make choices and influence household decisions regarding the use of fuels. Creating self-help groups, promoting energy entrepreneurship and ensuring income generation opportunities for women as part of household energy strategy are the approaches that may improve rural living standards.
- The effective household energy programmes should address the range of sustainable livelihood and poverty needs of both women and men. In poor households, energy and time use for consumption and production are closely interrelated such as food and beverages may be prepared for family use as well as for sale; fuel wood may be collected for cooking and for sale etc. Increasing opportunities for women to earn income outside of the household may be the only way to reduce the use of fuel wood collected with unpaid family labour and therefore engagement in paid informal activities may generate income for the rural women. Programmes to improve household energy services and mitigate indoor air pollution need to address these aspects, by providing opportunities for income earning for women engaged in the informal economic activities.

REFERENCES

Armstrong, J. R. and Campbell, H. (1991), Indoor Air Pollution and Lower Respiratory Infections in Young Gambian Children. *Int J Epidemiol*, 20(2): 424-429.

Awasthi, S., Glick, H. and Fletcher, R. (1996), Effect of Cooking Fuels on Respiratory Diseases in Preschool Children in Lucknow, India. *Am J Trop Med Hyg*, 55(1): 48-51.

Barnes, D. F., Openshaw, K., Smith, K. R. and Van der Plas, R. (1994), *What Makes People Cook with Improved Biomass Stoves? A Comparative International Review of Stove Programs*. World Bank Technical Paper, Energy Series 242, Washington DC.

Behera, D., Jindal, S. K. and Malhotra, H. S. (1991), Ventilatory Function in Nonsmoking Rural Indian Women Using Different Cooking Fuels. *Thorax*, 46(5): 344-346.

Bhattarai, T. N. (1996), *Integrating Wood Fuel Production in the Implementation of Agriculture, Forestry and Rural Extension Programmes in South Asia*. Regional Wood Energy Development Programme in Asia, Report No. 26, Food and Agriculture Organization, Bangkok.

Bruce, N. (2000), *Global Technical Consultation on the Health Impacts of Indoor Air Pollution and Household Energy in Developing Countries*. USAID/WHO, Washington DC.

Bruce, N., Perez-Padilla, R. and Albalak, R. (2000), Indoor Air Pollution in Developing Countries: A Major Environmental and Public Health Challenge for New Millennium. *Bulletin of the World Health Organization*, 78(9): 1078-1092.

Chen, B. H., Hong, C. J., Pandey, M. R. and Smith K. R. (1990), Indoor Air Pollution in Developing Countries. *World Health Stat Q*, 43:127-138.

De Koning, H. W., Smith, K. R. and Last, J. M. (1985), Biomass Fuel Combustion and Health. *Bulletin of the World Health Organization*, 63(1): 11-26.

Ellegard, A. (1996), Cooking Fuel Smoke and Respiratory Symptoms among Women in Low-Income Areas in Maputo. *Environ Health Perspect*, 104: 980-985.

Ezzati, M, Saleh, H. and Kammen, D.M. (2000a), The Contributions of Emissions and Spatial Microenvironments to Exposure to Indoor Air Pollution from Biomass Combustion in Kenya. *Environ Health Perspect*, 108: 833-839.

Ezzati, M., Mbinda, B.M. and Kammen, D.M. (2000b), Comparison of Emissions and Residential Exposure from Traditional and Improved Biofuel Stoves in Rural Kenya. *Environ Sci Technol*, 34:578-583.

Ezzati, M. and Kammen, D. M. (2001), Quantifying the Effects of Exposure to Indoor Air Pollution from Biomass Combustion on Acute Respiratory Infections in Developing Countries. *Env Health Perspect*, 109:481-489.

Florig, H. K. (1997), China's Air Pollution Risks. *Environ Sci Tech*, 31(6): 276A-279A.

French, D. (1986), Confronting an Unsolvable Problem: Deforestation in Malawi. *World Development*, 14 (4): 531-540.

Gao, Y. T. (1996), Risk Factors for Lung Cancer among Nonsmokers with Emphasis on Lifestyle Factors. *Lung Cancer*, 14 (Supplementary 1): S39-S45.

Grosh, B. and Somolekae, G. (1996), Mighty Oaks from Little Acorns: Can Micro Enterprise Serve as the Seedbed of Industrialization? *World Development*, 24 (12): 1879-1890.

McCall, M. (2001), Brewing Rural Beer should be a Hotter Issue. *Boiling Point*, 47: 23-25.

McCracken, J. P. and Smith, K.R. (1998), Emissions and Efficiency of Improved Wood Burning Cook Stoves in Highland Guatemala. *Environ Int*, 24(7): 739-747.

Menash, S. A. (2001), Energy for Rural Women's Enterprises. In: *Generating Opportunities: Case Studies on Energy and Women*. United Nations Development Programme, New York.

Mishra, V. and Rutherford, R. (1997), Cooking Smoke Increases the Risk of Acute Respiratory Infections in Children. *National Family Heath Survey Bulletin* (8).

Mishra, V. K., Retherford, R. D. and Smith, K. R. (1999), Biomass Cooking Fuels and Prevalence of Blindness in India. *J Environ Med*, 1:189-199.

Pandey, M. R. (1984a), Prevalence of Chronic Bronchitis in a Rural Community of the Hill Region of Nepal. *Thorax*, 39:331-336.

Pandey, M. R. (1984b), Domestic Smoke Pollution and Chronic Bronchitis in a Rural Community of the Hill Region of Nepal. *Thorax*, 39:337-339.

Parik, J. (1996), *Poverty, Environment and Development Nexus*. Human Development Report, United Nations Development Programme, New York.

Ramakrishna, J., Durgaprasad, M. B. and Smith, K. R. (1989), Cooking in India: The Impact of Improved Stoves on Indoor Air Quality. *Environ Int*, 15: 341-352.

Reddy, A. K. N., Williams, R.H., Johansson, T. B. (1996), *Energy after Rio: Prospects and Challenges*. United Nations Publications, New York.

Robin, L. F., Lees, P. S. J., Winget, M., Steinhoff, M., Moulton, L.H., Santhosham, M. and Correa A. (1996), Wood Burning Stoves and Lower Respiratory Illness in Navajo Children. *Pediatr Infect Dis J*, 15: 859-865.

Saksena, S. and Dayal, V. (1997), Total Exposure as a Basis for the Economic Valuation of Air Pollution in India. *Energy Environment Monitor*, 13(2): 93-102.

Samet, J. M., Marbury, M.C. and Spengler, J. D. (1987), Health Effects and Source of Indoor Air Pollution Part I. *Am Rev Respir Dis*, 136:1486-508.

Sarin, M. (1984), *Nada Chula: A Handbook*. Voluntary Health Association of India, Delhi.

Sarkar, S. (2004a), Air Pollution: Its Perilous Chronic Hygienic Impacts. *J Hum Ecol*, 16(2): 129-132.

Sarkar, S. (2004b), Theorising in Informal Sector: Concept and Context. *Social Action*, 54(40): 359-373.

Schwartz, J. (1994), Air Pollution and Daily Mortality: A Review and Meta Analysis. *Environ Res*, 64:36-52.

Smith, K. R., Aggarwal, A. L. and Dave, R. M. (1983), Air Pollution and Rural Biomass Fuels in Developing Countries: A Pilot Village Study in India and Implications for Research and Policy. *Atmos Environ*, 17: 2343-2362.

Smith, K. R. (1987), *Biofuels, Air Pollution, and Health. A Global Review*. Plenum Press, New York.

Smith, K. R. (1993), Fuel Combustion, Air Pollution and Health: The Situation in Developing Countries. *An Rev Energy Env*, 18: 529-566.

Smith, K. R., Apte, M. G., Yoqing, M., Wongsekiarttirat, W. and Kulkarni, A. (1994), Air Pollution and the Energy Ladder in Asian Cities. *Energy*, 19(5): 587-600.

Smith, K. R. (1996), *Indoor Air Pollution in Developing Countries: Growing Evidence of its Role in the Global Disease Burden*. Organizing Committee of the 7th International Conference on Indoor Air Quality and Climate. Seec Ishibashil Inc., Japan.

Smith, K. R. (2000a), Indoor Air Pollution Implicated in Alarming Health Problems. In: *Indoor Air Pollution-Energy and Health for the Poor*. Newsletter Published by World Bank.

Smith, K. R. (2000b), The National Burden of Disease in India from Indoor Air Pollution. *Proc Nat Acad Sci*, 97: 13286-13293.

Smith, K. R., Samet, J. M., Romieu, I. and Bruce, N. (2000), Indoor Air Pollution in Developing Countries and Acute Lower Respiratory Infections in Children. *Thorax*, 55:518-532.

Smith, K. R. and Mehta, S. (2003), The Burden of Disease from Indoor Air Pollution in Developing Countries: Compared of Estimates. *Int J Hyg Environ Health*, 206:279-289.

United Nations (2000), *World Energy Assessment: The Challenge of Sustainability*. United Nations, New York.

Wickramasinghe, A. (2003), Gender and Health Issues in the Biomass Energy Cycle: Impediments to Sustainable Development. *Energy for Sustainable Development*, VII (3): 51-61.

World Bank (1993), *Investing in Health*. World Development Report, Oxford University Press, New York.

World Bank (1997), *Clean Water, Blue Skies: China's Environment in the New Century*. World Bank 114, Washington DC.

World Bank (2000), *Household Energy, Air Pollution and Health*. UNDP/ ESMAP.

World Health Organization (1997), *Health and Environment in Sustainable Development*. Geneva.

World Health Organization (1999), *Guidelines for Air Quality*. Geneva.

World Health Organization (2002), *Reducing Risks, Promoting Healthy Life*. World Health Report, Geneva.

World Resource Institute (1999), *1998-99 World Resources: A Guide to the Global Environment*. Oxford University Press.

Wu, J. M. and Du, Y. X. (1996), Overview and Highlights of the Panel Discussion. *Lung Cancer*, 14 (Supplementary 1): S3-S8.

Zodpey, S. P. and Ughade, S. N. (1999), Exposure to Cheaper Cooking Fuels and Risk of Age Related Cataract in Women. *Ind J Occupational Environ Med*, 3:159-161.

8

ACCELERATING WOMEN ACCESS TO JUSTICE

JAMILA AHMED CHOWDHURY

INTRODUCTION

Bangladesh, one of the poorest South-Asian countries having an estimated population of 144 million[1] and ranked as 72 out of 95 developing countries in the world[2] is facing numerous problems in its development pursuit. But now-a-days one-issue getting increased deliberation in its development agenda is the empowerment of its women, a group constitutes fifty percent of its national population,[3] ignoring whose equal rights and participation a broad based development goal can not be materialized. Although Article 27[4] and Article 31[5] of the *Constitution of the People's Republic of Bangladesh*[6] have ensured people's equal right to access justice, the gap between theoretical entitlement and practical access is immense in the country. The formal state-court system in Bangladesh is inundated with exorbitant costs, a huge backlog of cases, excessive delay in disposal etc. (Hasan 2003) in *general* and lack of integrity among judicial personnel, corruption, uneven geographical distribution of formal courts in the urban and rural areas, diversified and complex economic and social order, pro-male gender biases etc. in *particular*. More importantly, women's backward socio- economic condition in the society, some religious obscurity, and discriminatory social taboos, made Bangladeshi women to stand in a much vulnerable and disadvantageous position than that of its male counterpart (Chowdhury 2005). So, most of the time it is women who are deprived of getting access to justice even through formal courts.

One alternative of availing formal justice is of course the use of some traditional adjudicative systems available in out-court settings. The practice of out-court dispute resolution through traditional and informal system of justice administered by local elites is prevailing in the Indian sub-continent from the time immemorial and is so deep tooted that sometimes it is said that, the *'villages self-governance is as old as the villages themselves'*.[7] In earlier ages, terms like mediation or arbitration were not at all common, rather the corresponding term *'Panchayet'*, later on *'Shalish'* was used to mean this type of informal dispute resolution systems (Islam 2002). But under current socio-economic condition, this form of traditional adjudicative systems is also inundated by corruption, political influence, pro-male bias etc.

Because of that, now a days, Out-court mediation conducted under the supervision of various NGOs is getting increased popularity among the vulnerable groups of the society, especially among women as an alternative means to provide justice to all. A handful number of NGOs are proving these mediation (local term *Shalish*) services to the people. This service can well be called as a modified version of Shalish or Traditional Shalish (TS). The main objective of these NGOs is to ensure that lawful and just decisions are made through out-court mediations conducted by local leaders or other local elites. Although NGOs are working for this modified form of TS for a long time, still not much research works have done in this field. So, this paper is constructed to give a brief idea about what NGO mediation is all about, and to identify its existing status, attained successes, and remaining limitation from the side of both service provider NGOs and of its recipients. For the purpose of this paper, data has been collected from both

NGO Mediation Workers (MWs) and NGO clients. MWs are employed by NGOs who work as coordinator in NGO mediation sessions and sometimes work as mediators. In this paper, NGOs providing mediation services are termed as practicing NGOs and if not otherwise mentioned, mediation means NGO mediation.

NATURE AND PROCESS OF NGO MEDIATION IN BANGLADESH

NGO mediation is actually an improved version of TS usually made by village heads and other local elites relating to various disputes in their respective villages, which resembles more to arbitration than mediation. In case of TS when general people in the locality make complaint to village heads, they organize a meeting to settle disputes in presence of the village community along with other local elites. In most of the cases, these village leaders act as arbitrators while making decisions in TS. But the two basic difference between NGO mediation and TS is that, in NGO mediation, *Shalishkars* (local term for mediators) act like mediators rather arbitrators and that all the process i.e., from filing of a complaint to the compilation of mediation agreement is documented by the NGO MWs, while in case of TS there is no formal, written entry of complaint or any written document about the decision made in *Shalish*. In case of NGO mediation, local brunch offices of respected NGOs receive written complaints of disputes from the aggrieved party and record complaint in a prescribed form including personal information about both the parties, details about and nature of the disputes i.e. whether the dispute is related to dower, maintenance or divorce etc. After that, MWs make field visit to collect information about the authenticity of the complaint and subject to the genuineness of the complaint, a notice is served under general post to the alleged accused informing about the complaint and inviting him to attend a mediation session along with his guardians for settling the dispute, specifying the date and time thereof. The aggrieved party and other mediators are also informed accordingly.

To conduct mediations on their behalf, practicing NGOs form different Community Based Organizations (CBOs) consisting of members from local leaders such as Union *Parishad* (UP) chairman, UP members, and other local elites including teachers, *Imam* (religious priest), social workers etc. Practicing NGOs provide various legal and social training to their CBO members to raise them as para-legals who can conduct mediation according to the rules and regulations provided under contemporary laws and are also motivated for conducting mediation sessions in an unbiased manner, with equal importance to women. If the accused does not attend the mediation session on specific date and time, the MW sends second or third notice as required. If the accused even fails to respond, a final notice under registered post is sent giving him a last chance to resolve the dispute through mediation, specifying the date, time and location thereof, notifying that after the expiry of such date the concerned NGO is gong to institute a formal suit in the court on behalf of the complainant. Receiving such notice, accused parties generally approach to the CBO members or concerned NGO offices for the resolution of said dispute and attends the mediation sessions accordingly.

On the day of mediation, one MW begins the session by outlining the ground rules and by creating an informal, congenial and non-confrontational environment within which both parties especially women can feel relaxed and express their grievances freely. In order to make the environment friendly for women, practicing NGOs also encourage more participation of women in their mediation sessions and include women mediators as well. After the starting of the session, a Mediation Committee (MC) is formed comprising CBO members and representatives from both sides. Disputant parties are said to choose the committee member on a consensual basis and if they cannot reach any consensus by themselves then the MW helps them to reach a settlement on choosing members and to form the committee thereof. After that, MC heard both the parties giving an equal opportunity to all and finally an attempt is made by the MC to reach a settlement agreement, which is amicable and acceptable, by both the parties.

After such settlement is reached, it is reduced into writing by the MW and signed by the representatives from both the parties, by the MC members attending mediation, and also by the MW as representative from the NGO. Under NGO mediation, depending on the policy of particular NGO concerned, the status of the settlement reached by the parties during the mediation session and its implementation are monitored by the monitoring cell of respective NGOs at a regular interval such as after every three months etc. or after receipt of any further complaint regarding the non-execution of mediated agreement. During monitoring if it is found that parties are not complying with the agreement, the MW choose a later date to re-open the proceedings and inform all the concerned parties accordingly. If such further mediation attempts do not become successful or if the accused does not attend mediation sessions, then the next step is to institute a suit in the formal court by the NGO on behalf of its client. As a matter of fact, sometimes the mere knowledge that a lawsuit in the formal court is the next and ultimate step that will be taken by the respective NGO is sufficient to make parties voluntarily comply with the mediation agreement reached [8] (Chowdhury 2005).

SUCCESSES AND LIMITATIONS OF NGO MEDIATION IN BANGLADESH

Following the brief discussion about the nature and process of NGO mediation in Bangladesh, the current section has been written based on the questionnaire survey made on three different NGOs from three different districts of Dhaka division. These are *Madaripur* Legal Aid Association (MLAA) at Madaripur, Women Development Organization (WDO) at Netrokona and Bangladesh Legal Aid and Services Trust (BLAST) at Narayanganj. While choosing these three NGOs, the main criteria was the different levels of their maturity i.e. the matured one which is conducting mediation for a long time, a moderately matured one, and a relatively newer one to cover any diversity of problems faced by NGOs depending on their level of maturity. The main objective of making the questionnaire survey was to verify the success of NGO mediation in Bangladesh and also to find out some existing limitations on NGO mediation eliminating which can ensure more access to justice to women through it. Responses were collected using a structured questionnaire comprising both open-end and close-end questions.

Successes of NGO mediation in Bangladesh: In Bangladesh, NGO mediation has by now attained considerable accolade from the grass-root people for its praiseworthy features, which ensures more efficacious access to justice especially to its women. Followings are the main points identified by NGO MWs and NGO clients about the success of NGO mediation in Bangladesh

NGO mediation is free from backlog problem unlike formal courts: The most important logic provided for the wide uses of NGO mediation in out-court settings is its complementary nature to reduce the huge backlog of cases in formal courts. So, one initial enquiry under this research was to know whether NGO mediation is free from this backlog problem or not. Results obtained in this regard, considering responses from different NGO workers conducting mediation in their respective localities, is quite impressive.

As shown in Table 1, three different NGOs surveyed can solve as much as 60% of the disputes they receive per month for mediation[9]. But the performance becomes much better and the rate of disposal reaches as much as three fourth of the disputes received per month when we exclude the least matured NGO i.e. BLAST at Narayanganj and consider only MLAA and WDO of Madaripur and Netrokona districts respectively. Since Narayanganj is different from Madaripur and Netrokona in another respect of its being adjacent to the capital city, it can be an interesting research question for the future researchers that whether the success rate of NGO mediation varies between city areas and rural areas and if so, how NGO mediation in city areas could be made more effective etc.

Table 1[10]
Rate of Disposal under NGO Mediation

	With BLAST	*Without BLAST*
Average number of cases received per month	3.83	3.00
Averages number of cases resolved per month	2.28	2.21
Average rate of disposal per month	59.48%	73.53%
Average percentage pending every month	40.52%	26.47%

Source: Primary Data.

Zero or Minimal Cost Involvement: One of the prime reasons identified by the NGO MWs (Table 5) for clients to come for NGO mediation rather going to the formal court is 'no cost' or 'only minimal cost' involved in NGO mediation. The same point has also been reflected on the opinion of NGO clients while asked by the same question during the survey (Table 2 and Table 3).

Table 2[11]
Advantages of NGO Mediation over Formal Court

No.	*Reason*	*Percentage*	*Rank*
1	No cost	68.18%	1
2	Faith on NGO that they will make justice	22.73%	2
3	Less time consuming	4.55%	3
4	No guardian to go to formal court	4.55%	4
	Total	100.0%	

Source: Primary Data.

Table 3[12]
Clients' Cost Involvement in NGO Mediation

No.	*Cost of NGO mediation*	*Percent*	*Rank*
1	No cost	75.00%	1
2	Very minimal cost	25.00%	2
	Total	100.0%	

Source: Primary Data.

As shown in Table 3, three fourth of the clients replied that they don't have to spend any money for getting NGO mediation while few others mentioned that they have to spend only the transportation cost or a minimal charge of 10/20 Taka (15/30 cents) for registering their case in the NGO for making mediation.

Quick Access to Justice without Harassment: Beside exorbitant cost of formal court, some other limitations of the formal court system raised by the clients are its time consuming nature and the harassment they have to face there because of their lower knowledge about the formal trial process. In case of formal court, rural illiterate women cannot understand the complex process and are faced with much harassment from corrupt court officials and other fraudster roaming in the court ground.

But while asked regarding their capacity to understand NGO mediation, cent percent clients reply that they can fully understand NGO mediation (Table 4). The issue of lower time involvement can also be recognized from the higher percentage disposal of disputes through NGO mediation, as indicated in Table 1.

Table 4[13]

Women Understands to NGO Mediation Process

No.	*Whether women can understand NGO mediation*	*Percentage*
1	Yes can understand fully	100.00%
2	No can not understand fully	0.00%
	Total	100.00%

Source: Primary Data

From Table 5, it is evident that the main reason identified by NGO clients for choosing NGO mediation rather than formal

Table 5[14]

NGO MWs' Perceptions on Clients' Urge to Come to NGO rather Formal Court

No.	*Reasons Identified*	*Percent*	*Rank*
1	No or minimum cost involved	24.59%	1
2	Faith and confidence on NGO to get justice	23.77%	2
3	Less time involved	13.93%	3
4	No harassment	13.11%	4
5	Establish harmony between parties	9.02%	5
6	Acceptability	9.02%	5
8	More voice to women	3.28%	6
9	NGOs are sincere to resolve disputes	3.28%	6
	Total	100.00%	

Source: Primary Data.

court is its zero cost accessibility to clients while the second most important reason is clients' faith and confidence on respective NGOs that they will get justice from them. The same question while asked to the NGO MWs also showed the no cost, and faith and confidence features as the first two reasons for women's coming to NGOs rather going to formal courts. A more comprehensive and well judged list mentioned by NGO MWs as reasons for women's coming to NGOs rather going to formal courts is as follows.

So, according to NGO MWs' perception, the main three reasons for which women especially the poor illiterate women living in rural areas come for NGO mediation rather going to formal courts are the zero cost involvement in NGO mediation, quick disposal, and the faith and confidence in the respective NGOs that they will get justice there.

NGO Mediation Enhancing Social Harmony and Preserving Family Ties: Two other reasons comes in with a moderate importance is the acceptability of NGO mediation in the society and that NGO mediation tries to establish harmony between disputing parties rather providing decree in favor of one while vanquishing the other as is in case of formal courts. Since the women of Bangladesh, especially those in rural areas, value their family tie above all, this type of harmonious decision is very much acceptable by them. In reality, they don't want to get divorced or tear off their marriage relation if not compelled to do so.

Table 6[15]

Cost incurred by NGOs to Dispose an Individual Dispute

Geographic area	Average cost of disposal (Tk.)
Netrokona	290.50
Madaripur	194.29
Narayanganj	366.67
Average	268.00

Source: Primary Data.

Lower Overall Social Cost in NGO Mediation: In case of NGO mediation, not only the personal cost of clients remains low, but also the overall social cost to resolve disputes through NGO is also very low. Answering the question about their average cost to resolve cases NGO MWs replied for only Tk. 268 (Table 6) or equivalent to 4 USD (approximate) under the current exchange rate. So, on the basis of this lower cost and prompt resolution of disputes, NGO mediation can be considered as a very effective complement to reduce pressure in the formal courts and thereby to reduce the backlog of cases in formal judiciary. In all of the NGOs clients don't have to spend even a single penny for getting this mediation service while in Netrokona only, clients have to bear Tk.75 (1US$ and 10 cents) to purchase a non-judicial stamp on which the terms and conditions of the settlement reached will be written down so that later it can be produced in the formal court, as evidence, if required.

Table 7[16]
Features of NGO Mediation Most Liked by Women

No.	*Feature most liked by women*	*Percentage*	*Rank*
1	Can speak freely about problems	47.37%	1
2	No cost	21.05%	2
3	Sincere and cordial cooperation	15.79%	3
4	Justice	15.79%	3
	Total	100.00%	

Source: Primary Data.

But although clients have to spend some money this practice is a good practice that ensures higher abidance of mediation decision by the parties.

Enhancing Women Voice to the Society: Besides lower cost, another criteria of NGO mediation for which women like it most is their ability to express opinion freely, which is not possible for them in case of TS usually, performed in their villages. So, while making opinion about the criteria of NGO mediation most favored by them, almost half of the female NGO clients responded (Table 7) that it is because of their increased voice ensured in NGO mediation, lacking of which is a top most reason for their dissatisfaction on TS. Some other reasons identified by female NGO clients for their preference of NGO mediation over TS are outlined in Table 8.

Although considering the current socio-economic structure of Bangladesh, where almost all the positions of social elites are still held by men, it is not possible for NGOs to maintain parity in the number of mediators engaged in mediation sessions and accordingly 72.5% of the NGO MWs mentioned that, men-women parity is not maintained in their mediation session,[17] still women can raise their voice freely. Their opinion and idea are heard carefully and judged equally with those come from men.

Table 8[18]
Reasons for Preference of NGO Mediation over TS

No.	*Advantage*	*Percentage*	*Rank*
1.	No cost	44.00%	1
2.	Justice	40.00%	2
3.	More voice	12.00%	3
4.	No harassment	4.00%	4
	Total	100.00%	

Source: Primary Data

Table 9[19]
NGO MWs' Perception on how Women Voice is raised in NGO Mediation

No.	*Means of raising women equal voice in NGO mediation*	*Percentage*	*Rank*
1.	Facilitating their right to express opinion freely	48.44%	1
2.	Patient hearing and proper evaluation of their opinion	18.75%	2
3.	Participation in decision making	14.06%	3
4.	Right to attend	12.50%	4
5.	Explaining about their right to voice to the attendants	4.69%	5
6.	Opportunity to ask question to others	1.56%	6
	Total	100.00%	

Source: Primary Data.

So, the best practice with regard to women's equal voice at mediation is to facilitate their expression of opinion during mediation. Other strategies used by the NGO MWs to enhance women voice during mediation are to facilitate women to participate in the decision making process, explain to others present in the mediation session about why women should have an equal voice in the mediation process and proper evaluation of opinions come from women's side to make them more inspired to express their opinion freely (Table 9).

Table 10[20]

Success Rate of NGO Mediation in Terms of Permanent Settlement

Area concerned	*Success rate*	*Future complaint*
Netrokona (WDO)	88.56%	11.44%
Madaripur (MLLA)	94.91%	5.09%
Narayanganj (BLAST)	84.17%	15.83%
Overall	89.71%	10.29%

Source: Primary Data

NGO Mediation Ensures Higher Rate of Permanent Settlement: Although NGOs are making mediation at a very lower cost, mediations made by them seems to be very much effective in the sense that only a very few percentage of clients have to go to formal court with the same complaint once mediated under NGO mediation. Although the rate varies for different practicing NGOs, the overall rate of such complaints of non-abidance is only about 10% of total disputes resolved through mediation as shown in Table 10. In Madaripur although it is only about 5%, in two other regions it is more than 10% or even above 15%. So, although NGOs have a satisfactory overall rate, something could be done to enhance the effectiveness of NGO mediation at least for those NGOs who have not yet reached the benchmark level set by MLAA at Madaripur.

EXISTING LIMITATIONS TO ENHANCED EFFECTIVE-ENESS OF NGO MEDIATION IN BANGLADESH

For a mediation to be effective, both parties should abide by the settlement reached under it. Since the women clients have a perception that NGOs make just and fair mediation without showing any biasness against them, as is already mentioned in Table 7 and Table 8 and since they can express their opinion freely during the mediation session, it is very unlikely that women have some discontent on the decision made under

NGO mediation. So, the factor remaining for a mediation to be effective is its abidance by the male counterparts or especially by the husbands. During the survey various factors have been identified by NGO MWs and NGO clients, poor implementation of which causes lower abidance to NGO mediation. The most important of these factors identified as limitations to more effective NGO mediation in Bangladesh are as follows.

Inadequate or Non-cooperation from Local Government Bodies: Sometimes it is argued that the presence of representatives from local government bodies in NGO mediation sessions increases its effectiveness in the sense that local people usually not dare to disregard any mediation decision made in presence and under the guidance of local representatives such as Union Parishad member, ward commissioner etc. This is because of the influential image of those local leaders in their respective locality. To find out the strength of such argument, during the questionnaire survey, NGO MWs were asked about the involvement of local government representatives and local administration in their mediation sessions and the answer given by them shows a very interesting correlation with their rate of success.

Table 11[21]
Types of Cooperation Practicing NGOs Received from Local Government Authorities

No.	*Type of cooperation / non-cooperation*	*WDO*	*MLAA*	*BLAST*
1.	Make cooperation to organize mediation	90.00%	20.93%	nil
4.	No cooperation	10.00%	nil	100.00%
5.	Be present/ conduct mediation	Nil	30.23%	nil
6.	Make parties to attend mediation	Nil	27.91%	nil
7.	Help to implement mediation decision	Nil	16.28%	nil
8.	Legal support when necessary	Nil	2.33%	nil
9.	Campaign in favor of mediation	Nil	2.33%	nil
	Total	100.00%	100.00%	100.00%

Source: Primary Data.

According to Table 11, four important types of cooperation NGOs receive from local Government bodies to make their mediation more effective include the presence/conduction of mediation by local government representatives, pressure from local bodies to make the parties attend mediation, make cooperation to organize mediation and cooperation to implement mediation decisions. Moreover, from the local government representatives, NGOs also get necessary legal helps and cooperation through positive campaigning in favor of NGO mediation etc.

One reason for the higher rate of pending disputes and therefore a lower rate of disposal in Narayanganj can be found from the analysis of Table 12. While answering the question, *'What co operations and facilities do you expect from local administration and police to make NGO mediation more effective?'* respondents from all different NGOs put emphasis on a non-partial behavior from local Government bodies to all. Moreover, they also urge for the presence of local government authorities in mediation sessions and in some cases suggested to have their opinion and other services to conduct mediation peacefully and also sought help from local bodies to implement the mediation decisions later (see Table 12).

Table 12[22]

Ranking of Cooperation Sought by NGOs from Local Government Authorities

No.	*Nature of cooperation sought*	*Netro-kona*	*Mada ripur*	*Nara-yanganj*	*Over-all*
1.	Non partial behaviour	1	2	3	1
2.	Presence of local administration during mediation	2	5	2	2
3.	Prompt action	5	2	1	3
4.	Make disputants attend mediation sessions	3	4	nil	4
5.	Help to avoid any threat from disputing parties or outsiders	5	3	nil	5
6.	Campaign in favor of NGO mediation	nil	1	nil	5
7.	Help to monitor and implement the settlement reached	4	nil	nil	6
8.	Refer to NGO mediation before taking police case	nil	6	nil	7

Source: Primary Data

In case of Madaripur, we see that they are already receiving various types of services from the local Government authority as is indicated in Table 11. Local government representatives are being present in their mediation sessions and even conduct mediations; help to implement the mediation decision reached and provide other legal supports when necessary. In Netrokona, even though they haven't mentioned about the availability of variety of services from the local government bodies as it is in case of Madaripur, but 90% of the total responses mentioned that they get cooperation form local government authorities to organize mediation sessions. Unfortunately in case of Narayanganj, all the respondents unanimously opined that they do not get any cooperation from the local government authorities relating to their mediation.

So while asking about what other helps they require from local Government authorities, both WDO at Netrokona and BLAST at Narayanganj showed their urge for higher presence of local government bodies at their mediation sessions, while MLAA at Madaripur showed a lower urge because it is already getting various cooperation from local bodies as listed in Table 11. The logic behind this urge is that, if local government authorities show their consent on the decision made through mediation, either by conducting the mediation or even by providing necessary supports etc, then for the local people it is very hard to ignore the decision made under such mediation and for practicing NGOs it also becomes very easy to implement those decisions afterwards. Comparison of data on Table 1 and Table 11 shows that rate of disposal varies depending on the involvement of local government bodies in NGO mediation. So, support from local government bodies is very important for the effectiveness of NGO mediation although more in-depth research could be done in future to prove the accuracy of this hypothesis and to determine what are the most appropriate fields in which these support services should be provided.

Lack in Laws and their Proper Implementation: Besides the urge for higher local government participation, another point raised

Table 13[23]
Legal Changes Suggested by NGOs to Make their Mediation More Effective

Practicing NGOs		*BLAST*		*WDO*		*MLLA*		*Overall*	
Type	*Broader area identified*	*Rank*	*(%)*	*Rank*	*(%)*	*Rank*	*(%)*	*Rank*	*(%)*
L	Legalize NGO mediation and their actions	1	57. 14	2	7.14	nil	nil	3	9.72
S	Pass stringent law or increase punishment to stop repression on women	nil	nil	1	92.86	2	39.13	1	66.67
E	Passing laws for women equal right	2	28.57	nil	nil	3	17.39	4	8.33
R	Improvement of overall rule of law in the country	3	14.29	nil	nil	1	43.48	2	15.28

Source: Primary Data.

by the respondents is the necessity of some changes in existing laws to make NGO mediation more effective. A variety of opinions and suggestions comes up from NGO MWs while asked specifically about what laws they want to be changed for making NGO mediation more effective, but after compiling those under some broad heads the nature of their responses can be categorized as in Table 13 above. Changes of laws suggested under 'L' includes laws to make parties attend NGO mediation sessions, laws necessary to implement the decision of NGO mediation, laws prohibiting parties to file law suit when thy are asked to attend NGO mediation etc. Laws suggested under category 'S' includes the increment of punishment for dowry, wife battering, improper maintenance, non-payment of dower, remarry without taking permission from existing wife/wives etc. Type 'E' includes changes in laws relating to marital and inheritance right, and in other areas where women's equal right is not yet established through law. Type 'R' is self-explanatory.

Form Table 10 and Table 13 it seem that, the more cooperation NGOs are getting from the local authority to conduct and implement their mediation, the higher is their success, and the lower they have to urge for the passing of any law to give NGO mediation any legal footing or to enforce NGO mediation decisions by passing laws. NGOs those are getting better co-operation from local bodies are rather emphasizing more on the passage of stringent provisions under existing laws so that they can motivate clients to come for NGO mediation or otherwise to follow those stringent legal punishment under trial of formal courts. The most successful NGO MLAA is emphasizing more on the implementation of fair and speedy trial under the existing laws rather passing new laws because the more speedy the trials in formal courts are, the higher is the possibility that, for violating the fair decision made under NGO mediation or for not attending NGO mediation as an alternative to formal trial, defendants have to face the legal punishment under formal court trial in a near future.

Absence of Professional Monitoring System: Besides the presence of some external factors such as local Government support, passing of stringent laws, and quick and proper execution of existing laws etc. one internal factor of NGOs which can also contribute to the increased effectiveness of NGO mediation is the existence of a proper monitoring system to monitor the execution of decisions made under mediation. As delineated in Table 14, according to 85% of total respondents, NGOs have monitoring system to follow up whether the settlements made them through mediation are being implemented or not. In Netrokona, for example, monitoring is made mostly if any complaint comes in with a further complain or if the mediation committee thinks some events important to be monitored even after a settlement is reached through mediation. But in Madaripur, they have a formal monitoring team to monitor how the decisions made through mediation held under the supervision of their MWs are being implemented by the disputant parties concerned. Actually these monitoring reports are considered to judge the effectiveness of the mediation workers. So to prove their enhanced efficiency, MWs themselves also make individual follow-up that in fact increases the overall rate of success made by the NGOs. This follow-up mechanism, therefore, can be used as a good practice among other practicing NGOs to strengthen their mediation process.

Table 14[24]
Quantitative and Qualitative Features of Monitoring in NGO Mediation

Area concerned	*Percentage* *Netrokona*	*Madaripur*	*Narayanganj*
Monitoring	100.00%	100.00%	66.67%
No monitoring	0.00%	0.00%	33.33%
Separate monitoring team	-	-	-

Source: Primary Data.

In Narayanganj, although two-thirds of the respondents informed about the existence of a monitoring system, there the monitoring system is bit weaker, held once in six months and they do not have any separate monitoring team to conduct monitoring etc. So, as we compare between Table 10 and Table 14, both the quantity and quality of monitoring shows an important correlation with the success of NGO mediation.

Lack of Required Training: Another important factor that can be provided by NGOs internally and was identified by many MWs as an important factor to enhance the effectiveness of their mediation is to organize training for them and necessary supply of legal materials to make them well versed on laws relating to various disputes they have to resolve usually. For developing these training programs and for supplying training and legal materials to them, one important aspect is to know about the type of disputes they usually receive for mediation (Table 15) and the rate of difficulty they face in resolving these different types of disputes (Table 16) etc. So, while making the survey for this research, NGO MWs were asked about these issues and the information revealed through their answers are summarized as follows.

So, from Table 15, it can be deduced that improper maintenance by the husband, wife battering, dowry, child marriage etc are the primary reasons for rural women of Bangladesh to get recourse of NGO mediation. Although the ranking of different reasons vary in their weight among different regions, the first few reasons mentioned earlier got higher preference in almost all the regions covered under this survey. The moderately important reasons are dower and

Table 15[25]
Nature of Disputes Received Most by NGOs for Mediation

No	Types of disputes received / Nature of complaints	Area Concerned NK (%)	MD (%)	NJ (%)	Total (%)	Rank NK	MP	NJ	Over all
1	Dowry	28.41	23.91	31.58	31.37	1	1	1	1
2	Maintenance	20.45	30.43	31.58	24.84	3	2	1	2
3	Child marriage	21.59	nil	nil	12.42	2	nil	nil	3
4	Dower	5.68	10.87	15.79	8.50	5	4	2	4
5	Polygamy	9.09	nil	10.53	6.54	4	nil	3	5
6	Restitution of conjugal life	0.00	13.04	10.53	5.23	nil	3	3	6
7	Divorce	3.41	8.70	nil	4.58	6	5	nil	7
8	Fraudulent love	5.68	nil	nil	3.27	5	nil	nil	8
9	Family dispute & others	5.68	nil	nil	3.27	5	nil	nil	8
	100%	100%	100%	100%					

Source: Primary Data.

restitution of conjugal life, while the least important reasons include divorce, polygamy and other family disputes etc.

From the scale drawn in Table 16, we can divide the complexity of resolving various disputes received by NGOs into three different groups. The most complicated ones are divorce and maintenance, those that are moderately complex to resolve involves custody of children and recovery of dower money; and the simplest ones include restitution of conjugal life and other family disputes etc. Custody and dower is easier to solve because in the contemporary laws the rules relating to custody of children is very specifically mentioned where as in case of registered marriage, dower is included in the marriage contract.

Table 16[26]
Perception of NGO MWs on the Complexity to Solve Disputes

Ranking	1	2	3	3	4	5
Category	Maintenance	Divorce	Custody	Dower	Restitution	Others
Complexity	High		Moderate		Low	

Source: Primary Data.

In case of maintenance, the contemporary law says about 'reasonable maintenance' depending her husband's status which is a very vague term and also very hard to monitor. In case of divorce, though Muslim women can divorce her husbands on certain grounds under the *Dissolution of Muslim Marriage Act of 1939,* with the intervention of the court, nonetheless the proof of which is most of the time difficult. Thus, a woman cannot divorce her husband without the intervention of the court, unless the right to divorce is delegated to wife on the marriage contract. So, proper trainings should be organized to train mediators on those issues where they are still facing much complexity to resolve disputes.

Inadequate Social Awareness Program: Another important issue for effective mediation is the attitude of the society as a whole towards NGO mediation and people's willingness to resolve disputes through mediation without going to the formal courts first. One question asked to NGO mediation clients was about the response or attitude of their neighbors towards their coming to NGOs for getting mediation. The finding of this issue is incorporated in Table 17.

Table 17[27]
Attitude of the Society towards Women Access to NGO Mediation

No.	*Response*	*Percentage*	*Rank*
1	Help and encourage to get NGO mediation	45.00%	1
2	Neither help nor shame	40.00%	2
3	Shame because of coming to NGO	15.00%	3
	Total	100.00%	

Source: Primary Data.

From the analysis of neighbors' responses as compiled under Table 17, it is revealed that only 45% of the respondents get cooperation and encouragement from their neighbors for coming to NGOs and 55% either got shamed or not getting any cooperation from their neighbor for getting recourse to NGO mediation.

Getting social encouragement is very important for the wider access of justice to women through NGO mediation because as shown in Table 18 almost half of the total clients come to know about NGO mediation from their neighbors or other people from their locality. Source of this first hand knowledge is important because being a source means to give suggestion that NGOs could be a place where you can go for getting justice etc.

Table 18[28]
Sources of Information about the Existence of NGO Mediation

No.	*Means to first introduction about NGO mediation*	*Percentage*	*Rank*
1	NGO awareness program	30.00%	2
2	From neighbours/other people in the locality	45.00%	1
3	From NGO lawyer/client	20.00%	3
4	From local administration	5.00%	4
	Total	100.00%	

Source: Primary Data.

One way to increase social response in favor of NGO mediation is to organize various social awareness programs to make people more aware and interested about NGO mediation. But, the lack of such social awareness programs in practicing NGOs becomes evident when NGO MWs were asked about the existence of this type of program in their respective NGOs. As shown in Table 19, in only 55% cases NGOs have various social awareness programs to make NGO mediation more acceptable to the society. Along with their existing awareness programs, all of the respondents suggested various forms of training programs and seminars, symposiums, street shows, discussion in various social programs and in mosques about the utilities of mediation, organizing drama, and providing legal training and legal materials to MWs etc.

Table 19[29]
Existence of Social Awareness Programs in Practicing NGOs

	Existence of social awareness/ motivational program	
Area concerned	*Yes*	*No*
WDO, Netrokona	70.00%	30.00%
MLLA, Madaripur	50.00%	50.00%
BLAST, Narayanganj	16.67%	88.33%
Overall	55.00%	45.00%

Source: Primary Data.

Here one important point is that although more mature NGO like WDO in Netrokona and MLAA in Madaripur have some social awareness program to popularize their mediation among local community, in Narayanganj only less than 20% respondents informed about the existence of such type of social awareness program to popularize mediation.

Despite all these limitations remaining for the creation of an environment under which a more effective mediation can be attained by the practicing NGOs, still the majority of women accessing mediation services from different NGOs are very much confident about the restoration of their rights through NGO mediation. So, while asking the question about whether they think that the other party will abide by the decision made under NGO mediation[30], 55% women respondents asserted very confidently that their opponents will abide by the decisions made. Although the remaining 45% respondents are rather suspicious, all of them very confidently declared that otherwise they will file suit in the formal court taking help from their respective NGOs, since this time they know that they are not alone.

Recommendation going to any detail or providing any specific recommendation for the improvement of out-court mediation performed under NGO burden in the formal court system, ensure quick and cost free justice to the women, and at the same time make it free from all the excessive formalities those will drag its way in exchange of few extra benefits generated from these increased rules and procedures. The following specific recommendations for the improvement of out-court mediation, especially for the improvement of NGO mediation; have been made taking this general point in mind.

Local Government Bodies should Cooperate More for Organizing, Conducting and Executing the Decision of NGO Mediation: From the analysis earlier it is evident that proper cooperation from the local government authorities is very important for making NGO mediation more effective. According to the NGO MWs surveyed, as included in Table 20, local government representatives and local administration should be affiliated more in NGO mediation activities and should be motivated more to make impartial decision regardless of gender, political identity, religion, or cast etc.

Table 20[31]
Types of Co-operations Required from Local Government Authorities and Police

No.	*Types of cooperation required*	*Percentage*	*Rank*
1	Non partial behavior	27.14%	1
2	Presence of local administration during mediation	17.14%	2
3	Prompt action	15.71%	3
4	Make disputants attend mediation	14.29%	4
5	Help to avoid any threat from parties or outsiders	10.00%	5
6	Campaign in favor of mediation	10.00%	5
7	Help to monitor implementation of mediation decisions	4.29%	6
8	Refer to NGO mediation before taking police case	1.43%	7
	Total	100.0%	

Source: Primary Data.

Arrangements can also be made so that NGOs conducting mediation get help from local administration to remove any threat to mediators during, before, and after the mediation session, get help to make the disputant parties attend mediation, help to monitor the implementation of mediation decision made, and to make campaign in favor of NGO mediation etc.

More Stringent Laws should be Passed against Women Repression: More stringent laws should be passed on those issues[32] where harsh punishment under contemporary laws does not exists and so male counterpart disregard mediation decision thinking that they do not have to face any rigorous punishment even if their misdeeds are proved in formal courts.

Table 21[33]
Ranking on the Need for More Stringent Laws

No.	*Priority of stringent laws required to stop repression against women*	*Percentage*	*Rank*
1	Restrict polygamy and improper maintenance	40.91%	1
2	Restrict child marriage	36.36%	2
3	Restrict wife battering and dowry demand	15.91%	3
4	Others	6.82%	4
	Total	100.00%	

Source: Primary Data.

From the Table 21, it can be remarkably noticed that stringent laws to restrict polygamy and improper maintenance to prior wife is the primary area of concern for NGO MWs in which more stringent laws are required to compel husbands making proper maintenance to all of their existing wives and children even after getting married again. The second primary area of concern is the restriction of child marriage, while the third one is the restriction on the demand for dowry realized through physical and mental torture on women.

Fair and Speedy Trial Needs to be Ensured: Existence of stringent laws will have no value if these laws cannot be executed in a speedy manner with iron hands. So, along with the passage of stringent laws for restraining negligent and violent husbands to repress their spouses' lawful rights, a quick and just execution of these laws is also very consequential to create an impression on husband's mind that if they violate their wives rights then they have to face stringent legal punishment very soon.

Table 22[34]

Changes in Law Suggested for Higher Effectiveness in NGO Mediation

No.	*Broader area of change identified*	*Percentage*	*Rank*
1	Passage of stringent laws or increase of punishment to stop repression on women	66.67%	1
2	Improvement of overall rule of law in the country	15.28%	2
3	Pass laws to legalize NGO mediation and their actions relating to mediation.	9.72%	3
4	Passing laws for women's equal right	8.33%	4
	Total	100.00%	

Source: Primary Data.

Actually the fear to be executed under a specific law depends on the degree of stringent punishment suggested under that law multiplied by the probability of execution under the said law. So, a law with a 90% probability of being executed with speedy trial and follow a 5 year imprisonment might create higher pressure on the mind of violating husbands against a law suggesting 10 years imprisonment but only have a 10% probability of execution. Overall opinion of NGO MWs on necessary changes in laws also ranked this fair and speedy execution of laws in the second position as manifested in Table 22.

Higher Monitoring with Better Quality is Required: Since women in Bangladesh, lacking education and economic power, are very much vulnerable while staying in their husband's/in-laws' houses, without proper monitoring it is very much possible that they will again face the same or even higher degree of torture and harassment as they reveal the fact of prior torture and harassment to others through NGO mediation. Another reason for which an impartial monitoring system is required is to check whether any mediation committee assigned by an NGO is making mediation in a partial or prejudiced way so as to create some gross discontent in the mind of women seeking justice.

In Madaripur, MLAA has an independent monitoring team to collect field level data on the success of mediation. This could be taken as an example of exemplary practice because as MLLA evaluate its mediation workers on the basis of the success rate of mediation collected from these filed level survey, mediation workers becomes more enthusiastic to make high quality mediation and make follow-ups of accomplished mediation cases in their own initiative to get higher grade in these survey.

Table 23[35]

Clients' Perception on Benefits of Neighbours' Presence at Mediation

No.	*Clients' perception*	*Percentage*	*Rank*
1	Beneficial	65.00%	1
2	Harmful	20.00%	2
3	Neither beneficial nor harmful	15.00%	3
	Total	100.00%	

Source: Primary Data.

But another type of natural monitoring about the quality of mediation and its execution can be made by encouraging the neighbors of disputant parties to attend mediation. It increases the transparency of the mediation decision made at the presence of others and so, minimizes the probability of any discontent created in any party thinking that the decision is biased to others. On the other hand, it becomes difficult for any of the disputant parties to violate settlement agreement when such agreement is made by a consensual decision in presence of all of their neighbors who can make a continuous vigilance to the actions of the disputing parties concerned.

This natural monitoring system is cost effective and hasn't been objected by the clients while asking about the benefits or problems of their neighbors being present at their mediation. In fact, according to 85% of the clients, as featured in Table 23, attendance of their neighbors during NGO mediation is either beneficial or at least not harmful for them. So, beside the use of separate monitoring team, practicing NGOs should also encourage higher number of neighbors to attend the mediation session so that they can monitor the post effect of mediated agreement reached.

Training should be Organized for Both Mediators and Clients: Training on mediation techniques is indivisible part for the making of a successful mediation. Training is required on both the legal issues and also on social and religious issues those might come up while making mediation. More intensive training may be provided on some specific types of family disputes which most of the mediators indicated as more difficult to resolve, such as maintenance, divorce etc as included in Table 16.

Table 24
Types of Training Suggested by NGO MWs

Types of training suggested	*Percentage*
Training to general public about NGO mediation	37.93%
Legal Training to NGO MWs and other social elites	62.07%
Total	100.00%

Source: Primary Data.

Training to general people get less emphasis as shown in Table 24 because according to NGO MWs, other social awareness program such as seminar, group meeting etc as discussed later, seems to be more effective for making general people encouraged towards NGO mediation.

More Social Awareness Program Required: From Table 19, it is visible that on an average only 55% of the cases practicing

NGOs have separate social awareness program to make mediation more popular in the society. An increased popularity of NGO mediation in the society is very much important for a stronger natural monitoring system as discussed in section 4.4 above and thereby attaining a higher rate of implementation of NGO mediation decisions through social pressure on defying parties. It is important because the highest percentages of women still get their first hand information from their neighbors or other people from the locality (Table 18). So, society could be a proficient channel to disseminate the success story of NGO mediation among women who are still not aware about it but in need of a service provided through NGO mediation.

Table 25[36]
Tools of Social Awareness Programs Suggested

Types of social awareness programs suggested	*Percentage*	*Rank*
Work shop, seminar, and group meeting	26.39%	1
Legal training to mediators and other social elites	25.00%	2
Training to general public about mediation	15.28%	3
Leaflet, signboard, poster, advertisement in media	12.50%	4
Other motivational programs	12.50%	4
Street show, rally etc.	8.33%	5
Total	100.00%	

Source: Primary Data.

NGO MWs, while asked about the type of social awareness programs required for making NGO mediation more effective, identified various tools as presented in Table 25. From the above table, the most effective method suggested to train local elites and other local Government representatives such as UP chairman, UP members etc along with NGO MWs who usually coordinate or conduct mediation is to arrange legal training for them to get them more acquainted with the contemporary laws relating to various disputes they mediates.

To aware general people who usually seek mediation service from NGOs, the most effective awareness program suggested is the organization of various workshops, seminars, and group meetings to highlight the benefit of NGO mediation among the participants. Beside this, other social awareness programs can be the organized through different street shows, rally, distribution of posters, leaflets, or making advertisement through media or signboards etc. Although street show, drama etc. have not got much emphasis on NGO MWs' choice, street show, drama etc. can be a worthy medium to communicate the benefits of mediation among general people especially among the poor and illiterates. To accomplish this task, successful NGO mediations made on different types of disputes most common to a locality can be demonstrated through street shows, drama etc.

CONCLUDING REMARKS

From all the observations and analysis made through out this paper, the prime objective sought was to find out the achievements made and limitations remaining for out-court NGO mediation in Bangladesh under its current settings. The research tried to collect a broad based idea about the topic from both NGO clients, and NGO MWs and so the recommendations made could be used by the policy-makers to formulate a comprehensive policy suggestion for the further development of out-court NGO mediation in the country. While judging objectively, the most limiting factors for attaining an increased effectiveness of NGO mediation is the lack of proper cooperation from the local government bodies and lack of stringent laws and their proper and quick implementation through formal courts. So if these major limitations can be vanquished by adopting carefully designed policy options as suggested at the end of this paper, NGO mediation can be established as a competent complementary to formal court justice and so the day will not be far enough when access to justice will no more be a far cry for the women in Bangladesh and that they can participate in the development process of the society in a more vigorous way, having more empowerment, and an equitable share in the overall development pursuit of the country.

NOTES

1. The World Fact book (July 2005), CIA at *http://www.odci.gov/cia/publications /factbook/geos/bg.html;* last retrieved on February 23, 2006.
2. Bangladesh ranked 72 out of 95 developing countries of the world. Human Development Report 2004, UNDP at *http://hdr.undp.org/reports/global/2004/pdf/hdr04_HDI.pdf;* last retrieved on March 16, 2006.
3. According to July 2005 estimate, in Bangladesh total number of male is 74005714 and total number of female is 70313914. So, male/female ratio is 1.05:1 .The World Fact book, CIA at *http://www.odci.gov/ cia/publications/factbook/geos/bg.html;* last retrieved on September 20, 2005.
4. Article 27 of the Constitution of the Peoples Republic of Bangladesh states that, 'All citizens are equal before law and are entitled to equal protection of law'.
5. Article 31 enumerates equal protection of law as an inalienable right of every citizen of Bangladesh by stating that, 'To enjoy the protection of the law, and to be treated in accordance with law, and only in accordance with law, is the inalienable right of every citizen, wherever he may be, and of every other person for the time being within Bangladesh....'
6. Article 7(2) of the Constitution of Bangladesh provided that, 'This constitution, as the solemn expression of the will of the people, the Supreme law of the Republic and if any other law is inconsistent with this Constitution that other law shall, to the extent of the inconsistency, be void'.
7. Kudrat-E-Elahi Panir v Bangladesh, 44 DLR (AD) (1992), p. 326.
8. Based on information gathered under intensive interviews made with Ms. Aarif Jesmin, Executive Director, Nari Progoti Forum (NPF), a local NGO perform mediation at Netrokona, Bangladesh. She is also a renowned lawyer, secretary of Netrokona Bar Association, and women activist. This part has enriched further by another intensive interview made with Advocate Khan Md. Shahid, Program Director, Mediation Cell, Madaripur, Legal Aid Association (MLAA), Madaripur, Bangladesh, and Ms. Zahanara, Excutive Director, Women Development Organization (WDO), Netrokona, Bangladesh.
9. Calculated on the basis of the answers collected from NGO MWs against the question-now a days on an average how many

disputes they record for making mediation and on an average how many disputes they solve per month.

10. While the column 'with BLAST' shows the aggregate performance of different NGOs, the column 'without BLAST' has been included to show that mature NGOs have a much better performance than the average.
11. NGO clients were asked the question why they haven't gone to formal court rather came to NGOs for making mediation.
12. As responded by the NGO clients to answer the question about how much they have to spend by themselves for get NGO mediation.
13. NGO clients were asked whether they can fully understand the rules and procedures of NGO mediation.
14. NGO MWs were asked, according to their opinion for what reason clients come to NGOs for making mediation rather going to formal courts.
15. NGO MWs were asked about how much expenditure they have to make on an average to solve a dispute through mediation.
16. Based on responses of NGO clients about what feature of NGO mediation is liked most by them.
17. Most of the NGO MWs responded "No" while asked about whether they maintain parity between man and women mediators in their mediation sessions.
18. *Supra 118.*
19. Responses were collected according to the responses from NGO MWs about how they ensure women's equal right to express their opinion during mediation.
20. NGO MWs ware asked about after mediating disputes from their NGO in what percentage of cases clients again go to family court with the same complain.
21. Information in this regard has been collected by asking NGO MWs about what type of cooperation they receive from local Government authorities. In the table NK means Netrokona, MP means Madaripur, and NJ means Narayanganj.
22. NGO MWs were asked about what more cooperation and facilities they expect from local administration and police to make NGO mediation more effective.

23. NGO MWs were asked according to their opinion about what are the modification/additions needed in existing laws to make NGO mediation more effective.

24. NGO MWs were asked about whether they have any monitoring system to monitor whether the settlement decision made by their mediation is being implemented or not.

25. NGO MWs were asked about the type of disputes to resolve which female clients usually go to their NGO.

26. Respondents were asked Among various types of disputes like divorce, maintenance, custody of children, dower, restitution of conjugal life, and others which are the most complicated to solve, asking them to put a rank one for the most complicated one, 2 for the next complicated one and so on.

27. NGO clients were asked about whether neighbours cooperate or criticize when they come to make mediation on NGOs relating to their family issues. What cooperation they get or how they are criticized.

28. Clients were asked about how they could first come to know about NGO mediation.

29. NGO MWs were asked about whether they have any social awareness program to make NGO mediation more acceptable and popular in the society.

30. NGO clients were asked whether they think that the other party will abide by the mediation decision made.

31. *Supra*127.

32. The issues on which more stringent laws are needed to be passed are determined by asking NGO MWs about what changes/ modifications are necessary to make NGO mediation more effective.

33. *Supra* 125.

34. *Supra* 128.

35. NGO clients were asked about whether it is beneficial or harmful for them if neighbours and others being present during their mediation sessions.

36. NGO MWs were asked about what type of social awareness programs they think most appropriate for making NGO mediation more acceptable and popular to the society.

REFERENCES

Chowdhury, J. A. (2005), Women's Access to Justice in Bangladesh through ADR. In: M. Shokry Eldakak (ed.). *Family Disputes: Present Limitations and Remedial Measures with Some Lessons from Egypt*. Modern Bookshop, Alexandria.

Hasan, K. M. (2003), *Introducing ADR in Bangladesh: Practical Model*. Paper Presented at Workshop on the Mediation Techniques: Alternative Dispute Resolution (ADR) in Civil Justice System in Bangladesh, Dhaka.

Islam, F. (2002), *The Madaripur Model of Mediation: A New Dimension in the Field of Dispute Resolution in Rural Bangladesh*, Unpublished Research Work, Dhaka.

9

YOUTH UNEMPLOYMENT AND EMPOWERMENT STRATEGIES

DONATILLA K. KAINO & MARTIN P. NTONGANA

INTRODUCTION

In Botswana youth is defined as young males and females aged between 12-29 years (Botswana Government 1996). The United Nations defines youth as people between the ages 15 and 24 years and these accounted for 18 percent, 25 percent of the world population and labour force respectively (United Nations 1992). It was found that between the years 1993 and 2003 the number of unemployed youth increased steadily and the youth share of the total unemployment in 2003 stood at 47 percent (ILO 2004). The situation was even worse in developing countries where youth growth rate was higher and 85 percent of more than one billion young people in the world lived. In these countries youth accounted for 21.8 percent of labour force compared to 14 percent in industrialized economies. As a result, young people were 3.8 times more likely to be unemployed when compared with older workers. In industrialized economies, youth were 2.3 times more likely to be unemployed. Worldwide, young people were also more likely to be working for long hours, on short-term and/or informal contracts, with low pay and little or no social protection (ILO 2004; United Nations 2003).

Causes of youth unemployment have been established by different researchers. It was suggested that young people couldn't get jobs because they are demanding high wages and therefore 'pricing themselves out of jobs'. They do not have basic skills and right attitudes towards work, e.g. they are not punctual, do not dress properly etc. Generally, employers compare young job seekers to older workers and past generations (Jackson 1985).

Quality of labour in terms of education and training has been cited as the main contributing factor to youth unemployment. It is argued that the 'education system is failing to adapt to the changing labour demands' (Brian and Main 1987). It has been observed that, normally, youth unemployment problem was seen as a temporary predicament, hence, the remedies to this problem were also of short-term basis (ILO 1998). The findings by ILO suggest that the opportunities for young people to obtain a decent job are limited by inadequate aggregate demand for labour which is disproportionately affects young people, who are more vulnerable to the business cycle and, therefore, more exposed to social exclusion; increase in the young people cohort size increase in the share of youth in total population rise youth unemployment and reduce their wages relative to adults; low youth wages and strict employment protection legislation (EPL); low literacy rate of young people and the mismatch between qualification and skills or occupations in demand; lack of work experience which is highly valued by employers; youth are less active in entrepreneurship than adults as they have less capital in terms of skills, knowledge and experience, savings and credit, business networks and sources of information and; lack of / low presentation by youth in trade unions or employers' associations as well as in political parties (ILO 2004)

Youth normally find themselves worse off than any other group as they do not have any or proper training and capital to start projects. On leaving school, many youth face bleak prospects of employment as a result they feel lonely, worthless, rejected in the society. They tend to lose all hopes after repeatedly being turned down by employers and lose self-esteem when remain unemployed for a long-term. They usually experience some form of depression and frustration, which create psychological problems.

The youth stage is seen to be critical in the psychological development of young people, and unemployment may hinder such development. Unemployment can result in problems like racism, juvenile delinquency particularly property crime and theft, just to mention a few (Gurney 1980, Jackson 1985)). A study by Brenner showed that a 1 percent sustained increase in the level of unemployment led to 4.1 percent increase in suicide cases, 3.4 percent more state mental hospital admission, 4 percent more prison admission, 5.7 percent more homicides and 1.9 percent more deaths from cirrhosis of the liver, cardiovascular or kidney diseases five years later (Brenner 1984). Depending on the assumptions, ILO (2004) estimates a 4.4 percent to 7 percent increase in global gross domestic product (GDP) if youth unemployment is halved (i.e. reduced from 14.4 percent to 7.2 percent). Sub-Saharan Africa is expected to have the largest relative gain, with an estimated 12 percent to 19 percent increase in GDP. Therefore it is important for the governments to find ways of solving the problem of youth unemployment.

To deal with youth problems the government of Botswana set up Botswana National Youth Council (BNYC) in 1994 and later established the Department of Culture and Youth (DCY) under the ministry of Local Government, Lands and Housing. In 1996 the department published a Policy on National Youth and a National Action Plan for Youth The department gives grants to BNYC, which gives grants to all youth organizations (non-governmental organizations) that are working to empower young people either through training or starting enterprises. However, apart from all these measures, the problem of youth unemployment has continued to persist. In Botswana the statistics show that youth unemployment is on the rise in spite of the good performance of the economy. For example, youth accounted for 36%, 73% and 72% of total unemployed population in 1991, 1999 and 2001 respectively. From gender perspective female accounted for around 52% and 55% of unemployed youth in 1999 and 2001 respectively (Central Statistic Office 1999 and 2003). In trying to find out why government's efforts to reduce youth unemployment have failed, this study uses both qualitative and quantitative methods to examine the problems and challenges faced by the youth, and youth organizations in solving the problem in Botswana. Due to time and financial constraints only the Department of Culture and Youth is considered.

OBJECTIVES

The general objective of the study is to examine the problems and challenges faced in solving the problem of youth unemployment in Botswana.

Specifically the study:

(i) Determines the problems and challenges DCY faces in running out-of-school youth program

(ii) Finds and analyses the problems and challenges faced by youth in generating self-employment through out-of-school program and their self-initiatives.

Trend in Unemployment in Botswana

Table 1 shows that unemployment in Botswana fell by 5.5% between 1993/94 and 2000 and rose by 3.8% between 2000 and 2001 then fell by 0.3% between 2001 and 2002. BIDPA (2003) forecasted that unemployment rate would fall further by 0.2% and 0.3% in 2003 and 2004 respectively. Some of the reduction in unemployment rate is attributed to the government's expansionary policy. The 2004 budget speech indicated that employment grew by 2.7% per annum between 2001 and 2003 compared to 2% experienced between 1991 and 2001. On the other hand, the total labour force between 1991 and 2001 grew at an average annual rate of 2.5 percent per annum (Siphambe 2003).

Table 1
Trend in Total Unemployment, 1993 -2001

Year	General unemployment rate (%)
1993/94	21.6
1995/96	21.5
1998	20.8
2000	15.8
2001	19.6
2002	19.3
2003	19.1[f]
2004	18.8[f]

Source: Ministry of Finance and Development, Government of Botswana [2003] and Botwsana Institute for Development Policy Analysis[f] (BIDPA)[2003]

Unemployment and Participation Rate by Age Group in Botswana

Data in Table 2 and Figure 1 show that youth participation rate is lowest for the age group 12-14 years. This may be due to the fact that, youth between 12 and 14 years tend to be new

Table 2
Unemployment and Participation Rate by Age

Age	*Actively seeking work*	*Total labour force*	*Unemployment rate*	*Participation rate*
12-14	752	122735	23.88	2.57
15-19	17397	293705	48.94	17.45
20-24	38478	170614	38.03	59.31
25-29	22206	147766	20.57	73.05
30-34	11135	113755	13.14	74.52
35-39	7458	95343	10.95	71.43
40-44	4635	76373	9.02	67.31
45-49	3092	63480	7.86	62.01
50-54	1653	45100	6.68	54.86
55-59	994	33305	6.33	47.15
60-64	580	28615	5.98	33.89
65-69	311	25474	5.15	23.73
70-74	173	21130	4.52	18.10
75+	224	36640	5.61	10.90
Unknown	430	5653	13.08	58.15
Total	109518	1189688	19.60	46.97

Source: Siphambe [2003].

in the job market and do not posses the required experience and skills. The participation rate improves with age up to age group 30-34, indicating that more young people are being integrated into the economy as age rises.

Figure 1: Unemployment and Participation Rates by Age

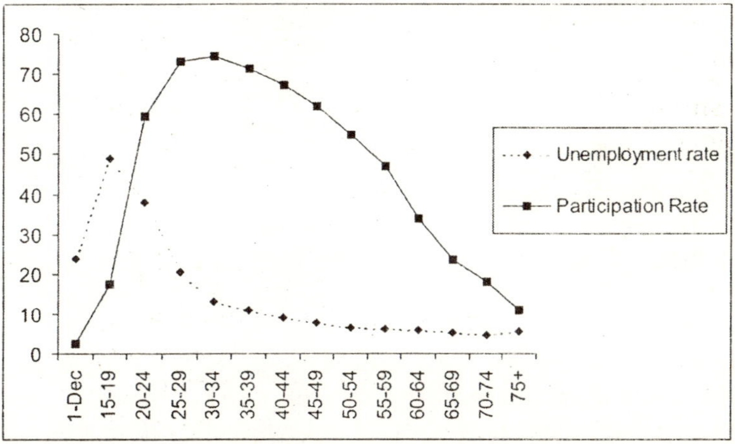

After reaching a maximum of 74.52 percent at the 30-34 age group, the participation rate starts falling slowly, implying that more elderly people are also less integrated into the economy. The data further shows that youth account for 61.8% of the total labour force of 1, 189 688. This indicates that Botswana's labour force is mainly composed of youth. Of the total youth labour force (those aged between 12 and 29) only 44.4 percent or 247, 830 are economically active. This also indicates that youth participation rate in the economy of the country is low relative to the aggregate youth labour force. Table 2 and Figure 1 show that unemployment rate rises initially and reaches a maximum at the 15-19 cohorts and falls quickly for the subsequent three cohorts and falls slowly for the rest of the ages.

CONCEPTUAL FRAMEWORK

Several studies have been done to determine the effectiveness of youth employment strategies, both for in-school and out-of-school youth. Ly *et al.* (1991) found that past employment strategies for young people in Africa were not successful due to their

bias, as they focused mainly on rural youth. The strategies formulated therefore intended to increase agricultural production in order to reduce rural-urban migration. These strategies involved 'occupational training programs' and were expensive and thus were not successful and could only attract a small number of youth. The programs were also not integrated with the whole economy and the training itself was more civic than productive, and could not secure jobs for all young people involved.

Burns and Thomas (1996) examined youth programs in Canada, United States, Australia and United Kingdom and identified the following five lessons that could be learned about what works in the field of employment-related programs and services for youth. First, there is a correlation between educational attainment and labour market success. This is because the skills learned in school were vocationally relevant and the possession of higher degree implied the possession of other qualities, i.e. intelligence, motivation, persistence and the capacity for hard work – that are useful in the labour market. They suggested that within the school system, emphasis needs to be placed on providing more clearly articulated pathways in and out of formal education, trying to reduce the stigma attached to vocational training, and providing innovative opportunities for young people to combine work and schooling.

Second, even when programs are successful, their impacts are generally modest in size. Therefore, in launching any initiative it is important not to oversell it. They argue that programs with small impact do not mean that are not worthwhile as they may be cost effective having positive returns and may be critical turning around the lives of particular young people. They suggest that no single intervention program and service that has to be called on because the needs of young people are many and vary. This means that the program that works for some youth would not work for others. Furthermore, knowing for which program works best allows the program to be more appropriately targeted. Since the impacts of the programs are generally modest, it is important to decide whether it is more important to provide programs with broad coverage or to provide help to those who need it the most.

Third, the key factors for most effective programs for young people are that there is ongoing contact with an adult (teacher, mentor, counselor, supervisor etc.) over an extended period of time and that it includes elements of monitoring, as well as support. This helps to provide the participants with structure and the motivation to do well. For disadvantaged out-of-school youth the most effective strategy would be one that is multifaceted i.e. combining a training component with strong links to the employer community, more formal training linked to on-the-job training and work experience, and, job search assistance and transitional wage subsidies for the most disadvantaged ones.

Fourth, for young people who drop out of school there is a need of quick intervention in order to prevent them from facing many other hardships that will make the problem almost insurmountable.

Fifth, 'better preparation for labour market increases the probability that young people will obtain and retain employment – but only if jobs exist. Therefore, supply - side measures cannot on their own, solve youth labour market problems. The state of the economy – the availability of jobs – is an important determinant of the program effectiveness. Parallel strategies on the demand – side, to ensure the availability of and access to employment opportunities, must be part of any coherent set of labour market policies. In this respect government needs to engage the private sector in the provision of job opportunities for youth'.

For out-of-school youth programs, which are the main focus of our study, Burns and Thomas found that there are six general approaches that have been used to help them overcome their employment related problems. They include: (a) help in finding a job (b) projects to provide periods of temporary work experience (c) wage subsidies to encourage hiring by employers (d) support to self employment (e) training, and (f) encouragement to return to school. In Canada, Australia and several European countries, these programs are typically run as an extension of the unemployment insurance systems. The qualitative studies conducted in these countries pointed out the importance of combining financial assistance with other types of support, such as management training and business planning help. The evidence suggests that well-designed training programs can make a difference. They can be more effective if they are combined with other services, such as job search help and work experience opportunities. The most successful training programs for disadvantaged youth have tended to be those that are relatively intensive and provide support services together with the training. However, such programs are expensive and complicated to operate and hence they will always be limited to helping relatively small number of people.

Finally, Burns *et al.* concluded that putting effective programs in place is not easy. This is due to the variation in impacts across similar programs that have been implemented in different places and different times. They suggested that a good program design is not, on its own any guarantee of success. It also needs sufficient time and resources for its implementation, to develop operational procedures, train staff, to work out initial start-up problems prior to full implementation. It is also important to have well-trained and motivated staff, effective program management, and early and continuous monitoring of program implementation and operation. The variability of outcomes may also reflect differences in economic environments.

This study differs from the aforementioned studies in that, instead of comparing the different effectiveness of youth employment programs across countries over a decade, it focuses only on problems and challenges faced by youth and government department of youth, in trying to deal with the problem of youth unemployment in Botswana. It focuses only on out-of-school youth who have been assisted financially with grants to be self-employed. Oral interviews with structured questionnaires were used to collect data and information from DCY and selected youth. The information and data obtained are presented in tables and graphs. Panel discussions with youth and other stakeholders were conducted in order to get more information on the problems.

RESEARCH QUESTIONS

Has the Department of Culture and Youth attained its objectives?
What are the problems and challenges faced by the department in solving youth unemployment problem?
What are the problems and challenges faced by the youth in solving the youth unemployment problem?
What are the suggestions from DCY on how to improve the situation?
What are the suggestions by the youth on how to improve the situation?
What are the views of other stakeholders on youth unemployment problem?

RESULTS

While the information colleted from youth and officials of DCY helped to answer research questions 1 to 5, information obtained from panel discussions helped to answer question 6 above.

Problems and challenges Faced by unemployed youth in generating self-employment.

The study interviewed 40 randomly selected unemployed youth in Gaborone, trying to find out problems and challenges facing them in generating self-employment. The findings presented in Figure 2 show that 45% of the respondents did either thought of having self-employment or had started some projects but collapsed later. The other 55% had never thought of having self-employment but concentrated on looking for someone to employ them. Youth in first group pointed out that lack of financial capital and skills were major constraints in creating self-employment.

Figure 2: Those who Tried Self-Employment or not

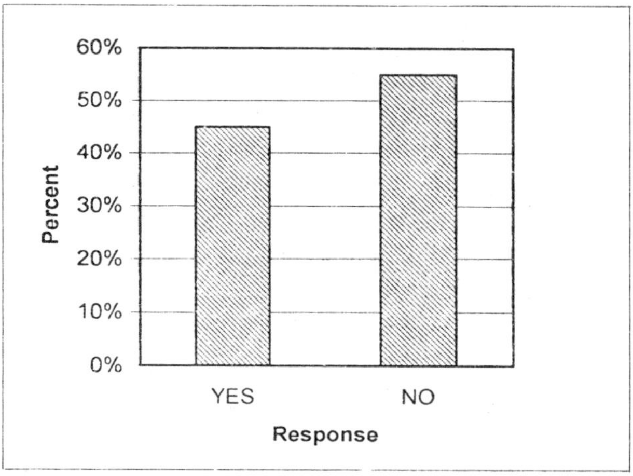

Data obtained showed that 60% of the respondents had some skills, and 40% did not have any skills. Those who had some skills got them from different jobs they were doing before. Most women had skills in tailoring, hairdressing and secretarial services. Men possessed skills in brick-laying, mechanic and generally considered themselves as laborers.

Out of 40 youth interviewed 27.5% knew the existence of department and its youth programs, the rest 72.5% said had never heard of it. Out of the 27.5% who knew the program, only 27.3% had made efforts of getting the grant to start different enterprises. The rest did not apply for the grant mainly because they did not have any skills or an idea on the projects they could invest the money. The main thing they wanted was to get some training or go for further studies, which could enable them, get employment or be self-employed. Some did not even attempt to apply for the grant because they knew some people who applied and whom they thought qualified for the grant but was not granted the fund. They thought that those who got the grant either bribed the Youth officers or belonged to families known/related to the officers. Others did not apply for the grant because they did not know how to prepare the project write-ups.

Functions and Achievement of DCY

The Ministry of Labour and Home Affairs, through the Department of Culture and Youth (DCY), is responsible for youth affairs in the country and as such is responsible for the coordination, implementation and evaluation of the National Youth Policy. DCY is charged with overall responsibilities of the national coordination of youth and cultural affairs and to oversee the implementation of the policies, programs and services. The government through DCY provides financial assistance for out-of-school marginalized and unemployed young people to venture into income generating projects. The broad objective of the financial provision is to empower youth through participation in the socio-economic development of the country.

Assistance is available to youth aged 12-29 years, out-of-school and unemployed disabled/marginalized/ disadvantaged youth. However, activities like running bars, bottle stores, cash loans, brothels/night clubs, transport operators and infrastructure development are not funded under the program. Youth Officers, one in each district, have to do the monitoring of the projects and ensuring that funds are used for purposes stated in their project proposals. But district youth officers can only deal with projects requiring funds of not more than P20, 000. Any project requiring between P20, 000 and P50, 000 is forwarded to DCY Headquarters. Youth officers can invite Project Officers to assist with their expertise on projects that give them problems. Lack of data on the number of applicants, beneficiaries, the value of projects financed, number of failed projects etc. made it impossible for this study to assess the performance of DCY as far as out-of-school program is concerned.

Problems Experienced by the Beneficiaries of Out-of-School Grant

A sample of ten young people, who benefited from the out-of-school youth program or grant, was studied. A larger number could have been studied, but it was not possible because it was difficult and sometimes impossible to track the beneficiaries. It was unfortunate that DCY had no other way of contacting the beneficiaries apart from mobile phones, which in most cases could not be reached. The 10 projects surveyed fell into three categories, namely; manufacturing, services, and tourism that accounted for 40%, 50%, and 10% respectively. A structured questionnaire was used to interview the beneficiaries.

One of the problems encountered by the beneficiaries is inadequacy of funds provided by DCY. Out of 10 beneficiaries only 4 got exact amount of money that was applied for; the other 6 beneficiaries said that the amount of money requested was cut significantly. As a result, some of the projects intended could not be established, and the meager funds provided were diverted to other uses unknown to DCY. Additional funds were applied for the project to start and some for expansion purposes in order to compete with already established companies. Another problem experienced by beneficiaries was the time taken by BCY to process and release funds. Of 10 beneficiaries, 30%, 20%, 10%, 30% and 10% respectively, got the grant within three, four, six, seven and nine months. On average, each applicant had to wait for 5.3 months to get the funds. Only 20% of respondents perceived the time taken to be short, and 80% considered it to be long.

Beneficiaries also had a problem of getting the right place for business operations. Figure 2 below shows that 50% of the beneficiaries interviewed had their projects located at their parents' homes because they were not making enough profits that could enable them rent a suitable place. However, 40%

Figure 3: Place of Operation in Percentage

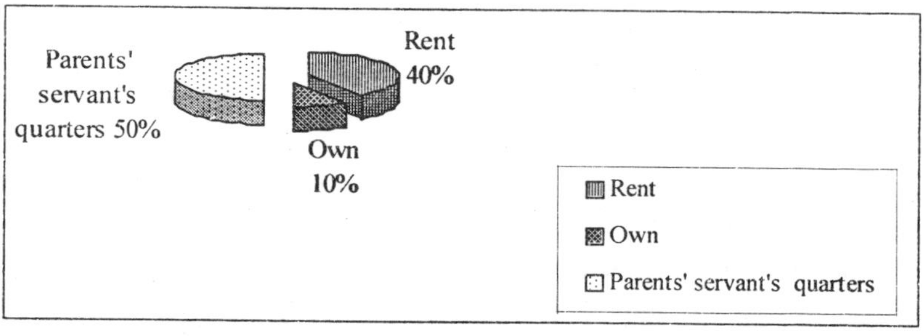

could afford to pay rent, and 10% owned the premises in which they were operating.

Across all ten projects surveyed, there were only 40 employees. This makes an average of 4 workers per project. Results show that, out of the 40 workers, 85% were youth aged between 12 and 29 years the rest 15% were people aged 30 years and above. This shows that very few people were employed in the established youth projects. The reason given for not employing more people was the lack of enough capital to establish big enterprises. Most of the manufacturing enterprises employed family members because the income generated was not enough to pay monthly salary and other benefits to an outsider like employees in established companies do.

Due to shortage of funds, youth had to establish enterprises whose inputs could be easily obtained from domestic suppliers and whose products could be domestically consumed. For example, out of 5 service-oriented enterprises surveyed, 4 were in the music and entertainment industry. As a result of concentration in this industry, these enterprises could not make enough returns to sustain themselves and therefore had to find other activities for extra income. The main cause of this situation was the lack of new ideas among youth and as a result they tended to copy from each other. On the other hand youth claimed that music and entertainment was the easiest thing they could do because it depended on their talents and do not need much of the training. Of 10 beneficiaries surveyed, 80% got their inputs from the local retailers, and only 20 percent imported their inputs from the Republic of South Africa and all of them produced for the domestic market

Shortcomings of the Out-of-School Youth Program

Lack of proper training was seen as one of the major problem by 30% of interviewed beneficiaries. They asserted that, a proper training before getting money could reduce the failure rate of many youth businesses. They argued that a one weeklong seminar on business management, they attended, was not enough if it was not useful at all. Another 50%

complained that DCY was under-staffed. There was only one district youth officer doing the administrative, funding and monitoring duties. This resulted in late provision of funds and poor monitoring. They alleged that the youth officers are in most of the time out of their work premises and can only be contacted through phone calls. They wondered how DCY could ever know if the disbursed funds were not diverted to other uses. The beneficiaries felt that the monitoring of projects is important in order to know the progress and problems of the projects. This could also build a healthy relationship between DCY and their clients. In addition to that the rest 10% claimed that DCY was being run by old women and old men who did not know or even comprehend the needs of young people. They do not really take it as their responsibility to help the youth. Their suggestion is such that, older people be replaced with younger, enthusiastic and appreciative people. They also alleged that the majority of the youth population in the country was unaware of the existence of DCY and the services it provided. They said the services of the department are confined to urban and semi-urban areas. This encouraged rural-urban migration and hence increased the problem youth unemployment in the country.

Finally, another 10% claimed that officers in the DCY lacked knowledge about youth economic empowerment. They suggested that DCY should employ people and mainly youth with relevant qualification e.g. economists since are knowledgeable about economic issues.

For them to perform better they suggested the following: (1) An intensive training of beneficiaries on how to invest and run business efficiently (2) Regular monitoring by DCY officers (3) DCY should employ more employees but with relevant qualification and who are committed to solve youth problems (4) To let more youth, especially those in rural areas know about DCY and its programs (5) DCY should avoid unnecessary reduction in applied fund for the projects (6) The government should allocate more funds towards this program for suggestion (1) to (5) to be implemented

Problems Encountered by DCY

Officials in the DCY pointed out four main problems that were encountered in the provision of the grant as: the absence of Act that could enable them to take legal action against youth who misuse funds; the shortage of manpower at district level which resulted in some activities like the monitoring of the projects funded not be done properly; the majority of applicants did not have new ideas as far as projects were concerned. They usually copy from what has been done and as a result, they fail to get funds and; the majority of youth who apply for the grant seemed not mature enough to understand how precious it was to have such opportunity in life. This also contributed much to the diversion and misuse of funds provided.

In order to improve its performance DCY officials suggested that more people be employed and more funds be provided as there were a lot of things that had to be done and the demand for the grant was so high. They thought that there was a need of having youth seminars in order to educate them on different issues that affected their life. Most of youth aged between 12 and 29 seemed not serious with life and did not appreciate whatever government did in trying to make their life manageable. They wanted everything to be done for them without knowing that the resources available are so limited and cannot meet all of their needs. They wanted the government to look into ways it could to help expand investment ideas among youth.

Findings from Panel Discussion

From panel discussions, youth mainly complained about inaccessibility of youth programs. They also complained about shortage of staff in DCY offices. As mentioned earlier-on, they argued that the district DCY office was run by one youth officer and who had to service too many young people. Given that the size of the district is large and that the officers do both administration and monitoring duties, they were hardly found in their offices. The officers were also required to attend workshops and seminars. This discouraged some of young people who needed their services in many issues. Some youth complained of not being empowered despite of having attained higher levels of education. They placed the blame on the education system that lacked specialization and hence on completion of studies, youth had no basic skills to engage in self-employment.

Stakeholders argued that youth empowerment is a long-term process and as such, cannot happen overnight. They pointed out that youth empowerment, however, should lead to acquisition of skills and employment opportunities for young people. In addition, the skills should be sustainable and relevant to the changing demands of the labour market. They further suggested that economic empowerment should result in the generation of income. The feeling was that youth were not a priority to government due to the fact that the funds allocated to youth empowerment activities were the lowest compared to other government ministries/departments, while youth constituted more than 60% of the total population. This meant that the amount of money that was allocated for empowerment of each youth was too small if not insignificant. They thought that the government lacked commitment because the concept of empowerment originated from groups that were forcing it to empower people. They claimed that, what stakeholders were doing was not empowerment, but rather, just paving way for empowerment. They pointed out that as much as empowerment is a process, it should be a process that seeks to change the way power is distributed among different groups in the society. Leaders were blamed for being reluctant to give power to young people. Consequently they did not see the importance of government investing in empowering youth. The discussion established that youth empowerment should be a process that moves from one phase to another, and there should be conditions that have to be met to achieve it. The two conditions were stated as;

1. There should be effective national machinery in the form of empowerment organizations that must be well equipped because working within government structures was merely a job and thus there was no real commitment in solving the problems of youth.

2. Those who are to be empowered should within themselves be psychologically liberated. They have to know and understand the whole empowerment process and the expectations.

DISCUSSION OF RESULTS

The study findings show that unemployment in Botswana is decreasing at a decreasing rate. Young people are the most affected since they constitute over 60% of the country's labour force. Since the rate of job creation is almost the same as the rate of population growth the prospects of solving the problem of youth unemployment in the near future are limited. Youth projects under out of school programme could not generate enough employment because the funds provided by the DCY were small and did not reach the majority youth. In most cases the money provided was not enough to establish the intended projects by the youth and consequently it was diverted to other unknown uses. Some of those who started the projects had to operate in premises that were not conducive for their activities in order to minimize operation costs.

Though DCY officials were aware that some of beneficiaries diverted funds to other unknown uses, they could not take any legal action against such people as there was no Act that gave them powers to do so. DCY failed to monitor the progress of the projects because it employed few workers due to shortage of fund. This made the diversion of funds to other uses by beneficiaries be easily done and some projects collapsed due to lack of professional advice. These findings concur with the findings by Burns *et al.* (1996) that if there is no sufficient time and resources a good program cannot be successful because it will not be implemented, essential procedures will not be developed, staff will not be trained and initial start-up problems prior to full implementation will not be worked out; unsuccessful good program can also be due to lack of early and continuous monitoring of program implementation and operation.

Youth lacked new ideas in establishing projects and therefore ended up copying activities that already existed in the market. This led to stiff competition among themselves and hence low returns on their projects. Lack of intensive training also contributed to the failure of many youth projects. A one-week training given to youth before getting the grant was considered by youth as useless as it did not give them even basic knowledge of running business. This problem could also be associated with the type of education offered in Botswana schools, which the youth and stakeholders said it was not preparing youth for self-employment. Burns *et al.* found a correlation between education attainment and labour market success because the possession of higher degree implies the possession of capacity and other qualities for hard work. They suggested that in order to reduce the stigma attached to vocational training, and to provide innovative opportunities for young people to combine work and schooling, the emphasis within the school system should be placed on providing more clearly articulated pathways in and out of formal education.

Furthermore, the study found that many youth did not apply for out-of-school grant due to lack of information on the existence of DCY and its programs; lack of appropriate skills and ideas on projects that could be established; bad experience by other youth whose applications for fund were turned down and; inability to prepare proposals for the projects. All these reflect the lessons from the study by Burns *et al.* (1996).

Stakeholders also pointed out that DCY had shortage of staff and therefore could not perform its duties as expected. Each district had one youth officer who was responsible for all duties including monitoring of the projects. They agreed that not only DCY offices were under-staffed, but were also run by old employees whom the panel suspected had no relevant qualification and who had no commitment to solve youth problems. The government was also blamed for its low commitment towards solving the problem of unemployment among young people. It allocated meager amount of money for youth empowerment activities while youth accounted for more than 60% of the country's labour force. Burns *et al.* argue that for a good program to succeed it is important to have well trained and motivated staff, and the state of economy where jobs are available. The best approach is to have both labour supply and demand strategies running concurrently. The demand-side strategies can be achieved if the government engages the private sector, which could provide job opportunities for youth.

In addition to that, stakeholders observed that out-of-school program concentrated more in towns and cities than in villages. This bias encouraged rural-urban migration and intensified the problem of unemployment in the country.

CONCLUDING REMARKS

Based on the study findings and the discussion presented above the following are the recommendations:

- DCY needs to review its grant limits and criteria of allocating funds to projects. This may solve the problem of under-financing and financing unviable projects and hence the problem of diverting funds to other unknown uses. This means that training DCY officers in these areas is crucial.
- As suggested by both DCY and out-of-school grant beneficiaries, it is important that the identified beneficiaries are intensively trained on how to run and manage business before given the funds. This also may help to reduce project failure rate.
- Furthermore, start-up problems prior to full implementation need to be worked out by the beneficiaries together with DCY officers in order to avoid the failure of some of the projects. This may also help DCY understand the problems and allocate some more funds for the project to solve such unforeseen problems.
- Elsewhere, research has shown that most successful projects were those that the parents had had significant input into their children's projects. The moral support given by parents in addition to financial resources encouraged youth to work harder. Therefore this study suggests that parents and the community should be involved in the empowerment of youth. Hence the public should be educated on the importance of empowering youth in the economy.

- In order to provide innovative opportunities for young people, schooling could be combined with work and the emphasis within the school system could be placed on providing more clearly articulated pathways in and out of formal education.
- Youth in rural areas need to be considered equally as youth in urban areas as far as the schemes to empower youth are concerned. This may help to reduce the growing rural-urban migration and consequently high unemployment among youth. Projects which can help to reduce participation of youth in agricultural sector need to be identified and funds be provided for establishment of such projects.
- As stakeholders suggested it is important to have an independent youth organization, which will deal with youth problems, unemployment inclusive. This organization should not be within government structure. Then it will be easier to determine the commitment by the government towards youth empowerment and other issues.
- In order to implement recommendations mentioned above, the government needs to allocate more resources towards out-of-school program and youth empowerment strategies at large.

REFERENCES

Botswana Government (1996), *The National Youth Policy*. Gaborone.

Botswana Government (2003), *Ministry of Finance and Development*. Gaborone.

BIDPA (2003), *BIDPA Briefing*, 2nd Quarter, Botwsana Institute for Development Policy Analysis, Gaborone.

Brenner, H. (1984), *Estimating the Effects of Economic Change on National Health and Social WellBeing*, A Study Prepared for the Subcommittee on Economic Goals and Intergovernmental Policy of the Joint Economic Committee, Joint Committee Print 98-198. US Government Printing Office, Washington DC.

Brian, G. and Main, M. (Ed.) (1987), *From School to Unemployment: The Labour Market for Young People*. Macmillan Press Ltd., London.

Burns, A. J. and Thomas, V. (1996), Evidence on the Effectiveness of Youth Labour Market Programs in Australia and the United Kingdom in Evaluating the Effectiveness of Employment-Related Programs and Services for Youth. Department of Human Resource and Social Development, Canada.

Central Statistic Office (1999), *Labour Statistics.* Government Printer, Gaborone.

Central Statistic Office (2003), *Labour Statistics 2001.* Government Printer, Gaborone.

Gurney, R. M. (1980), Does Unemployment Affects the Self-esteem of School-leavers? *Australian Journal of Psychology,* 32(3): 175-182.

ILO (2004), *Global Employment Trends for Youth,* Geneva.

Jackson, M. P. (1985), *Youth Unemployment.* Croom Helm Ltd., London

Ly, B. *et al.* (1991), *Facing the Future: Young People and Unemployment around the World.* UNESCO, Paris.

Siphambe, H. K. (2003). Economic Activity and Labour Force, Paper Presented in the Population and Housing Census Dissemination Seminar, Gaborone.

United Nations (1992), *Statistical Charts and Indicators on the Situation of Youth 1970 - 1990.* New York.

United Nations (2003), *World Youth Report 2003.* New York.

10

WOMEN AND THE NUCLEAR ISSUE

ADLURI SUBRAMANYAM RAJU

INTRODUCTION

A number of studies divulge that women are more peace loving than men ((Boulding 1984; Caldicott 1984; Elshtain 1987; Hamilton *et al.* 1987; Jensen 1987; Lamare 1989; New Comb 1986; Putney and Russel 1962; Silverman and Donald 1987; Whitworth 1994) and they do not like war. Ruddick (1983) describes 'there is a real basis for the conventional association of women with peace. Women are daughters who learn from their mothers the activity of preservative love and the maternal thinking that arises from it. These lessons from her mother's house can shape a daughter's intellectual and emotional life even if she rejects the activity, its thinking, or, for that matter, the mother herself. Preservative love is opposed in its fundamental values to military strategy. A daughter, one might say, has been trained to be unsoldierly'. Compared to women, men are more aggressive, hierarchical, and power seeking. Woman opposes more than man to the spread of nuclear weapons (Barke *et al.* 1997; Brody 1984; Conover 1987; Goertzel 1993; Gutteling and Weigman 1993) because she will be more vulnerable victim than man, as a mother, as a wife and as the one who takes enormous responsibility of the family. However, there are studies, which show that there is no difference between men and women in their attitudes toward nuclear issue (Fiske *et al.* 1983; Tyler and McGraw 1993). The above-cited studies are largely related to women attitude towards nuclear issue in the Western countries and we find very a few works in India. The author had done a research project on Indian women scientists' perceptions of the nuclear issue. The research revealed that their perceptions of nuclear issue are determined by their position and their area of study, rather than by virtue of being women (Raju 2005).

India tested its first nuclear device in 1974. After 24 years, it again carried out a series of tests in May 1998. Pakistan considered India's nuclear programme and its tests a threat to its security. It reacted immediately by conducting its nuclear tests in the same month. The sub-continental nuclear adventurism not only reflected the mutual strengths of both the rivals in atomic ability, but it broke the myth of nuclear non-proliferation. The Chinese factor weighs in India's nuclear policy and India in Pakistan's nuclear policy. If India and Pakistan continue their nuclear weapon programme South Asia may witness a potential conflict in the years to come. To avoid such a dangerous scenario, restraint is necessary on the part of both the states. Restraint, however, may become possible in the region if the people, state and the international community work to achieve it. However, the international community will work only with the help of people and states. But states seem to lack interest in working for restoring peace in the region. The only hope for us is the participation of people to work towards a peace process. Public opinion is one of the instruments through which people may express their concern over the development and may influence their governments on such sensitive issues. If there is a nuclear war or leakage in a nuclear plant or nuclear accidents, woman would be more vulnerable victim than man. In this context, the paper tries to explore the attitudes of Indian women on the nuclear issue.

SURVEY DESIGN

The study focuses on the following objectives:

- To understand the views of Indian women on the nuclear issue
- To analyze whether India's nuclear policy is consonant with the opinion of women.

A survey was carried out in Kolkata, Delhi, Hyderabad and Mumbai following the Pokhran II explosions in 1998, to elicit the views of young women, belonging to the age group of 20-35. The sample size was 106. A questionnaire was provided to the respondents from a cross section of society - lawyers, teachers, journalists, people working in Non Governmental Organizations, students and political leaders to elicit their views on the problems, based on the snowballing method. A statistical package for Social Sciences was used for cross tabulation and analysis and to ascertain the pattern of response.

FINDINGS

Importance and Knowledge of the Issue

India, as one of the developing countries, faces many problems. The respondents were asked to give priority in their preferences regarding the problems being faced by India. Only six per cent of the respondents considered the nuclear issue as being the most important concern facing the country. Poverty, terrorism, communalism and liberalization ranked above the nuclear issue for the majority of the respondents (Table 1). Since they are pre-occupied with many problems like unemployment, nuclear issue is in no way a cause of concern for them. However, in response to a separate question, majority of them, 31 per cent and 35 per cent of them treated the issue as very important and important respectively (Table 1). There is no consistency between respondents rating the nuclear issue and the importance of the issue.

Majority of the respondents (52 per cent) are 'just informed' (i.e. had a bare knowledge) about the nuclear issue, 44 per cent were well informed, whereas each 2 per cent of them were not informed and never paid attention respectively (Table 1). Since

Table1
Knowledge of the Issue

Problem	*%*	*Importance*	*%*	*Knowledge*	*%*	*Influence*	*%*
Poverty	60	Very imp	31	Well informed	44	Newspaper & magazines	42
Terrorism	13	Imp	35	Just informed	52		
Commu-nalism	9	Imp to extent	28	Not informed	2	TV	21
Liberali-zation	7	Not imp	4	Never paid attention	2	Books	25
Nuclear	6	Neither/ nor	3			Other	12
Kashmir	5						

the source of information is an important tool to understand the problem, respondents were asked to reveal their source of information: 42 per cent are influenced by newspapers and magazines; 25 per cent of them by books and 21 per cent by television. The rest (12 per cent) are influenced by many factors such as parents and elders, teachers, friends, political leaders and NGO's (Table 1).

India and Nuclear Programme

After China acquired the atom bomb in 1964, India considered it as a threat and sought to obtain an assurance for its security from the nuclear powers. However, nuclear powers did not give any assurance to India. A series of nuclear tests conducted by China since 1964 made India uncomfortable. Its alleged transfer of nuclear weapons and design to Pakistan has brought a different dimension to the security of South Asia. India felt that nuclear threat from China looms large with a possibility of India being blackmailed in future. Thus its nuclear programme is linked with China's nuclear policy. There is a few issues related India's nuclear programme.

Nuclear Issue for India

Twenty five per cent of them felt that nuclear issue is a political issue; whereas 23 per cent and 19 per cent of them felt that it is a national pride and an attempt to divert people's attention respectively. Majority of them (33 per cent) gave preference to all the above (Table 2).

Nature of India's Nuclear Programme

Majority of them (58 per cent) opined that Indian nuclear programme is a beneficial one and did not violate any treaty pertaining to non-proliferation. However, remaining 42 per cent of the respondents were of the opinion that it is harmful (Table 2).

Table 2
Opinion on India's Nuclear Programme

Nuclear issue for India	%	*Nature of nuclear programme*	%
A political issue	25	Harmful	42
An issue of national pride	23	Beneficiary	58
An issue to divert people attention	19		
All the above	33		

Reasons for Conducting Tests

The reason for India testing nuclear devices according to majority of the respondents (54 per cent) was to enhance India's international status. They felt that the nuclear tests conducted are more for status, than security needs and were an attempt to challenge the nuclear hegemony of the select few and to put an end to nuclear apartheid. Twenty three per cent of them felt that India perceived danger equally from both Pakistan and China, whereas 8 per cent of them considered that threat might come from other nuclear weapon powers, 3 per cent from Pakistan and 1 per cent from China. Eleven per cent of the respondents gave the following reasons (Table 3).

- It was long overdue.
- To keep going towards scientific advancement and self-sufficiency.
- It was a political strategy of *Bharatiya Janata Party* (Indian People's Organization) coalition government to capture votes and to create a sense of national pride among the people.
- India realizes the fact that it can play a role in international affairs if it becomes nuclear weapon state because no one listens to a weak state.
- It is meant to be a deterrent in avoiding war.

Stance on Further Nuclear Tests

Majority of the respondents (73 per cent) opposed India going nuclear tests in 1998, whereas remaining 27 per cent supported the tests (Table 3).

Strained Relation with whom

When India conducted nuclear tests, there was an opposition from different parts of the world. Respondents were asked whether India had strained relations with any country as a result of the nuclear tests. Eight per cent of the respondents felt that nuclear tests strained relations with Pakistan; 4 per cent said with China; whereas 17 per cent felt with US and 38 per cent stated that with all the above countries. Another 30 per cent were of the opinion that with most of the countries and 1 per cent did not respond. Remaining 2 per cent (others) (Table 3) maintained that India's strained relations with many countries were not because of nuclear tests.

Opinion on India's Peaceful Nuclear Programme

Forty seven per cent of the respondents felt that Pokhran-II tests marked a departure from the continuation of India's peaceful nuclear policy, whereas 39 per cent did not agree and some of them gave the following reasons: (a) The tests only

Table 3
Opinion on India's Nuclear Tests

reasons for conducting tests	%	*Opinion on further tests*	%		%	*Did India cahnge its policy*	%
Nuclear powers	8	Yes	27	Pakistna	8	Yes	47
Pakistan	3	No	73	China	4	No	39
China	1			U.S	17	difficult to say	12
Pakistan & China	23			All the above	38	No response	2
Enhance status	54			Most of the countries	30		
Others	11			Others	2		
				No response	1		

end the question of a continuation of ambiguity on nuclear issue and (b) Because India offers no-first use for avoiding war. Twelve per cent felt that it is difficult to comment and 2 per cent did not respond (Table 3).

Opinion on Conducting Nuclear Tests with the Public Support

Overwhelmingly, respondents (85 per cent) did not want Indian government to conduct nuclear tests without the support of public. It means they seek transparency over the nuclear issue. Since India is democracy, they felt that importance should be given to public opinion. Remaining 15 per cent opposed it (Table 4). They argued that since the majority of people are illiterate they couldn't adequately comprehend security issues. Therefore policies pertaining to national security require some element of secrecy. However, they maintained that the question of security matters and information about the nuclear issue should be made public. It is important to note that the Indian government, under the Atomic Energy Act of 1962, under section 18 (1) of the Act, can restrict the disclosure of information.

India's Superiority over Pakistan

Opponents of India going nuclear argued that India is superior to Pakistan in conventional weapons; hence there was no need for nuclear tests. They argued that India's nuclear tests were followed by Pakistan's, which resulted in Pakistan attaining parity with India. The majority of the respondents (68 per cent) expressed that India did not lose its superiority over Pakistan, whereas 12 per cent of them felt that India lost the supremacy. The remaining of them (20 per cent) opined that it is difficult to assess the strength of both countries (Table 4).

Table 4
Opinion on India's Nuclear Policy

Public support	*%*	*Did India lose superiority over Pakistan*	*%*
Yes	85	Yes	12
No	15	No	68
		Difficult to say	20

The Possible Use of Nuclear Weapons

With reference to a question as to under which circumstance could India use its nuclear weapons, respondents gave different options: (a) the majority of them (42 per cent) were of the opinion that under no circumstance should India use its nuclear weapons because in a nuclear war no one is a winner. Twenty six per cent felt that India could use them if Pakistan uses nuclear weapons against India. Twelve per cent wanted to use them if China attacks and 13 per cent said if the US does. However, in another question, the respondents (23 per cent) opined that the reasons for India testing devices were due to threat equally from both Pakistan and China (Table 3). Here regarding using nuclear weapons against both countries, perceptions of respondents vary. Only 12 per cent of them wanted to use weapons against China, whereas 26 per cent of them wanted to use against Pakistan. The respondents might have thought that India is yet to get parity with China. Remaining 7 per cent are not in a position to respond to the question (Table 5).

Table 5
Opinion on when to use Nuclear Weapons

Opinion	%
If Pakistan attacks	26
If China attacks	12
If US attacks	13
Under no circumstance	42
Difficult to say	7

Impact of Nuclear Tests on Kashmir

Kashmir is the major source of tension between India and Pakistan. Though three wars were fought and a number of talks were held between the two countries much progress could not be made towards finding a solution to Kashmir dispute. The failure resulted in mutual distrust and suspicion over the years. To a question whether the tests conducted by both the countries would increase tension between them, 33 per cent of the respondents maintained that the tests increased the tensions between them, 13 per cent opined that the tests ruled out the Indo-Pak war on the Kashmir issue. Perhaps they agreed with Kenneth Waltz's argument that international stability would be possible by nuclear proliferation and more nuclear weapon states would create less international aggression. Another 17 per cent felt that the tests internationalized the issue, whereas 24 per cent argued that both the countries adopted an unnecessary course of action. Thirteen per cent opined that there was no impact on the Kashmir issue (Table 6) (For more details about their perceptions along with men see Raju 2001)

Table 6
Impact of Nuclear Tests on Kashmir

Opinion	%
Test increased tension between Indo-Pak	33
Ruled out war	13
Tests internationalized the issue	17
Both countries adopted unnecessary course	24
No impact	13

Opinion on India Signing the Nuclear Non-Prolifration Treaty (NPT) and Comprehensive Test Ban Treaty (CTBT)

With regard to signing the NPT and CTBT, majority of the respondents (57 per cent) opposed India signing the treaties. For, 26 per cent of them, India should sign, whereas 8 per cent supported signing only NPT, 9 per cent for only CTBT (Table 5). Among the majority, some of them gave the following suggestions: (a) Certain biased clauses of the treaties should be amended; (b) India should sign with due safeguards. (c) India should sign if it is included in the nuclear club.

The respondents were asked under which circumstance; India can/ should sign the treaties. Thirty two per cent of them wanted to sign unilateral, 27 per cent maintained that it should sign only if Pakistan adheres to the treaties. Thirty per cent did not support to ratify the treaties under any circumstances, whereas the rest 11 per cent did not respond (Table 7).

Table 7
Opinion on India Signing NPT and CTBT

India should sign the treaties	%	*If India should sign, it should be*	%
Yes	26	Unilateral	32
No	57	If Pakistan signs	27
NPT only	8	Under no circumstance	30
CTBT only	9	No response	11

Pakistan and Nuclear Issue

Pakistan has linked its nuclear policy with India's approach towards nuclear proliferation. Pakistan regarded India's nuclear development and nuclear tests as a threat to its security. Pakistan was involved in an armed conflict with India in 1948, 1965 and 1971 and perceives that India would attack it in future too. Following factors can be cited as reasons for Pakistan launching a nuclear programme: India's nuclear test in 1974 being reckoned as a security threat to Pakistan; to develop a nuclear programme as a bargain tool, which would increase Pakistan's bargaining power so that it can compete India to join a mutually binding agreement against the production of nuclear weapons, strengthen its position in any future arms control and disarmament talks involving India; to gain parity with India; reduce India's superiority; to use it as a deterrent against India; 1979 Afghanistan crisis forced Pakistan to have nuclear weapon capabilities; not signing the NPT and link it up with India; and using the NPT as a diplomatic tool to establish its nuclear non proliferation credentials. Pakistan sought to legitimize its nuclear programme. With reference to Pakistan's nuclear policy, respondents gave the following options: (a) It is a political issue (16 per cent); (b) It is an issue of national pride (19 per cent); (c) It is an issue to divert people attention (22 per cent); (d) All the above (43 per cent) (Table 8).

South Asia and Nuclear Issue

Majority of the respondents (53 per cent) expressed that India, Pakistan, China and US are equally responsible for the nuclear proliferation in the South Asian region. Opinion of others: (a) Seven per cent opined that India was responsible, 4 per cent

Table 8
Pakistan and Nuclear Issue

Opinion	%
A political issue	16
An issue of national pride	19
An issue to divert people attention	22
All the above	43

felt that Pakistan was responsible, whereas 16 per cent said that China was responsible and for 17 per cent of them, it was US, which was responsible. However, 3 per cent did not respond to the question (Table 9).

Table 9
South Asia and Nuclear Issue

Opinion	%
India	7
Pakistan	4
China	16
US	17
All the above	53
No response	3

US and South Asian Nuclear Proliferation

In the earlier question, 17 per cent of the respondents felt that US was responsible for nuclear proliferation in the region. Further respondents were asked to list out the motives behind US attempts to make the region free from nuclear weapons. Majority of them (84 per cent) opposed the US involvement in the region. In other words, they maintained that US does not want to maintain peace but to show its hegemony in the region. However, 4 per cent of them felt that US wants to establish peace in the region, 7 per cent said that US does not want India and Pakistan spending on military instead of economic development in their respective countries. Remaining 5 per cent gave the following reasons (Table 10): (a) It wants to market its weapons in the region where its requirements have no place after the collapse of the Soviet Union. (b) It cannot tolerate the rise of a nuclear power in the region. (c) It is just part of its global policy.

Table 10
US and South Asian Proliferation

Opinion	%
US wants to establish peace in the region	4
US does not want to spend on military	7
Us wants to show its dominance	84
Other reasons	5

Global Disarmament

On the question of disarmament, respondents were divided into three groups: (a) 39 per cent of the respondents were of the opinion that it is possible to achieve global disarmament, whereas 43 per cent felt that it is not possible. Remaining 18 per cent maintained that they were not in a position to say anything (Table11). Probably, the respondents, who are optimistic, must have felt that there are only few states (India, Pakistan and Israel) which are capable of using nuclear weapons and it would not be a problem in achieving global disarmament. They hoped that in the era of globalization, the states would act together in the common interest and work for global disarmament. Others, who did not see the hopes in achieving disarmament, felt that the nuclear weapon states did not show sincerity in ending arms race and did not respond to time bound plan proposed by India to end of arms race by 2010. For them, it is politically not possible and is difficult to conceive a world without any arms. In an anarchical system, where conflicts are inevitable, it would not be possible to achieve disarmament. They maintained that theoretically one can talk about disarmament but practically it is not possible.

Table 11
Opinion on Global Disarmament

Opinion	%
Yes	39
No	43
Difficult to say	18

ANALYSIS

The following is more detailed analysis of the survey.

Variations

Regional Variations: There were some differences in opinion across region. The following are the views of respondents of different cities in India on nuclear issue.

Majority of the respondents from Kolkata (35 per cent) and Mumbai (34 per cent) considered the issue very important whereas majority of the respondents of Mumbai (33 per cent) and Hyderabad (35 per cent) considered it as important (Table 12). Regarding the knowledge about the issue, majority of the respondents of Delhi (68 per cent) were well informed, whereas majority of others from Kolkata (65 per cent), Hyderabad (58 per cent) and Mumbai (51 per cent) were just informed (Table 12).

Table 12
Regional Differences on Knowledge of the Issue

Issue	*Kolkata %*	*Delhi %*	*Hyderabad %*	*Mumbai %*
Importance				
Very important	35	32	23	34
Important	32	36	35	33
Important to an extent	24	28	31	29
Neither nor	3	4	7	-
Not important	6	-	4	4
Knowledge				
Well acquainted	35	68	35	41
Just acquainted	65	32	58	51
Not informed	-	-	7	-
Never paid	-	-	-	8

Regarding the nuclear issue, for both India and Pakistan, the respondents of the different places gave the reasons: respondents of Kolkata (21 per cent) considered nuclear issue for Pakistan having a political nature whereas only 16 per cent felt nuclear issue for India as a political (Table13). Respondents of Delhi (24 per cent) maintained that nuclear issue as a political issue for Pakistan whereas 30 per cent considered nuclear issue as a political for India (Table 13). Among the respondents, majority of the respondents of Hyderabad (27 per cent) felt that for Pakistan nuclear issue as a national pride, whereas, majority from Kolkata (31 per cent) felt it is a national pride for India. When a comparison is made among the respondents of Delhi: 24 per cent of them felt that nuclear tests are to divert people attention from the nuclear issues (Table 13), whereas only 15 per cent of them felt in the similar way in case of India. Respondents from Hyderabad (13 per cent) felt it was to divert attention of people, whereas 20 per cent felt in the same way in case of India (Table 13). There was hardly difference among the respondents of Kolkata and Mumbai regarding the nuclear issue for Pakistan and India. Whereas respondents of Delhi: 24 per cent of them felt that nuclear issue for Pakistan was to divert attention of people, however 15 per cent felt same way in case of India. And respondents of Hyderabad felt other way round. Where 13 per cent of them viewed in the same way in case of Pakistan and 20 per cent in case of India.

Majority of the respondents of Kolkata (61 per cent), Delhi (60 per cent) and Hyderabad (58 per cent) felt that India's nuclear programme is beneficial, whereas respondents of Mumbai equally felt that India's nuclear policy is harmful as well as beneficial (Table 13). In comparison with the majority of the respondents of Kolkata and Mumbai, majority of respondents of Delhi opined that the Pokhran-II tests did mark a departure from the continuation of India's peaceful nuclear policy (Table 13). For the respondents of Hyderabad, majority (43 per cent) did not see departure, but respondents of Kolkata (45 per cent) were more than others (Table 13). Majority of the respondents from Hyderabad (46 per cent) felt that it is possible to achieve global disarmament, whereas majority of others felt other way (Table 13).

Biographical Characteristics

Regarding the question about the nuclear issue for Pakistan and India: lawyers (32 per cent) felt that the nuclear issue for Pakistan was to divert attention of people whereas in case of India only 20 per cent felt in the same way. Only 17 per cent regarded nuclear tests as a national pride in case of Pakistan

Table 13
Regional Differences on Some Nuclear Issues

Issue	*Kolkata* %	*Delhi* %	*Hyderabad* %	*Mumbai* %
Nuclear issue for Pakistan				
A political	21	24	26	29
National pride	18	21	27	23
Divert people's attention	18	24	13	23
All the above	43	31	34	25
Nuclear issue for India:				
A political	16	30	28	30
National pride	31	18	24	22
Divert people's attention	16	15	20	22
All the above	37	37	28	26
Stance on further tests:				
Yes	26	32	24	26
No	74	68	76	74
India's nuclear programme				
Harmful	39	40	42	50
Beneficiary	61	60	58	50
Opinion on departure of *India's peaceful nuclear policy*				
Yes	52	60	31	46
No	45	36	43	29
Do not know	3	4	26	25
Global disarmament				
Possible	36	40	46	33
No	48	48	31	42
Difficult to say	16	12	23	25

whereas 25 per cent of them felt in case of India. It is interesting to note that 28 per cent of political leaders considered that it was a political issue for Pakistan and in case of India no one treated the issue as a political (Table 14). Majority of teachers (78 per cent), NGOs (87 per cent), journalists (83 per cent), students (71 per cent) and political leaders (71 per cent) did not support for further tests, but it was lawyers (52 per cent) who wanted India going further tests (Table 14). It should be noted that in the survey conducted among men, lawyers were constituted more in supporting the further tests.

Except majority of respondents of NGOs, majority in all other groups did not support India signing the NPT and CTBT (Table 16). Regarding the question under which circumstance India should sign the treaties, majority of respondents of lawyers (60 per cent), journalists (38 per cent) and students (35 per cent) felt that it should not sign at all. However, in other fields – teachers (41 per cent), NGOs (54 per cent) and political leaders (35 per cent) argued for signing them. It is important to note that the sample of political leaders was very small (only seven respondents) and they belonged to Congress (2), Communist party (3) and BJP (2). Except majority of lawyers, majority of others were of the opinion that India should not use nuclear weapons under any circumstances (Table 14).

Table 14
Respondents of the Different Fields Views on Various Issues

Issue	*Lawyers %*	*Teachers %*	*NGOs %*	*Journalists %*	*Students*	*Politicians*
Nuclear issue for Pakistan:						
Political issue	22	31	13	31	22	28
National pride	17	26	20	22	30	23
To divert people attention	32	5	17	14	12	36
All the above	29	38	50	33	36	13
Nuclear issue for India:						
Political issue	15	35	30	29	40	-
National pride	25	21	26	14	22	30
To divert people attention	10	4	24	24	13	29
All the above	40	40	20	33	25	41
Justify further tests:						
Yes	52	22	13	17	29	29
No	48	78	87	83	71	71
India should sign NPT & CTBT						
Yes	5	32	44	29	26	20
No	88	52	24	60	74	44
Only NPT	7	7	8	4	-	22
Only CTBT	-	9	24	7	-	14
Under which circumstance India should sign:		41	54	21	31	35
Unilateral	10	27	28	37	27	22

Contd...

Issue	*Law yers %*	*Teac- hers %*	*NGOs %*	*Journal- ists %*	*Stude- nts*	*Politi- cians*
If Pakistan signs	21	8	13	38	38	22
Under no circumstance	60	24	5	4	4	21
No response	9					
Did India change its nuclear policy:						
Yes	27	57	34	52	42	69
No	57	26	43	32	46	30
Difficult to say	11	16	22	16	6	1
No response	5	1	1	-	6	-
Possible use of nuclear weapons:						
If Pakistan attacks	31	29	16	25	25	29
If China attacks	16	11	5	5	20	15
Is US Attacks	21	6	6	6	23	16
Under no circumstance	20	45	52	64	32	40
Difficult to say	12	-	21	-	-	-

With reference to question whether Pokhran II tests marked a departure from the continuation of peaceful nuclear policy, majority of the respondents divided into two groups: majority of lawyers (57 per cent), NGOs (43 per cent) and students (46 per cent) did not feel the there was a shift, however majority of teachers (57 per cent), journalists (52 per cent) and political leaders (69 per cent) felt in other way round (Table 15).

Table 15
Opinion on Respondents of Different Fields Views on US Policy & Disarmament

Issue	*Law yers %*	*Teac- hers %*	*NGOs %*	*Journal- ists %*	*Stude- nts*	*Politi- cians*
US involvement:						
Wants to establish peace	-	11	6	-	6	-
Wants to spend money on economic development	-	-	17	13	12	-
Wants to show dominance	100	79	62	87	77	100
Others	-	10	15	-	5	-
Global Disarmament:						
Possible	36	41	54	31	43	30
Not possible	43	24	31	54	51	55
Do not know	21	35	15	15	6	15

The majority of the respondents of all fields were of the opinion that US wants to show its dominance in the region. But all the respondents of lawyers and political leaders pointed out that the US has hegemonic ambitions in South Asia (Table 15). Majority of lawyers (43 per cent), journalists (54 per cent), students (51 per cent) and political leaders (55 per cent) did not think any possibility of achieving global disarmament, whereas majority of others - teachers (41 per cent) and NGOs (54 per cent) were of the opinion that it is possible (Table 15).

CONCLUDING REMARKS

The survey reveals a diffused pattern of response on some issues by the respondents on the basis of region and occupation. Whether the results of the survey of four cities in India tally with the views of youth (women) in other parts of India is a matter of conjuncture. The study is more of exploratory attempt to study how the young women understand and analyze the nuclear issue.

For majority of the respondents, poverty and economic instability have higher salience than nuclear issue. Instead of spending on nuclear/ military capability, they suggested that resources should be diverted to improve social development. They felt that India changed its policy from peaceful to military purposes. The tests conducted by India and Pakistan increased tensions further between them, t hey maintained. Majority of them said that under no circumstances should India use nuclear weapons against any country and it should not carry out further tests. However, they disagreed India signing the treaties (NPT and CTBT). It may be because; they must have felt that even if India signs, preventing proliferation at global level is not possible. So, for them, without signing any treaty India should stick to disarmament. They maintained that India, Pakistan, China and the US were responsible for exposing South Asia to arms race and found fault mainly with the US and China. From the above analysis, one can conclude that the respondents are peace loving.

REFERENCES

Barke, Richard P. *et al.* (1997), Risk Perceptions of Men and Women Scientists. *Social Science Quarterly*, 78 (1): 167-176.

Boulding, E. (1984), Focus on: The Gender Gap. *Journal of Peace Research*, 12 (1): 1-3.

Brody, Charles J. (1984), Differences by Sex in Support for Nuclear Power. *Social Forces*, 63 (1): 209-228.

Caldicott, Helen (1984), *Missile Envy: The Arms Race and Nuclear War*. William Morrow, New York.

Conover, Pamela Johnston (1988), Feminists and the Gender Gap. *Journal of Politics*, 50 (4): 985-1010.

Elshtain, Jean B. (1987), *Women and War*. Basic Books, New York.

Fiske, Susan T. *et al.* (1983), Citizens' Images of Nuclear War: Content and Consequences. *Journal of Social Issues*, 39(1): 41-65.

Goertzel, Ted G. (1983), The Gender Gap: Sex Family Income and Political Opinion in the Early 1980s. *Journal of Political and Military Sociology*, 11: 209-222.

Gutteling, Jan M. & Wiegman, Oene (1993), Gender Specific Reactions to Environmental Hazards in the Netherlands. *Sex Roles*, 28 (7-8): 433-447.

Hamilton, Scott B. *et al.* (1987), In the Eye of the Beholder: Accounting for Variability in Attitudes and Cognitive/Affective Reaction toward the Threat of Nuclear War. *Journal of Applied Social Psychology*, 17(11): 927-952.

Jensen, Mark P. (1987), Gender, Sex Roles and Attitudes toward War and Nuclear Weapons. *Sex Roles*, 17 (5-6): 253-267.

Lamare, James W. (1989), Gender and Public Opinion: Defence and Nuclear Issues in New Zealand. *Journal of Peace Research*, 26(3): 285-296.

Newcomb, Michael (1986), Nuclear Attitudes and Reactions: Associations with Depression, Drug Use and Quality of Life. *Journal of Personality and Social Psychology*, 50 (5): 906-920.

Putney, Snell and Russel, Middleto (1962), Some Factors Associated with Student Acceptance or Rejection of War. *American Sociological Review*, 27 (5): 655-667.

Raju, A. Subramanyam (2001), *Third Generation Indian Perceptions of the Kashmir Issue*. Regional Centre for Strategic Studies, Colombo.

Raju, A. Subramanyam (2005), *Indian Women Scientists' Perceptions of the Nuclear Issue*. WISCOMP, New Delhi.

Ruddick, Sara (1983), Pacifying the Forces: Drafting Women in the Interests of Peace Signs, *Journal of Women in Society and Culture,* 8 (3): 471-489.

Silverman, Jane M. & Donald, Kumka S. (1987), Gender Differences in Attitudes toward Nuclear War and Disarmament. *Sex Roles,* 16 (3-4): 189-203.

Tyler Tom R & McGraw, Kathleen (1983), The Threat of Nuclear War: Risk Interpretation and Behavioral Response. *Journal of Social Issues,* 39 (1): 25-40.

Whitworth, Sandra (1994), *Feminism and International Relations*. St. Martin's Press, New York.

11

WOMEN IN KENYA: A SECOND CLASS CITIZEN

TABITHA W. KIRITI-NGANGA

INTRODUCTION

Despite worldwide progress in promoting women's rights, in no country are women free from discrimination. This discrimination feeds and is reinforced by violence against women (Amnesty International 2002a and 2002b). This has led to marginalization of women and lack of political and economic empowerment.

Empowerment implies the creation of an enabling environment for individuals to fully use their capabilities to take charge of their lives. Empowerment also implies the building or acquiring of capacity to accomplish certain tasks and attain specific goals. In the case of women, empowerment involves creating conducive environment so that women can use their competencies to address the fundamental problems of society at par with their male counterparts. Therefore, true empowerment should show that women are increasingly breaking the traditional boundaries and stereotypes in Kenya and in the world at large.

This paper first looks at the issue of sex discrimination in Kenya. I then look at women's contribution to Kenya's social and economic development. In section four I look at women participation in politics and decision-making in Kenya. After that the issue of access to contraception among women in Kenya is discussed. This is followed by a discussion of access to education and employment to women in Kenya. Section 8 looks at the intra-family allocation of resources in the Kenyan situation, followed by a discussion of gender violence in Kenya. I then look at the economic policies and programs initiated by the government for women empowerment in Kenya. After that I conclude and give policy recommendations.

SEX DISCRIMINATION

Women constitute 52 percent of Kenya's population, but the majority of them are among the illiterate and poor in the country (United Nations Economic and Social Council 1995). Majority of the women are still affected by customary laws and practices, which for so long have perpetuated their oppression and enhanced sex based discrimination. Kenya being a patriarchal state, fears the illegalization of sex discrimination because it may lead to countless court suits by women. This fear has therefore meant that women, who are most likely to be affected by such provisions, are denied constitutional protection from sex based discrimination.

Even where the *dejure* process has been made in achieving equality, women continue to be discriminated against as a result of conflict between laws in Kenya and customary practices and the economic situation. Women experience a wide range of discriminatory practices, limiting their political and economic rights. They are *de-facto,* second-class citizens. Customary law disadvantages women, particularly in property rights and inheritance. Under the customary law of most ethnic groups in Kenya, a woman cannot inherit land and most live on the land as a guest of male relatives by blood or marriage. Customarily, women do not own property, or the land they work on, which causes them economic hardship and places them in a position of dependence.

The traditional inferior status of women is reinforced by the predominance of marriages under some form of customary law that limits women's rights. There are several laws governing marriage and divorce based on the different religions in the country; namely customary, Christian, Hindu and Muslim laws. The marriage bill has to date not gone into force that is expected to harmonize these laws. The constitutional legitimization of sex discrimination has far reaching consequences for women in Kenya as will be seen in this paper. This has meant that in the area where women are most affected, the constitution offers them no protection.

The majority of the poor in Kenya are women and it means that legal services are in most cases out of reach for a majority of them. This means that special legal aid arrangements are necessary to enable them to challenge discriminatory practices inherent in personal law. For example under customary law there is a general principal that the husband should manage the wife's property, except for movables such as personal effects. There are also divergent practices on the position of the woman, as regards to her property rights and dissolution of marriage.

The responsibility to care for a child born out of wedlock is placed squarely on the mother, who has to provide for its education and other necessities of life. This is discriminatory. An unwed mother has no remedy, save for pregnancy compensation, which is recoverable by parents under customary law. The compensation of Ksh. 1000, (13 US Dollars) sanctioned by the law, is contemptuous and would not even go halfway to defray medical expenses related to the child's birth. In any case it is recoverable by parents for the lost honour of their daughter and not necessarily for the maintenance of the child.

In the Law of Succession Act, there is a distinction between rights of married and unmarried daughters. It has been argued and held that married daughters are not entitled to inherit. This means that an unnecessary number of women headed households in urban centres that are exposed to extreme poverty, overcrowding, unemployment and health hazards are as a result of this Act. Women have rarely inherited land and other property in their rural homes. This maybe the reason why more female household heads move to urban areas in search of employment as they seek other means of production and survival.

Poverty and traditionalism remain two serious obstacles to women's equal rights in Kenya. The United Nations Economic Commission for Africa (1998) noted that poverty in general inhibited the full employment of women rights and that the situation meant that women have unequal access to resources ensuring continued discrimination.

The draft constitution, rejected on the 21st November 2005, had provided for the equal treatment with men, including the right to equal opportunities in political, economic and social activities and the equal right to inherit, have access to land and control property. The draft had prohibited any law, culture, custom or tradition that undermined the dignity, welfare interest or status of women.

SECOND CLASS CITIZENS

Although Kenya's various ethnic groups have different cultures and traditions, some of which contribute to promoting women's rights, in general the status of women in Kenya is that of second-class citizens. Section 82 (3) of the Kenya constitution, denies women protection outside their homes (e.g., in the workplace) whilst section 82 (4) (6) further denies them protection in their homes. The effect is that at no time are women guaranteed protection from sex based discrimination.

Section 82 (4) (b) legitimizes the traditional position, which accorded women fewer privileges than men in matters concerning their families, marriage, divorce and succession. Other than this, The Marriage Bill (1985) gives equal rights to spouses in a marriage in matters concerning custody of children, divorce, or division of matrimonial property. But this bill has failed to pass through parliament for reasons including objections to interference with a man's right to chastise his wife, objections to adultery made a reason for divorce proceedings and objections to a wife having a right to object to her husband marrying a second wife.

Forced marriage is customary in some communities in Kenya. In other communities in Kenya, on the death of her husband, a woman is 'inherited' by his brother or close male relatives. The woman's consent to this new marriage or to sexual relations with her new 'husband' is not sought.

CITIZENSHIP

The world organization against torture (Organisation Mondiale Contre la Torture) (OMCT 2003) raised the issue of gender discrimination regarding citizenship in its alternative report to the committee on the rights of the child. As the OMCT report pointed out, the constitution of Kenya and the Kenya citizenship Act (Chapter 70, Republic of Kenya 1998) discriminate against children born to Kenyan mothers abroad but do not discriminate against children born to Kenyan fathers abroad. Children born to Kenyan mothers abroad have to apply for citizenship and are given entity permits for a limited duration upon entry into Kenya, while similar treatment is not accorded to children of Kenyan fathers born to non Kenyan mothers.

The law of domicile, The Domicile Act (Chapter 37, Republic of Kenya 1998) gives credence to and perpetuates the practice of discrimination against children born out of wedlock. In Kenya residence is different from domicile and domicile or origin refers to the home of the parents at the time of birth. In Kenya, this is often equated to the ancestral home that every person born within lawful wedlock is presumed to have. Children born out of wedlock are accorded the domicile of their mothers whereas those born within lawful wedlock acquire that of their fathers. Domicile determines other rights such as voting rights. In many cultures, children born out of wedlock do not belong in the mother's home (domicile) and have no rights to inherit property. As a result, many are often rendered without domicile.

According to the Kenyan constitution, a Kenyan woman marrying a foreigner does not pass on her citizenship to her husband, though it applies if a Kenyan man married a foreign woman. These laws are discriminatory and since Kenya is a signatory to the convention on the eradication of discrimination against women, it should live up to its obligation under the convention by repelling such provisions, which promote discrimination against women.

WOMEN'S CONTRIBUTION TO KENYA'S SOCIAL AND ECONOMIC DEVELOPMENT

The contribution that women make to economic, social and political lives of their nations, communities, families and the next generation, make them key actors in effective development. The basic objective of development is enlarging people's choices. The essential components of enlarging people's choices is the equality of opportunity for all people in society, sustainability of such opportunities from one generation to the next, and the empowerment of people so that they participate in and benefit from the development process. This entails equal access to basic social services, including education and health, equal opportunities for participation in political and economic decision-making, equal reward for equal work, equal protection under the law, elimination of discrimination by gender and equal rights of citizens at the workplace and at home (United Nations Development Programme 1995).

Women face discrimination not only at the household level where resources are unequally allocated but also at the national level where the systems (laws, culture, taboos and so on) are anti-women. More than 800 million women are economically active worldwide, in agriculture, small and micro enterprise and in export processing industries. However women's unemployment rates remain high relative to those of men and when employed, they are paid less than men for the same work.

Limitations on women's legal rights and participation in civil society are widespread. Political leadership positions are still mainly occupied by men. Although women have increasingly provided dynamic leadership in Non-governmental Organizations (NGO's) and small enterprise sectors, legal restrictions on women's land and property ownership continue to hamper women's ability to acquire productive assets to reduce their vulnerability to poverty. Girl's education has been shown to have a dramatic impact on women's economic power and on families' welfare but progress towards gender equality in education still lags behind, both in absolute terms and relative to those of boys. However, violence impedes women's ability to live full and productive lives. It restricts their contributions to family, societal and economic development.

WOMEN PARTICIPATION IN POLITICS AND DECISION-MAKING

The Kenyan society is a patriarchal society with widespread discrimination against women and a virtual absence of women in positions of power in the socio-economic and political spheres. Although women in Kenya are the majority of the voter population, they turn out to be under represented. Women in Kenya have achieved little progress since the Beijing Platform for Action was adopted. Women account for 52% of the country's adult population and 60% of the voting population. Their participation in the political and elective office is at a low level. Although some women have

Table 1
Distribution of National Assembly Members by Gender 1969- 2005

Year	*Elected Members*			*Nominated Members*			*National Assembly Members*		
	Men	*Women*	*Women %*	*Men*	*Women*	*women %*	*Men*	*women*	*women %*
1969	154	1	0.7	11	1	8.3	165	2	1.2
1974	152	5	3.2	10	2	16.7	162	7	4.1
1979	155	3	1.9	11	1	8.3	166	4	2.4
1983	157	1	0.6	10	2	16.7	167	3	1.8
1988	186	2	1.1	11	1	8.3	197	3	1.5
1992	182	6	3.2	11	1	8.3	193	7	3.5
1997	206	4	1.9	7	5	41.7	213	9	4.1
2002	201	9	4.3	4	8	66.7	205	17	7.7

Source: Republic of Kenya, Economic Survey [2004].

Table 2
Women Participation in Decision Making

Rank	June 2003				June 2005			
	Men	*Women*	*Women*	*Men*	*Women*	*women*	*Men*	*women*
Ambassadors	7	27	34	20.6	11	29	40	27.5
Permanent Secretaries	3	21	24	12.5	6	25	31	19.4
Provincial Commissioners	0	8	8	-	0	8	8	-
District Commissioners	3	68	71	4.2	2	69	71	2.8
Deputy Secretary	19	75	94	20.2	21	77	98	21.4
Councilors	377	2460	2837	13.3	377	2460	2837	13.3
Lawyers	1645	3179	4824	34.3	1708	3277	4985	34.3
District Officers	68	355	423	16.1	88	358	447	19.7
Chief Justice	-	1	1	-	-	1	1	-
Judges of Appeal	1	12	13	7.7	-	14	14	-
Commissioners of Assize	1	2	3	33.4	1	2	3	33.4
Chief Magistrates	6	8	14	42.9	6	9	15	40
Senior Principal Magistrate	9	13	22	40.9	11	15	26	42.3
Senior Resident Magistrates	32	55	87	36.8	38	63	101	37.6
Resident Magistrates	53	71	124	42.7	64	82	146	43.8
District Magistrates	85	121	206	41.3	92	126	218	42.2
Chief Kadhis	-	17	17	-	-	17	17	-
Total	2309	6493	8802	26.23	2425	6632	9058	26.77

Source: Department of Gender, Electoral Commission and Directorate for Personnel Management Compliment Statistics, Republic of Kenya

attempted to enter the political field, the numbers of women members of parliament are still very few. Table 1 shows the distribution of parliamentary seats between 1969 and 2002.

As Table 1 shows, women represent only 7.7% of the total members of the current parliament. Other than this, there has been no significant appointment of women into top-level ministerial posts in the government and in parastatals. Participation of women in political and public decision making is viewed as critical to the actualization of gender equality because women must command real political power if their concerns are to be prioritized and meaningfully included in the national agenda.

Table 2 shows the participation of women in decision-making in areas other than parliament.

Representation of women should also be effective at the district and location levels, as well as in the county, town and municipal councils. Unfortunately, participation of women is low and ineffective at the local and national levels as shown in Table 2. In the political process where women are significantly ignored in policies, policymaking and implementation, policies adopted to improve their lot will not be easily practiced.

As a result of poor representation, women in Kenya feel they lack a sufficient voice to push the enactment of laws that could enhance respect for women's rights and fight against their economic marginalization. The rejected draft constitution had provided affirmative action that required political parties to ensure that at least one third of their candidates for direct elections were women. As Kenya prepares to present its performance report on the Convention on the Elimination of All Forms of Discrimination against Women, it is evident that the country is far from meeting it s obligations to more than half of its population.

ACCESS TO CONTRACEPTION AMONG WOMEN

The rate of population growth in Kenya was until recently among the highest in the world. 3.7% in 1980, 3.1% in 1990, and 2.0% in 2003. Despite some decline in fertility, 7.7 children in 1980, 5.9 in 1990 and 4.4 in 2003 there is still need for sustained promotion of family planning services (Kiriti and Tisdell 2005). Women have a right to contraceptive information and services for them to be able to determine the number of children they would like to have. Certain laws restrict women in the exercise of these rights. No specific law governs family planning and dissemination of information relating to it. This requirement is constraining in that a woman who has made an independent and informed choice may be prevented from exercising her right by the spouse if he wants more children.

Abortion is illegal in Kenya, whether the woman herself performs it or whether someone else performs it. Under the Kenyan Law, abortion is only allowed where the operation is performed to save the physical or mental health of a pregnant woman. In this instance, at least two medical opinions have to confirm the necessity of the operation. The woman's consent and that of her spouse (if she is married) are a prerequisite to such an operation. This law is restrictive and interferes with a woman's right in so far as making decisions as to how to regulate her fertility. By making abortion illegal, the law makes the service unavailable to women who might find themselves unable to cope with the child they are expecting. Consequently, the law imposes compulsory motherhood on expectant women with all the attendant consequences.

Currently, 24% of married women in Kenya would like to limit or space their pregnancies, but are not using any method of contraception. Women in Kenya have on average 4.4 children, and for every 100,000 live births there are 1300 maternal deaths - a staggering figure. Nearly half of all the births are reported to be unwanted or unplanned and almost half of Kenyan women give birth before the age of 20. An estimated one-third of maternal deaths can be attributed to unsafe abortion (Republic of Kenya 2005).

According to UNAIDS (2004) there were an estimated 890,000 Aids orphans in Kenya as of 2001 as shown in Table 3, a number expected to increase to 1.5 million by 2010. Due to the socio-economic and cultural status of women in Kenya, they are twice as likely as men to become infected by HIV/AIDS; currently 60% of those living with HIV/AIDS are women.

Table 3
People Living with HIV/AIDS in Kenya

Year due	*Total Adults and Children*	*Adults (millions)*	*Adult rate (%)*	*Women 15-49 yrs*	*Men 15-49 yrs*	*Children <15 yrs*	*Orphaned to AIDS <15 yrs*
End 1999	2.1m	2.0	NA	1.1m	0.9m	0.078m	NA
End 2001	2.5m	2.3	NA	1.4m	0.9m	0.22m	0.890m
End 2003	1.2m	1.1	6.7	0.720m	0.380m	0.100m	0.650m

Source: UNAIDS [2004].

By the end of the year 2001, 2.5million people in Kenya were estimated to be living with HIV/AIDS. 1.4 million women in the age bracket 15-49 years were HIV-positive compared to 0.9 million men in the same category by the end of 2001. The HIV infection rate of all pregnant women aged 15-24 years was 9.8% in 2003 (Republic of Kenya 2004).

Women and girls are more vulnerable to HIV than men and boys because of their limited access to economic and educational opportunities, and the multiple household and community roles they are responsible for. Also women and girls are subject to social norms that deny them sexual health knowledge and practices that prevent them from controlling their bodies. The gender division of labour and male urban migration keeps men away from their wives for long periods leading to promiscuity and the spread of HIV. Women in the rural areas may also find themselves discriminated against when trying to access care and support when they are HIV-positive. In Kenya, women who are HIV-infected are divorced even when it is their husbands who have infected them. Family resources are more likely to be devoted to buying medication and arranging care for ill males than females. Because of lack of hospital facilities in rural areas and lack of income, those in rural areas affected by AIDS may find it difficult if not impossible, to obtain hospital care. Therefore, they mostly have to be cared for at home. Generally this is the burden of females (Kiriti and Tisdell 2005).

As the country loses young productive people to AIDS, the effects have an influence on all sectors of the economy. The loss of income of the breadwinner, increased medical expenses and increased time taking care of the sick persons may lead to reduced agricultural output. Households fall into deeper poverty and women are left bearing even larger burdens as workers, educators, and mothers and, ultimately as caregivers, as the burden of caring for the ill family members rests mostly with women and girls.

In Kenya, HIV/AIDS has become one of the major public health challenges facing the country and has been declared a national disaster. In the wake of HIV/AIDS, mortality and morbidity have increased, with a wide gender disparity in prevalence. Pregnant women are particularly prone to severe forms of malaria due to their reduced immunity levels; moreover, malaria in pregnancy is a major cause of anemia and low birth weight.

EDUCATION

Education is treated as a basic need by the government, and as such the government is committed to the position of equal education opportunities for all persons in Kenya. However, inequalities still persist in enrolments of girls and boys starting from pre-primary to the university level as shown in Table 4.

Table 4
Enrolment in Pre-Primary, Primary and Secondary Schools in Kenya (1999- 2004) ('000)

Year	*Pre*		*Primary*		*Secondary*		*University*	
	Male	*Female*	*Male*	*Female*	*Male*	*Female*	*Male*	*Female*
2000	636.8	609.8	3064.5	3013.6	402.5	356.5	37.4	21.8
2001	671.1	645.1	3079.6	3002.2	421.2	376.4	43.7	27.6
2002	738.9	708.6	3143.1	2988.0	431.3	387.9	51.1	29.9
2003	809.5	783.4	3653.5	3463.8	460.6	419.4	51.5	30.6
2004	815.8	788.8	3810.4	3574.4	481.6	431.0	57.9	33.6

Source: Republic of Kenya, Economic Survey [Various Issues].

Levels of education and literacy for women and men differ widely. Although the number of boys and girls is roughly equal at the primary level, men substantially outnumber women in higher education. In rural areas, families are more reluctant to invest in education for girls than in educating boys. Hence, 70% of the illiterate persons in Kenya are female.

The enrolment of girls in secondary schools is much lower than in primary schools. This is mainly due to early marriages, pre-marital pregnancies and poverty where parents would rather educate boys than girls. This means that the girls may eventually slip back to illiteracy. This trend continues to tertiary institutions where there are more boys than girls and translates to lack of empowerment for women in employment, decision-making and control of resources (Kiriti 2005). In 2004, female students in all universities in Kenya composed only 33.6% of the total number of students enrolled.

The Education Act does not make education a right for all Kenyans although current policy makers make it compulsory. Women's education is often curtailed by factors such as early pregnancies, discrimination and cultural practices. The education materials used in various institutions fail to depict women as role models whom school girls can naturally identify with. In various schoolbooks, there is continuous use of masculine words, illustrations and content. Women portrayed in schoolbooks are often known as mothers, cooks nurses or teachers. Most books fail to show them in technical positions.

EMPLOYMENT

Women make up about 75% of the agricultural work force, and have become active in small urban businesses. However, the average monthly income of women is about two thirds that of men and women hold about 5% of land titles (Republic of Kenya 2003). This marginalization of women in the work force means that most women are financially dependent upon husbands thereby making it extremely difficult for them to leave situations of domestic violence.

The participation of women in formal employment is quite low. In 2002, female participation remained low accounting for 29.6% of the total wage employment in the modern sector. The education sector remained the major female employer in

2002 engaging 136.3 thousand females with a share of 27.1% of total female employment. Of the total wage employees, 1381.1 thousand were on regular terms of employment of which 29.1% were females (Republic of Kenya 2004).

A number of reasons can be given for women's low participation in formal employment, such as lack of equal education and skills compared to men, cultural attitudes about women working, or family obligations. Kenya's employment law is provided by the Employment Act (cap 226), which does not specifically provide for employment as a right. However there is an underlying implication that it is gender neutral, but bearing in mind that the constitution condones sex discrimination, one can see that the gender neutrality of the employment law can be undermined by such a provision.

In the export processing zones (EPZs), women are often preferred due to the nature of work. They are often underpaid and overworked. No trade unions are permitted in such zones, which makes labour very cheap and working conditions fairly poor. Women employees are guaranteed maternity leave for 2 months, though they are supposed to forfeit their annual leave the year they take up maternity leave. Maternity has often been used as an excuse to deny women's appointment to certain posts for the simple reason that it would be uneconomical to employ them.

Although Kenya's employment laws are gender neutral, in practice women have not been sufficiently catered for. Deliberate measures are therefore important to ensure that practices, which tend to promote sex discrimination, are eliminated. If women are to fully participate in policymaking and implementation, it is important that impediments that prevent their participation are eliminated. A number of these arise from societal attitudes on the role and place of women and other roles, which place barriers to the advancement of women.

INTRA-FAMILY ALLOCATION OF RESOURCES

Access to critical resources provides an alternative way of conceptualizing determinants of women's second-class position. In Kenya, besides satisfying the family's need for food, clean clothes and a nice and tidy home, women's activities include participating in cash crop production and other income generating activities and tending livestock. Men's responsibility for taking care of the family is primarily fulfilled through provision of cash, mainly through wage labour, production and sale of cash crops such as tea, coffee and of livestock. This pattern of resource control heavily favours men. They control the major means of production, income and surpluses. To the extent that women control the resources and surpluses generated through their own production or family production, these are usually quite small and economically insignificant. Further, the few resources most rural women control (typically a vegetable garden, smaller amounts of maize, beans, finger millet, chicken and evening milk from goats) are almost entirely oriented toward providing for the home and family, or providing women with the means (i.e. cash) to acquire necessary family consumption goods on the market (Kiriti 2003).

In Kenya, although land now belongs to individuals, it can be bought and sold or used for purposes over which women have no control. Under certain circumstances, women can thus be denied access to land, and traditional rights of female kin give way to men's legally confirmed rights. The introduction of cash crops in Kenya increased gender inequality in the provision of credit since cash crops are male controlled. Credit schemes and extension services are geared towards male farmers, ignoring women and undermining their position as primary producers of agricultural products.

As revenue-generating cash cropping rises in importance, the proportion of resources controlled by women tends to diminish. This is largely due to the fact that household resources, such as land and inputs, are transferred away from women's crops in order to promote the production of cash crops (Davison 1988; Kiriti 2003). An increase in family income arising from cash crop production usually results in a new loss to women as in some Kenyan societies males take possession of any cash income earned by females, or most of it, and use it for their own ends (Kiriti 2003). Just as Sen (1981) demonstrated that famine could occur in the midst of an increase in aggregate food availability, poverty amongst women and children can increase with rising aggregate family income (Tisdell 1999).

Agricultural inputs and training are rarely provided to female farmers. Even efforts to reduce poverty through land reform have been found to reduce female income and economic status because they distribute land titles only to male heads of households (Todaro 1997). Cultural and social barriers to women's integration into agricultural programs remain strong because, women's income is perceived as a threat to men's authority. While men are taught new agricultural techniques to increase their productivity, women, if involved at all, are trained to perform low-productivity tasks that are considered compatible with their traditional roles, such as sewing, cooking, or basic hygiene. Women's components of development projects are frequently little more than welfare programs that fail to improve economic well being. Furthermore, these projects tend to depend on the unpaid work of women, while men are remunerated for their efforts (Todaro 1997).

Men's control over labour as a factor of production can translate into claims on women's labour for cultivation of the husband's fields. In effect the culturally determined rules of access to and control over resources may constrain women as much as external biases in providing access to farm support services (Palmer 1991). The cultural norms actually may predetermine unequal access to agricultural inputs, marketing services, and farmers' organizations because of the link between farm support services and land title, for which women are rarely eligible (Jiggins 1989).

Unequal access to resources means unequal barter or bargaining capabilities and sub-optimal resource allocations in the household. Male domination, perceived as embedded in cultural norms and institutions, characterizes intra-household power relations and resource allocation patterns. Kenyan women's agriculture is carried out within the confines of powerful and limiting constraints. For example, inputs such as fertilizer and insecticides, seeds, and credit facilities are channeled to men. Women do not qualify for loans unless a spouse or male relative represents them. After all they do not have the collateral needed for a loan. Through land adjudication and registration, land previously held by custom and over which simple use rights prevailed became the object of property rights. Land rights go to the male heirs while the daughters are almost entirely excluded. If a daughter is married, she cannot inherit land from her parents. If she is not married, she is treated like a pariah and can only be given a small portion of land in which to cultivate vegetables and other simple food crops but no cash crop since these crops means permanence. The land can never be registered in her name and she is there at the mercy of her brothers or other male relatives (Kiriti *et al.* 2004).

Where wives head households due to the continued absence of husbands (*de facto*) output may be low because women are not decision-makers. Men though absent want to make all the decisions concerning the household and the allocation of resources (Kiriti *et al.* 2003). They control the output, which they sell but do not buy the inputs. Women rely on remittances which come from their husbands and when it comes it is either too little or too late that it can't be used to buy inputs.

The diversity of needs and interests among family members and the allocation of the scarce resources are determined by the degree of decision-making power possessed by each negotiating party (Bennett 1983). Furthermore, not all household members have equal bargaining power to enforce their own definition of utility and therefore not all members benefit equally from the way resources are actually allocated. This view interprets observed inequalities in the distribution of household resources not as the most efficient reaction to the prevailing wage/price situation or as evidence of the household's maximizing behaviour, but as evidence of structural asymmetries in the economic, social, and legal position of men and women, which give the two unequal bargaining powers (Bennett 1983).

Bargaining power or a household member's ability to realize personal allocation priorities, can be influenced by the individual's contribution to the household income and some studies have shown that increases in women's income have given women more decision-making power and control over the distribution of resources within the household. Acharya and Bennett (1983) found that women's involvement in market activities gives them much greater power within the household in terms of their input in all aspects of household and resource allocation decisions. At the same time, confining women's work to the domestic and subsistence sectors reduces their power vis-à-vis men in the household.

The greater a woman's net control of income, the greater her leverage in other household economic and domestic decisions, and the greater her overall 'voice and vote' (leadership) in the relationship. Tisdell (1999) identifies five factors that may increase the threat power of a married woman in relation to her husband or partner; (1) her capability of finding independent employment and the level of income earned by her; (2) her ownership of property and ability to transfer, inherit and bequest property; (3) her rights to collective family assets in the event of dissolution of marriage; (4) her ability to institute divorce proceedings, especially if the legal hurdles to divorce are minimal; and (5) contacts with influential networks in a community.

However, legal, institutional, and social factors also affect bargaining power, for example, property rights could easily have a much bigger impact than changes in relative earnings of men and women (Folbre 1992). The World Bank (1996) says that women and children are more vulnerable because tradition gives them less decision making power and less control over assets than men, while at the same time, their opportunities to engage in remunerative activities, and therefore to acquire their own assets, are more limited.

Compared with men, women in Kenya are disadvantaged in their access to and control of a wide range of assets. With fewer assets and more precarious claims to assets, women are more risk-averse, more vulnerable, have a weaker bargaining position within the household, and consequently are less in a position to respond to economic opportunities. Access to land is not an end in itself. Access to land and other productive resources are critical in creating wealth and generating growth. The right mix of assets, including land, labour and financial services, is critical to ensure that women are economically empowered.

GENDER VIOLENCE

The experiences of women in Kenya show how the failure of the authorities to combat discrimination and in particular to prohibit, investigate and punish violence against women perpetuates suffering. Despite the moral and legal obligations, the government has not reformed Kenya's laws, to make all acts of violence against women criminal offences, nor has it addressed the discriminatory practices of the police force, prison services and court system. Some courts view any form of domestic violence as a private affair, which should be settled only by village elders.

Unequal power relations between men and women have led to the domination of and discrimination against women, which in turn leads to violence against women. Women in Kenya are specifically vulnerable. Violence against women is widespread and persists in all layers of society. In 1999 the attorney general of Kenya acknowledged that violence against women pervades all social and ethnic groups. It is a societal crisis that requires concerted action to stop its scourge.

Culture influences the relationship between the various groups in society and some cultural practices, beliefs and traditions have had the tendency to relegate women to second status in society thereby not only violating their rights as human beings but also leading the discrimination against women. Some customs and cultural practices have found their way not only into law but are also used as justification for violence against women.

The Committee on the Elimination of Discrimination Against Women defines discrimination as including gender-based violence, that is, violence that is directed at a woman because she is a woman or that that which affects women disproportionately. It includes acts that inflict physical, mental or sexual harm or suffering, threats of such acts, coercion and other deprivations of liberty. The committee stated that laws against domestic violence and abuse, rape, sexual assault and gender based violence should give adequate protection to all women, while promoting respect for their dignity and integrity. However, cases of gender violence still persist as shown in Table 4.

Kenya's combined third and fourth reports submitted under the convention on the elimination of all forms of discrimination against women leaves the issues of violence in the family, violence in the community and violence at the hands of state agents untouched.

Violence against women has been a problem in Kenya. This is mainly manifested in the number of rape or attempted rape cases, assaults and battering. In Kenya, women are physically and sexually abused everyday. Rape occurs in all social and ethnic groups. It is a crime that shocks and traumatizes the victim, but it is largely suffered in silence.

Victims of rape in Kenya often face huge obstacles in trying to bring the perpetrators to justice. Many rape victims are too intimated by cultural attitudes and state inaction to seek redress. To do so can lead to hostility from family, the community and police, with little hope of success. Those who seek justice are confronted by a system that ignores, demeans and even condones violence against women and protects perpetrators, whether they are state officials or private individuals. Table 5 shows the reported cases of rape, attempted rape, assault and battering on women between 2000 and 2004.

Table 5
Reported Cases of Rape, Attempted Rape, Assault and Battering on Women between 2000 and 2004

Offence	*Year*				
	2000	2001	2002	2003	2004
Rape and attempted Rape	883	933	984	1126	1419
Defilement/Incest	752	1094	1021	1182	1489
Assaults and Battering	6255	6648	7896	8544	8950
Total	7890	8635	9901	10852	11867

Source: Republic of Kenya, Economic Survey [2005].

Table 5 provides the number of reported cases of violence against women and girls for five years. Violence is a major factor in the subordination of women and it occurs in different arenas, including economic, political, social and private spheres of human life. Cases of rape including attempt have been on the increase over the five-year period. Between 2003 and 2004, the total number of reported cases of violence against women and girls increased by 9.4%. Cases of defilement and incest increased from 1,182 in 2003 to 1,489 in 2004. Battering and assault of women had the highest prevalence. Currently there is a pending Bill in Parliament on Sexual Violence and Assault which, if passed will pass harsh sentences to men who sexually assault women or girls. This is one way of empowering women where they can work and realize their potential without fear. The government of Kenya should reform both its laws and practices to end impunity for violence against women.

ECONOMIC POLICIES AND PROGRAMS FOR WOMEN EMPOWERMENT

Since the National Rainbow Coalition government came to power in 2003, it has strengthened the national machinery for promoting gender equality with the establishment of the Ministry of Gender, Sports and Culture and the National Gender Commission. However, the legal framework for promotion of gender equality remains weak and inadequate, despite Kenya having ratified the Convention on the Elimination of Discrimination against Women.

Kenya does not have a comprehensive gender and development policy that can guide the legislative reforms. There are a number of bills that have been pending for the last six years, which seek to protect women's human rights. These include the Affirmative Action Bill, Criminal Law Amendment Bill, National Gender and Development Bill, Equity Bill, Domestic Violence (Family Protection) Bill and the Gender and Development Policy Bill and Session Paper.

The National Commission on Gender and Development Act 2003 was passed and is operational to coordinate, implement and facilitate gender mainstreaming in national development. However, the government has not yet come up with a plan to implement the gender policy. The Gender Department has also been established in the Ministry of Gender, Sports, Culture and Social Services to oversee policy issues affecting women in Kenya. The Kenya National Commission on Human rights has been established through an act of parliament with its task, among other things, to observe the principle of impartiality and gender equity.

The Domestic Violence (Family Protection) Bill 2000 was published, but not introduced in Parliament. It is intended to provide for the intervention of court cases of domestic violence, including physical, sexual, psychological, harassment, intimidation, destruction of property and so on. This is an important bill to women of this country and efforts should be made to re-introduce it to parliament. The Government, civil society, and NGOs have been working very closely to provide women, who are subjected to violence, with access to the mechanism of justice and informing women of their rights in seeking redress. The government is also in the process of setting up the first police station to specifically deal with women and children, particularly on issues of violence. It also intends to establish gender desks at every district police station.

The Central Bureau of Statistics has also embarked on measures for including data on women's contribution to gross domestic product into the national account data. Most of the data on employment is currently collected and analyzed in a disaggregated manner to reflect gender contributions.

The government through the Ministry of Labour and Manpower Development has for the first time in the country's history formulated a comprehensive draft employment policy mainstreaming women in employment planning and discouraging child labour.

Despite these initiatives, women are under represented in decision-making levels in public employment, judiciary, and private employment and in statutory bodies. Women are still highly marginalized largely due to their relatively low levels of skills and weak empowerment, which are in turn due to disparities in educational, training and other opportunities caused by culture and institutional bottlenecks, gaps in laws and in socio-cultural attitudes and practices.

The Economic Recovery Strategy process attempts to link district priorities with government resource allocations and recognizes the increasing awareness and acceptance of the role of the community-based organizations, community empowerment and partnerships between the government and civil society in providing rural services. However, community empowerment does not necessarily reflect gender empowerment, or women's activities indicating gender equality. There is therefore need for special policies and programs to address these challenges to uplift women from their second-class status.

CONCLUDING REMARKS

From the discussion, I have shown that women in Kenya are regarded and treated as second-class citizens. Cultural and institutional impediments are found every step of the way preventing their empowerment and rise to the same status as their male counterparts.

Affirmative action should be taken to ensure that women are well represented in the government by appointing women to top leadership posts. Legislation may facilitate this by deliberately reserving a certain number of seats in parliament or the party for women. The same should be provided for in the local councils.

Policy interventions and legislative measures are necessary to ensure that women are empowered to have access to matrimonial property. More training and employment are some examples of the necessary interventions. Moreover, legislation is necessary to address rights of women involved in situations of cohabitation for a considerable number of years without going through a ceremony of marriage under any law.

The government should amend the Kenya Citizenship Act to ensure that every child born of either parent of Kenya citizenship is granted automatic citizenship. It should also amend the Domicile Act to ensure an end to discrimination against illegitimate children.

The principle of non-discrimination is not adequately implemented with respect to certain vulnerable groups of children, especially girls. Also, the constitutional guarantee of equal treatment does not cover various tribal, traditional customs and practices associated with, for example, fostering, marriage and divorce that constitute major challenges for the full realization of children's rights in the state.

The government should adopt an official policy to end the practice of early marriages, and include a minimum age, that is the same for boys and girls. It should also enact specific legislation ensuring the rights of girls to inherit property, particularly in those cultures that have traditionally denied this right to girls.

The Kenya government should fervently pursue the goal of achieving gender balance; create a mass of women leaders in strategic positions especially in managerial positions. It should also protect and promote women's equal rights with men and remove all discriminatory practice and prejudices in education, the electoral systems, at work and also sensitize men on the importance of involving women in decision-making. It should also encourage NGOs, the private sector and trade unions to achieve equality of men and women in their ranks including decision-making bodies and all negotiations.

Political parties should try to integrate women in elective and non-elective positions. They should take measures to ensure that party structures do not discriminate against women directly or indirectly. They should also incorporate gender issues in their political agenda and ensure that women participate in leadership on equal basis with men.

Measures should also be adopted to improve women's economic status. Affirmative action and other actions should be taken to redress gender imbalances. There should also be changes in the oppressive traditional and cultural practices. The government should reform its law and practices to end impunity for violence against women.

The government must demonstrate commitment to removing legal impediments and socio-cultural obstacles against women, especially in rural areas where the majority of women live and are economically active. The constraints on women's access to land, credit, and extension services, inputs and new technologies must be removed, and opportunities should be created for their enterprise. Measures to improve women's access through institutional reforms must be pursued and monitored for effectiveness.

Gender biases in the educational system, training and employment must be consistently attacked to give women new opportunities for achievement, while school curricula must incorporate concepts of gender equality so that students will incorporate them throughout their lives. Young women need role models to motivate them and must be given usable education and skills to play meaningful roles in society.

However, the most important thing is not to have many women in positions of decision-making who do not represent the wishes and aspirations of the common woman. A thousand jobs for middle class women out of touch with the reality of the ordinary woman does not constitute an improvement in the status of 16 million women. Better delivery on economic, social and cultural rights and better delivery on civil and political rights is the most important vehicle for the empowerment of women in Kenya

REFERENCES

Acharya, M. and Bennett, L. (1983), *Women and the Subsistence Sector: Economic Participation and Household Decision-Making in Nepal.* World Bank Staff Working Paper No 526, World Bank, Washington DC.

Amnesty International (2002a), *Kenya: Rape–the Invisible Crime.* Available at *www.web.amnesty.org/ai.nsf/index*

Amnesty International (2002b), *Women in Kenya.* Available at www.web.amnesty.org/web/wire.nsf/printMarch2002Kenya

Bennett, L. (1983), *Dangerous Wives and Sacred Sisters: Social and Symbolic Roles of High Caste Women in Nepal.* Columbia University Press, New York.

Davison, J. (1988), *Agriculture, Women, and Land: The African Experience,* West View Press, Boulder and London.

Folbre, N. (1992), Introduction: The Feminist Sphinx. In: Nancy Folbre, Barbara Bergmann, Bina Agarwal and Maria Floro (eds.). *Issues in Contemporary Economics, Vol. 4: Women's Work in the World Economy*, Macmillan Academic and Professional Ltd., Hong Kong.

Jiggins, J. (1989), How Poor Women Earn Income in Sub-Saharan Africa and What Works Against them? *World Development*, 17(7): 953-963.

Kiriti, T. (2003), *Gender Inequality in Agricultural Households in Kenya: An Economic Analysis*, Unpublished PhD Thesis, University of Queensland, Australia.

Kiriti, T. (2005), *Evaluating Public Policies for Poverty Reduction: Tools, Techniques and Process.* A Concept Paper Presented at a UNCRD Workshop at United Nations, Gigiri, Nairobi.

Kiriti, T. Tisdell, C. and Roy, K. (2003), Female Participation in Decision-making in Agricultural Households in Kenya: Empirical Findings. *International Journal of Agricultural Resources, Governance and Ecology*, 2(2): 103-124.

Kiriti, T. Tisdell, C. and Roy, K. (2004), Institutional Deterrents to the Empowerment of Women: Kenya's Experience. In: K. C. Roy (ed.). *Twentieth Century Development: Some Relevant Issues.* Nova Science, New York.

Kiriti, T. and Tisdell, C. (2005), Family Size, Economics and Child Gender Preference: A Case Study in the Nyeri District of Kenya. *International Journal of Social Economics*, 32(5): 492-509.

OMCT (2003), *Violence Against Women in Kenya.* Report Prepared for the Committee on the Elimination of Discrimination Against Women, The World Organization Against Torture, Geneva.

Palmer, I. (1991), *Gender and Population in the Adjustment of African Economies: Planning for Change*, International Labour Office, Geneva.

Republic of Kenya (1998), *Laws of Kenya: The Constitution of Kenya.* Government Printer, Nairobi.

Republic of Kenya (Various Issues), *Economic Survey.* Government Printers, Nairobi.

Sen, A. K. (1981), *Poverty and Famines: An Essay on Entitlement and Deprivation.* Clarendon Press, Oxford.

Tisdell, C. (1999), *Sen's Theory of Entitlement and Deprivation of Females: An Assessment with Indian Illustrations.* Social Economics, Policy and Development, Working Paper No. 2, University of Queensland.

Todaro, M. P. (1997), *Economic Development.* Addison Wesley Longman Limited, London and New York.

UNAIDS (2004), *Report on the Global HIV/AIDS Epidemic.* Geneva.

United Nations Development Programme (1995), *Human Development Report.* Oxford University Press, New York.

United Nations Economic and Social Council (1995), *Economic Empowerment of Women.* Economic Commission for Africa, Addis Ababa.

United Nations Economic Commission for Africa (1998), *African Women and Economic Development.* African Centre for Women, Addis Ababa.

World Bank (1996), *The World Bank Annual Report.* World Bank, Washington DC.

12

Development, Political Stability and Human Rights for Organized Workers

Lewis B. Dzimbiri

INTRODUCTION

Trade union rights, which include freedom of association, collective bargaining, and the right to strike are accepted as fundamental human rights since 1948. According to Anderman (1998) the rights of association underlying collective labour legislation are based on the basic political freedom of association of individuals, comparable to freedom of speech, assembly and religion in order to modify the prerogatives of the employer. Most governments have enshrined these rights in their national constitutions as well as labour laws. One aspect that becomes very clear when one reads industrial relations literature on trade unions in Africa is that these rights are severely repressed by governments. This paper attempts to explain why organized workers in Africa continue to experience uneasy relationship with governments. It starts by clarifying trade union rights as human rights, what trade unions are for and the potential role of trade unions in Africa.

It further discusses persecution of trade unions in Africa before examining reasons for the persecution. It later examines the role of the international donor community and the source of the discrepancy between legal provision and practical realities.

TRADE UNION RIGHTS AS HUMAN RIGHTS

On December 10, 1948 the General Assembly of the United Nations adopted and proclaimed the

Universal Declaration of Human Rights and Article 23 stipulates that a) Everyone has the right to work, to free choice of employment, to just and favourable conditions of work and to protection against unemployment; b) Everyone, without any discrimination, has the right to equal pay for equal work; c) Everyone who works has the right to just and favourable remuneration ensuring for himself and his family an existence worthy of human dignity, and supplemented, if necessary, by other means of social protection; and, d) Everyone has the right to form and to join trade unions for the protection of his interests. These form collective and individual labor rights. Collective trade union rights are reflected in the International Labour Organization's Convention No, 87 Freedom of Association and No. 98 the Right to Organize and Collective Bargaining. According to the International Confederation of Free Trade Unions (ICFTU) 130 countries have ratified convention No. 87 and 145 countries have ratified convention No. 98. In most countries, these conventions are reflected in their national constitutions and labour laws. For example, the Malawi constitution Section 31 gives the right to fair and safe labour practices, fair remuneration, the right to form and join trade unions or not form or join trade unions, fair wages and equal remuneration for work of equal value and the right to withdraw labour. Again, the Labour Relations Act (LRA) 1996 was enacted to promote sound labour relations through the protection and promotion of freedom of association, the encouragement of effective collective bargaining and the promotion of orderly dispute settlement conducive to social justice and economic development.

TRADE UNIONS AND WHAT DO THEY STAND FOR?

Trade union rights stem from the institutionalized relationship between employer and employee in paid employment: the ways in which employees are rewarded, motivated, trained and disciplined and the influence on these processes of the major institutions like management, trade unions and the state (Edwards 1995). A trade union is 'a continuous association of wage earners for the purpose of maintaining or improving the conditions of their working lives' (Webbs *et al.*1902). The concept of trade unionism like industrial democracy emerges from the premise that participation by workers in decisions that affect them is of vital importance to both employers and employees. Some would argue that this is an unnecessary diversion from the primary job of management which is to supply a profitable and cost-effective service to customers and that employers should have the right to make decisions without being forced to consider employee interests. Others would suggest that an unbridled managerial prerogative is quite contrary to the democratic ideals upon which developed societies are based and that employees ought to have say in decisions, which affect their working lives (Salamon 2000). It may also be argued that employees are more likely to co-operate in the process of change if they are aware of the circumstances confronting their company, the reasons behind the need for change and their knowledge of the alternatives. Increasing expectations on the part of working people, who have learnt from a more democratic socialization that they ought to have some influence over their conditions of employment and the quality of their working lives, is also an important factor.

Edwards *et al.* (1986) distinguish three types of western-style unionism. Unions, which act primarily as collective bargaining agents for particular groups of workers such in the United States and the United Kingdom, unions which serve as constituent elements in systems of 'political' unionism (as in France and Italy together with Spain where union organization is closely linked to political parties) and unions which operate as partners, within social-democratic government arrangement (such as the case of Australia and for a long period Sweden). Thus, trade unions may seek to achieve their objectives by collective bargaining, lobbying the legislature or by a more fundamental form of political action aimed at transforming the employment relationship.

In his comparative examination of industrial relations in French and British oil refineries Gallie (1978:313) describes French unions as *class - oriented* organizations which view contemporary western society in Marxist terms aspired to promote overall long-term worker interests rather than to defend particular and narrow craft or job interests. They interpreted their role as being one of heightening the consciousness and awareness of the workforce seeking to mould perceptions and mobilize workers ideologically towards a far-reaching structural transformation of what was seen as an exploitative and alienating society. On the other hand, British unions conceived their *role within the factory* as being basically one of continuing representation of work-force interests on *narrow bargaining* economist issues desired by workers themselves. These aims were to be accomplished by means of negotiation backed up by a powerful well-disciplined and cohesive trade union that would represent a potential threat to management if the dispute becomes unresolved.

The representational role of trade unions has five distinctive aspects (Salamon 2000). The first is that a union provides countervailing power to the employer and a pressure group within society. The second aspect is economic regulation through maximizing the wages and employment of their members within the framework of the wage/work contract of employment. The third aspect is job regulation through creating a joint rule making system to prevent arbitrary management actions. A trade union also plays a social change role as it expresses the social cohesion and aspirations or political ideology of its membership and seeks to develop a society, which reflects this view. Finally, a trade union provides a mechanism whereby individuals may develop outside the immediate confines of their jobs and participate in decision-making processes, thereby experiencing self-fulfillment.

ROLE OF TRADE UNIONS IN GOVERNANCE, PEACE AND SECURITY IN AFRICA

The need to have sound laws for the establishment of effective trade unions in Africa was important at independence because, 'for generations, the African worker had been ruthlessly exploited and condemned to sub-human conditions of work' (Chisiza 1961).

Apart from the bread and butter concerns of trade unionism, the Trade Union Congress in the UK is of the view that trade unions in Africa can potentially play a crucial role in good governance, peace and security. More importantly, they could play an important part in the development of effective states, good governance, popular participation, reduced corruption and increased transparency as well as building unity. This is so because unions tend to be multi-racial and interested in gender and other equalities issues. They can also promote peaceful resolution of disputes economically, politically and in the community. Strong, free and independent trade union movements are one of the cornerstones of democratic states. In advocating the core labour standards of the International Labour Organization, unions promote an approach based on practical human rights, and, where the core labour standards are implemented, societies are more equal, more open and tolerant and more effective at managing change peacefully.

Unions play a key role in civil society and ensure that working people and others have the opportunity to develop practical experience in democracy, problem solving, negotiation and other aspects of participation in public life. This is true around the world, but no less true of Africa where trade unions play major roles in civil society. In part, this is demonstrated by the reaction of dictatorships to trade unions, which is to try either to destroy them or take them over. Trade unions often act as the repository of democratic ideals. In many countries emerging from dictatorship, the trade union movement has played a key role in the transition to democracy, for example in South Africa, where trade union confederations like Congress of South African Trade Unions were central to the overthrow of apartheid and have played a major role in the transition process.

Trade unions are also an important part of combating corruption because of the function they can perform as examples of open and democratic activity, and because of the challenge function, which they present to government and business elites. The collective nature of trade unions gives them a tendency towards openness and honesty. Trade unions have shown, in many countries around the world but in particular in Africa, that they can play a major part in creating and maintaining effective states based on good governance and popular participation. Unions also have a vital role to play in promoting economic progress and decent work, and thus in poverty reduction and the promotion of decent standards of wealth distribution, equality, health and education. In Malawi, they have been instrumental in constitutional reforms, Labour Relations Act 1996 and Employment Act 2000; participated in national Vision 2020 consultations and have been critical of government policy on the price of the staple food crop and fuel. No wonder that the Trade Union Congress believes that the Commission for Africa needs to promote and assist the development of strong, free and independent trade unions in Africa, able to take up their proper role in social partnership with government and employers. Without such trade unions, civil society will never function properly in Africa, and the role of the African peoples will remain that of the passive observer or object of social progress.

PERSECUTION OF TRADE UNION RIGHTS IN AFRICA

The 1997 ICFTU report noted that 299 trade unionists were killed, nearly 2,400 workers were arrested and detained for their union activities; 50,000 lost their jobs for the same reason; 290 trade unionists received death threats, more than 3,000 activists were placed under police surveillance; 450 strikes were fiercely repressed and over 80 countries placed severe obstacles in the way of freedom of association. Giving a report on trade union rights violation in 1999, Bill Jordan, general secretary of the ICFTU was critical of the hypocrisy of government officials parading at international gatherings, ostensibly promoting basic workers' rights, while in practice harassing, attacking, threatening, sidelining or silencing trade unionists. This report noted that at least 140 trade unionists were assassinated, disappeared, or committed suicide after they were threatened, because they had the temerity to stand up for workers' rights against the state or unscrupulous employers. It says that nearly 3,000 people were arrested, more then 1,500 were injured, beaten or tortured and at least 5,800 were harassed because of their legitimate trade union activities. Another 700 trade unionists received death threats. Abuses compiled in the survey range from murder to subtle legislative arrangements that make trade union activities increasingly looking like a daunting obstacle race. Some 12,000 workers were unfairly dismissed or refused reinstatement, sometimes with the complicity of the government, because they were active members of a trade union. At least 140 strikes or demonstrations were repressed by governments, sometimes with the support of the employers using strikebreakers, while 80 of the 113 countries mentioned in the survey restrict the right to strike altogether. Similarly, the 2002 report had shown that 213 trade unionists were assassinated, 1,000 union activists attacked and beaten, 2,562 were detained and 30,000 trade unionists were sacked.

Africa is no exception in trade union repression. According to ICFTU 2002 report, nearly four out of five arrests worldwide took place in Africa; 80% of the world total of those given prison sentences for their trade union activities were in Africa; Strikes and demonstrations were also harshly repressed. The legislation of 23 of the 31 African countries covered contains restrictive measures on the right to strike. The survey lists 834 cases of trade union harassment in nearly two thirds of African countries, a higher average than any other continent in the world. The report gives examples of different experiences in several African countries: In Libya, Sudan and in Equatorial Guinea, the ban on independent trade unions remained. In Ethiopia, two leaders of the teachers' union Ethiopian Teachers' Association (ETA) died in prison because of poor conditions, while another received a 15-year prison sentence, as part of continual harassment of the ETA. The authorities in Djibouti imposed their own candidates at the top of the labour federations and froze their assets, claiming that the genuine organizations were illegal. In Morocco, 23 trade unionists were sent to prison for striking over labour law violations, 21 of whom had been tortured by police in detention. In Swaziland, trade unions continued to be repressed, and the Swaziland Federation of Trade Unions and its leaders were regularly harassed. The police detained the entire national executive committee of the Swazi Teachers Union, accusing them of 'un-swazi' behaviour because they had carried a coffin during a march. Despite some legislative improvements, the Kingdom of Swaziland remained one of the African countries most ferociously hostile to unions. Zimbabwe was another country where respect for trade union rights deteriorated dramatically, and three leaders of the Zambian Congress of Trade Union (ZCTU) were attacked following a strike. Strikes were declared illegal, and those taking party severely harassed. In the dead of night, a Zimbabwean trade unionist and his family were assaulted at their house by government agents. He was forced outside, beaten with chains, pipes and whips, then left for dead. Even though they were identified, the attackers remained at large, and the trade unionist had no choice but to go into hiding. The passing of a January 2002 law reinforced President Mugabe's powers and led to yet more arrests, detentions, beatings, kidnappings, death threats and other forms of anti-union repression. The Zimbabwean government does not recognize the ILO's Convention 87, which recognizes the right of workers to freely associate and organize themselves and has laws restricting freedom of assembly and allowing the interference of government in union affairs. Zambia is a signatory to the ILO's core conventions on labour rights, but instances of failure to comply with the conventions include discrimination in job selection and remuneration and government interference in the collective wage bargaining process. Nigeria has ratified five of the ILO's seven core conventions but has continued to violate some of them;

violations include the arrest of some union leaders and disruption of union rallies and has labour laws, which discriminate against women.

Trade union suppression in Africa goes as far back to the colonial and post-colonial period. The Secretary General - Organization of African Trade Union Unity wondered:

As a trade unionist, the question that worries me most is why trade unions which fought side by side with political parties to dislodge colonialists ... are not now accepted by African Governments ... trade unionists are in jail or in detention ... some under investigation, splits are being encouraged to weaken trade union leadership...some unions are facing threats of dissolution. There are trade unionists living in exile because they have displeased home governments' (Ananaba 1977:175).

At independence in 1964, the Zambian government restructured the industrial relation policies creating a policy of one industry one union; integrated the ZCTU with the ruling United Nations Independent Party and gave ZCTU a new role. It became an administrative arm of the government to communicate government policies to the workers- the conveyer belt role-consistent with economic development orientation.

In Kenya, 'by identifying and persecuting trade union leaders as communists the state had succeeded in postponing the effective organizations of African workers by many years' (Mihyo 1979:201). The first trade union 1947 was banned and its leaders deported. After independence the Kenyan state behaved like its colonial counterpart in labour controls. Although trade unions were allowed and the right to strike was included in the labour laws, strikes provoked the wrath of political elites, like Tom Mboya, the Minister of Labour who threaded to remove the right to strike (Mihyo 1979:234). The Central Organization of Trade Unions was created through a Presidential Decree of 1965 as a recognized umbrella of trade unions in the country and in 1974, strikes were officially banned.

Though there were 26 trade unions in Zimbabwe by 1962, they remained extremely weak due to state control, close police surveillance, breaking strikes, harassment and arrest of leaders. (Shadur 1994). The trade union congress was used as an administrative arm for interpreting and implementing government development policies. President Mugabe intervened like his Zambian counterpart by introducing extensive legislative powers, beating with button sticks, suspended sentences and arrests, detention of strikers, and dismissals aimed at neutralizing militant unions. In Tanzania, trade unions that mushroomed up to 1953 were repressed by the colonial state until the Tanganyika Federation of Labour (TFL) emerged in 1956 only to be re-organized by the new state at independence (Mihyo 1979). Strikes in the sisal plantations, mines and railway in the first decade of independence over rapid unconditional Africanization angered the state. The latter abolished TFL and created the National Union of Tanganyika Employees entrusted with studying wage structure annually, advising government on wages in accordance with income and wages policy, implementing these policies, settling disputes among workers and propagating and implementing the policy of the ruling party (Mihyo 1979). For Nyerere, first president of Tanzania, although one of the purposes of trade unions is to ensure for workers a fair share of the profits of their labour, such fairness would be judged in relation to the whole society (Nwabueze 1974: 375).

In Malawi, the preoccupation of the independent state with the role of economic development and political stability resulting from its colonial political and economic history made the state so determined to pursue economic development plans uninterrupted (Dzimbiri 2004). This created a hostile environment where trade unions and strikes were suppressed. As a single largest employer and actor in economic development the state weakened the labour movement by streamlining trade unions from 19 to 5, harassment and detention of unionists and the integration of unions into the then ruling Malawi Congress Party (Dzimbiri 2001). The latter created party branches at workplaces; witch hunted union activists and intervened in workplace disputes. The legal and institutional framework served the interests of the state to meet political stability and economic development at the expense of workers' individual labour rights, freedom of association, collective bargaining and the right to strike. Although the transition to democracy in the 1990s led to a significant transformation of industrial relations and the growth of trade unions to 25 by 2005, the multiparty state employs 'divide-and-rule' and 'hide-and-seek' tactics to weaken public service trade unions (Dzimbiri 2001). Such experiences have been reported in some southern African countries like Botswana, South Africa, Namibia, Zambia, Zimbabwe, Malawi, Lesotho and Swaziland (Madhuku 1997; Sibanda 1999).

WHY ARE ORGANIZED WORKERS PERSECUTED?

From the above brief survey of trade union suppression, we can discern two key issues that come to surface when state-labour relations are discussed.

Political Stability and Human Rights Suppression

Political elite in Africa are scared of a strong labour movement because the latter has the potential to take over government especially where trade unions forms a political party. The Labour party in Britain is one such example. Ruling parties are also uncomfortable to encourage alliances between unions and opposition political parties, as this would pose a formidable threat. In Africa, the Zambian Trade Union Congress began a campaign of strikes and politicization in 1991. Teachers, communication workers, university teachers, hotel and catering workers, health workers demanded good governance, transparency, accountability, and democracy besides pay and conditions of employment (Mihyo 1995:210-211). When Chiluba, ZCTU leader, led the Movement for Multiparty Democracy, he defeated Kaunda in the 1991 multiparty presidential elections. In Malawi for example, massive strike activity in the early 1960s were associated with the alliance between nationalist politicians and the labour movement to dismantle the colonial administration and speed up independence. In 1992, after three decades of industrial peace, underground pressure groups anxious to dismantle the one-party dictatorial regime used worker to mount concerted political strikes, which targeted business establishment of members of the political elite. Should this be surprising that even within the multiparty political system with generous civil liberties, the state should be implicated in behind the scene maneuvers to weaken the labour movement? The use of the strike as a political weapon has had a long history in Africa.

Although colonial authorities discouraged trade unions from participating in politics, trade unionists saw the struggle for independence as a national issue deserving the support of every organized group (Ananaba 1977). Workers organized political strikes, which on the surface appeared purely economic. Kwame Nkrumah's slogan 'seek ye first the political kingdom and everything else would be added unto you thereafter' became so popular that trade unionists throughout colonial Africa made reference to it in their efforts to help liberation struggles. After all, the fact that both employers and government in colonial Africa were foreigners, made workers view poor wages and conditions of work as a problem of foreign colonial domination as opposed to the capitalist logic (Davis 1966). That is why there were unorganized and organized strikes before 1945. Strikes at Sierra Leone Harbour and railways, those at South Africa's docks and railways and in Nigeria before 1945 were examples. When nationalist politicians and trade unionists saw the role of the strike as a political instrument, well co-coordinated strikes between nationalist politicians and trade unionists became frequent in Guinea, Ghana, Tanganyika, Kenya, Tunisia, Algeria, Mali and the Ivory Coast (Davis 1966: 96). Thus, political elites in Africa are too aware of the political role unions can play if they are not controlled.

Economic Development and Human Rights

The economic role of the state in Africa became enormous at independence. In developing societies where the state is the biggest employer through the civil service, local government and state controlled enterprises the state has many instruments at its disposal to influence employment relations. It could influence industrial relations through its terms and conditions of employment, attitude towards collective bargaining and trade unions through its legal and institutional framework. As noted above, the role of the political party was also very instrumental in authoritarian one-party states. As a provider of the legal framework and economic manager anxious to create employment, attract foreign investment, reduce the rate of inflation and raise the standards of the unemployed masses, it is not difficult for the state to make legislation that is in favour of the employer and wider economic considerations. Once the state is hostile towards trade unions and its wages and conditions of employment are poor, then the private sector will project anti-union attitudes and victimize union activists. As the regulator of incomes through its role of macro-economic management the state shall give high priority to the achievement of high employment, higher productivity, attraction of new investment, maintenance of low levels of inflation and expenditure. These policies influence collective bargaining, wage levels and the attitude of the state towards unions. Economic development considerations during the one-party states in Africa forced the state to restructure trade unions at independence, reassign them new roles and integrated them with ruling parties to ensure their behaviour conformed to the dictates of economic development. In Tanzania, the Chairman of TFL was the Minister of Labour, and in Malawi, the Chairman of Malawi Trade Union Congress was also Mayor of Blantyre City (Dzimbiri 2001).

There seems to be some tension between human rights and economic development. In Malawi for example, in the one-party and the multiparty period, like other developing countries in Africa, economic development became a major priority for the government. Because of the critical resource and material shortage in most poor nations, the state has been in the forefront of formulating and implementing economic development policies. Through its efforts in collaboration with the private sector and non-governmental organizations, the Malawi state has been concerned with increased productivity in order to enhance the welfare and standards of living of the rural people, alleviate poverty, and reduce infant mortality and other ills of society. The need to provide workers - who constitute 13 percent of the economically active – with a decent wage and conditions of employment in a context where the majority of the people live below the poverty line, is one of the most difficult challenges of the state in Malawi. Should it widen workers' rights to higher and better wages at the cost of scaring away private investors who would help the state in developing the country for the benefit of the majority? Should workers be given unrestricted freedom of association, collective bargaining and the right to strike in defense of their economic interests when the state cannot afford to meet such demands?

Governments in the third world believe that industrial relations have a direct bearing on the development process since unions are consumptionist in function and would therefore impede the rate of capital formation. Furthermore, industrial conflict may adversely affect productivity and exports especially in fragile economies. Strikes may not provide a good climate for foreign investors. It is not surprising therefore that many African governments had passed legislation to regulate strikes by public servants either prohibiting them or subjecting them to rather stringent conditions (Nwabueze 1974). The rationale for these restrictions, Nwabueze argues, is that apart from the loss of man hours involved, workers demands for wage increase can only be met at the expense of farmers and other self-employed persons who account for the majority of the population and would widen the income gap between the two classes. For Madhuku (1997) the multifarious restrictions and preconditions imposed on the right to strike in Southern Africa is due to the economic reasons which makes governments view the human rights dimension of strikes as a relative luxury.

Over the years the IMF and World Bank have insisted on reduction in government expenditure, the need to privatize some public services and corporations as part of economic reforms. These demands have in most cases run counter to workers demands for job security, higher wages and better working conditions. The consequence of this has been stunted wages and salaries, retrenchment and lay-offs, which have reduced the standards of living of the people. Again, unions have lost membership not only because of the massive retrenchment, but also their inability to protect workers from the ravages of IMF and World Bank conditionality. Both the national governments and trade unions are helpless. Collective bargaining under such austerity conditions is a waste of time and effort. With threats of dismissal amidst huge army of the unemployed standing nearby, threats of strikes or the most powerful weapon at the disposal of organized workers- the strike- becomes meaningless. Under these circumstances, it would not be surprising to observe that while the national constitution and labour laws have enshrined freedom of association, collective bargaining and the right to strike, the state restricts them either through 'hide-and-seek' and 'divide-and-rule' tactics or outright threats of dismissal. It can also use the law to threaten illegality of any strike to be called for and at times have used the police to teargas workers to break the strike.

In Malawi, the one-party state was notorious for the violation of human rights in general and workers' rights in particular in order to achieve political stability and economic development. This was particularly more pronounced after the cabinet crisis that led to the near-collapse of Government six weeks after independence. The president, the ruling party, members of the national executive committee, regional and district party officials including those at area and branch level, were in the forefront of 'preaching' unity. loyalty, obedience and discipline to workers. Heavy surveillance of pro-union activists at work by the youth wing of the party paralyzed any attempt to raise issues of terms and conditions of employment as well and wages at the workplace. The consequence was the total control of trade unions and the suppression of strikes. On the other hand, the period of the multiparty politics (from 1992 onwards) has witnessed open defiance from unorganized workers who have continued to mount both political and economic strikes in recent years. The fact that the multiparty state manipulates union leaders, creates splinter unions, delays recognition of some unions, uses the police and the law to control strikes (Dzimbiri 2004), suggests its dilemma in dealing with questions of human rights and economic development at the same time. Thus, tensions between the need to meet demands for human rights on the one hand and economic development and political stability on the other will remain the major challenge facing industrial relations in Malawi and similar states in Africa.

Thus the need for economic development and political stability becomes the major priorities of governments in Africa. However, because of the strings attached to foreign development aid in third world countries, good governance involves observance of human rights and labour rights are human rights. To be openly hostile as was the case during the cold war period, Governments are afraid that development aid might not be forthcoming. During the one party period, for example, Malawi was an ally of the Western capitalist nations because of her pro-capitalist stance. Western capitalist nations and donors did not want to antagonize by imposing penalties on Malawi for repressing human rights. After the collapse of communism in Eastern Europe, Western countries and donors began to emphasize good governance as a precondition for aid. That is why traditional donors withholding non-humanitarian aid to Malawi became a powerful force facilitating the collapse of the authoritarian one-party government and the democratization of Malawi during 1992-1994. The dilemma with late developers is how to handle both development imperatives and human rights tenets simultaneously.

Exogenous Influences: The Role of International Donor Community

In trying to understand various form of human rights violation in Africa and trade union rights in particular, the role of the international donor community needs to be understood. Why is it that most governments in Africa have national constitutions and labour laws which reflect the tenets of the international declaration of human rights, international labour organizations and other international instruments reflecting a modern democratic society when the practice is different? Are human rights viewed as an externally evolved thing or an internally hatched fashion? Why didn't human rights occupy significant space in the vocabulary of donors before the collapse of the Berlin Wall towards the end of the 1980s? In Malawi industrial relations reforms in the 1990s stemmed from the political reforms that led into the transition from the one-party to a multiparty state. This major state transformation was possible as a result of international pressure and in particular the withholding of Malawi's non-humanitarian aid and calls for democratic reforms. Since 1989 the World Bank has abandoned its previous economist interpretations of African crisis and advocated instead good governance, gender equality, decentralization of power, human rights, the need to check corruption and the involvement of local people in decision-making (Ihonvbere 2000:9). The consequence of this pressure led to the 1993 national referendum and the 1994 general election that in turn led to the formal creation of a multiparty state in Malawi.

The one-party state was not subjected to pressures for good governance and democratic reforms for close to three decades. Human rights violations such as detention without trial, forced donations to the president, murder of dissident, repression of freedom of speech and association, which Amnesty International documented, did not lead to an international outcry at the time. One reason for this had been Malawi's capitalist and pro-western stance during the Cold War period and Western capitalist nations saw Malawi as a good ally. As Lwanda (1993:76) noted, Banda's moderate policies of modest economic goals, slow Africanisation, stability, unity, loyalty obedience and discipline were viewed as likely to provide a climate of stability attractive to Western investment. Like other authoritarian Africa states, which received international financial support despite human rights violations (Ihonvbere 2000: 10), Malawi continued to receive financial aid from the donor community. The fact that such a position was maintained for three decades suggests that the international community indirectly helped the creation of a status quo in the role of the state in industrial relations. By reacting to human rights violations and imposing economic sanctions, the Western donor community facilitated the breakdown of an authoritarian one-party state and the creation of a multiparty state. The question that follows is how far externally- induced changes become institutionalized and sustained in practice. There are numerous examples of failures of democracies in Africa as evidenced by arguments over electoral results, voting along regional lines as the case of the 1994 and 1999 general elections in Malawi (Patel, 2000), lack of tolerance for dissenting views, and suppression of labour rights. This is symptomatic of deep-rooted problems, which would continue to confront democracy, human rights and therefore industrial relations in Africa.

Newspaper headlines confirm these symptoms: 'Democracy is failing in Sub-Saharan Africa' (Financial Times, 5 March 2002); 'Zambia's leader in crackdown on dissent' (Financial Times, 4 January 2002); Protests over Madagascar's poll (Financial Times, 30 January 2002); 'Madagascar dispute deepens as Ratsiraka rejects vote recount' (Financial Times, 30 April 2002); 'South African unions condemn Zimbabwe violence' (Financial Times, 5 March 2002); 'Only closest allies at Mugabe's inauguration' (Financial Times, 18 March 2002); 'Violence still rising since poll in Zimbabwe' (Financial Times, 30 April 2002). For Malawi, headlines include 'Catholics denounce United Democratic Front attack' (Daily Times, 29 October 2001); 'UDF draws up list of journalists to be beaten' (Daily Times, 1 November 2001); 'Young democrats implicated in intimidation' (Daily Times, 4 November 2001); 'World jurists protest removal of judges' (Daily Times, 30 November 2001).

What do all newspaper headlines tell us about democracy and human rights and by extension, workers' rights in Africa? While international structures and institutions of democracy and human rights can be imported from the Western advanced industrial nations to poor developing states like Malawi, is it possible to do the same with values and norms of democracy? Why should the state in Africa interfere with freedom of association, collective bargaining and the right to strike when national constitutions and the labour laws reflect international democratic principles and ILO norms? As analysts have noted, externally imposed state transformations through aid have the potential danger of 'propping up theoretically multiparty regimes' (Financial Times, 5 March 2002).

The implication of this is that externally imposed human rights traditions have the potential of being officially welcome on paper but most frequently forgotten in practice. Thus, until, and only, when internally developed structure and norms which might have sufficient anchorage within societal norms and traditions are created, there will still be significant degrees of discrepancy between what is provided and what actually happens on the ground. As it might be difficult to develop indigenous structures and value systems because of Africa's incorporation into the capitalist global political economy since the colonial period, industrial relations in Africa will continue to be characterized by discrepancies- the discrepancy between what is provided in the labour laws and national constitution and what happens in practice.

CONCLUDING REMARKS

This paper has examined how the need for economic development and political stability in Africa continue to create an industrial relations regime that suppresses workers' rights. In spite of the fact that governments have ratified ILO labour conventions, enacted various labour-friendly laws and enshrined pro-labour provisions in their national constitutions, trade union rights are suppressed through legal or administrative apparatuses, political incorporation, harassment, intimidation, detention without trial or murder of union leaders and sacking of union members. Strikes are heavily suppressed using teargases from the police, political intimidation, threats of dismissal from government and employers. It finally raises the problem of implementing international standards or principles, which are at loggerhead with the local situation on the ground. In other words, by being 'forced' to respect human rights and enact labour legislation, which is in accord with international democratic practices against real or perceived practical economic and political realities on the ground, governments opt to sacrifice the human rights dimension of the development menu.

REFERENCES

Ananaba, W. (1977), *The Trade Union Movement in Africa.* Hurst, London.

Anderman, S. (1998), *Labour Law: Management Decision and Workers Rights.* Butterworths, London.

Chisiza, D. (1961), *The Realities of African Independence.* The African Trust, London.

Damachi, U. G., Seibel, H. D. and Trachtman, L. (Eds.) (1979), *Industrial Relations in Africa.* Macmillan, London.

Davies, I. (1966), *African Trade Unions.* Penguin, Harmondsworth.

Dzimbiri, L (2001), Trade Union Rights in Malawi: Context, Past and Present. *International Union Rights,* 8 (3): 21-22.

Dzimbiri, L (2004), Trade Unionism under the One-party and Multiparty Political Systems in Malawi. *Malawi Journal of Social Science,* 18: 17-33.

Edwards, P. (Ed.) (1995), *Industrial Relations: Theory and Practice in Britain.* Blackwell, Oxford.

Edwards, R., Garona, P. and Todtling, F. (Eds.) (1986), *Union in Crisis and beyond: Perspectives in Six Countries.* Auburn House, Massachusetts.

Gallie, D. (1978), *In Search of the New Working Class, Automation and Social Integration within the Capitalist Enterprise,* Cambridge University Press, Cambridge.

Gertzel, C. (1979), Industrial Relations in Zambia to 1975. In: Damachi, U. G., Seibel, H. D. and Trachtman, L. (eds.). *Industrial Relations in Africa.* Macmillan, London.

Ihonvebere, J. (2000), Politics of Constitutional Reforms and Democratization in Africa. *International Journal of Comparative Sociology,* 41(1): 9-26.

Iwuji, E.C. (1979), Industrial Relations in Kenya. In: Damachi, U.G., Seibel, H. D. and Trachtman, L. (Eds.). *Industrial Relations in Africa.* Macmillan, London.

Lwanda, J. (1993), *Kamuzu Banda of Malawi: A Study in Promise, Power and Paralysis: Malawi under Dr Banda 1961-1993*. Dudu Nsomba Publications, Glasgow.

Madhuku, L. (1997), The Right to Strike in Southern Africa. *International Labour Review*, 136 (4): 509-530.

Mihyo, P. (1979), Industrial Relations in Tanzania. In: U. G. Damachi, Seibel, H.D. and Trachtman, L. (eds.). *Industrial Relations in Africa*. Macmillan, London.

Mihyo, P. (1995), Against All Odds: Trade Unions in Zambia. In: Henk, T. (ed.). *Globalization and Third World Trade Unions: The Challenge of Rapid Economic Change*. Zed Books, London.

Nwabueze, B. O. (1974), *Presidentialism in Commonwealth Africa*. Hurst, London.

Patel, N. (2000), 1999 Elections in Malawi: Challenges and Reforms. In: M. Ott, K.Phiri and N.Patel (eds.). *Malawi's Second Democratic Elections: Process, Problems and Prospects*. Christian Literature Association, Blantyre.

Salamon, M. (2000), *Industrial Relations: Theory and Practice*. Prentice-Hall, Hemel Hempstead.

Shadur, M. (1994), *Labour Relations in a Developing Country: A Case Study of Zimbabwe*. Avebury, Sydney.

Sibanda, N. (1999), Unions Still Fighting for Union Rights-for Human Rights. *Southern African Political Economy Monthly*, 12(5): 16-19.

Webb, S. and Webb, B. (1902), *The History of Trade Unionism*. Printed by the Authors, London.

13

Achieving Gender Equality through Gender Oriented Budgets

N. Narayana

INTRODUCTION

Although governments, all over the world, are involved to achieve gender equality, persistent gender inequalities are leaving women in a subordinated position to men. Existing gender hierarchies are both a result and cause of unequal power relations between men and women. Consequently, the type of social order currently witnessed indicates that the social, political and economic measures taken to keep women in an advantaged position appear to be inadequate. However, in recent years, governments are committed themselves to advance the status of women. It was also agreed in the International Conference of Population and Development, Cairo in 1994, the World Summit on Social Development, Copenhagen in 1995 and the Fourth World Conference on Women, Beijing in1995 to meet time-specific gender-related targets. But the progress, worldwide, made in reducing gender inequalities is limited (Elson 2002). In spite of increasing job opportunities, in recent years, for women in trade-related employment, low salaries and scant labour-related benefits prevail (Klein 2000 and Commonwealth Secretariat 2002).

Along with gender inequalities, the income inequalities have widened in majority countries. The world's richest 1 per cent of people receive as much income as the poorest 57 per cent (UNDP 2002). Those who support economic liberalization accept that millions of people's basic needs will go unmet as an unavoidable side effect of the global market. This situation of income inequalities can only offer limited redress for gender inequalities. Even in political representation, women hold only 14.3 per cent of all national parliaments' seats. The share of 30 per cent of women considered by governance specialists, as the percentage required to become a critical mass, is found in a handful of countries such as Sweden, Denmark, Germany, Finland, Norway, Iceland, the Netherlands and South Africa (Elson 2002). Furthermore, many states have left unchanged laws that discriminate against women and widen gender inequalities.

Most countries have realized the need to deal considerably with gender issues in the development process by bringing in suitable fiscal and monetary measures. Despite more recent efforts to enhance social policy as the driving force, economic criteria continue to dominate policy design. This poses a serious challenge to achieve the overall objective of reducing gender inequalities. As evident, gender inequalities can affect adversely overall macroeconomic performance of a country (Elson 2002; World Bank 2001). Macroeconomic policies have to ensure gender equality by allowing equal participation of male and females in income-generating activities and foster the development. Unpaid work predominantly carried out by women such as house keeping, cooking, cleaning, fetching fuel and water etc and their significant voluntary community work cannot be excluded from measures of Gross National Product. Women being outside the formal employment sector and engaged in subsistence production as unpaid labour on family farms, their employment in informal sector tends to be inadequately reported by statistical surveys. In 1995 UNDP estimated the value of women's unpaid labour globally to be $11 trillion per year (Elson 2002). If governments' commitments regarding the elimination of existing inequalities are taken seriously, the contribution of women to the economy both in their reproductive and productive roles has to be recognized.

The present paper brigs in analyses on how gender inequalities can be reduced by formulating gender oriented budgets (GoBs), which offer enough scope for governments to fulfill the broader objective of ensuring gender equality. As GoBs recognize the role of women in improving the national output and well being of the people, the strategies and programmes intended to strengthen the measures will contribute positively to reduce gender gaps.

GENDER ORIENTED BUDGETS

Budget is the most important policy statement made by the government in the course of a year, because it attaches financial allocation to the policies that are implemented. No government programme can be taken up seriously if it has not been allocated resources. Generally speaking, budgets are formulated to address the needs of everyone in a uniform and apparently neutral way. Policy makers tend to assume that all individuals are equal. These conceptions fail to acknowledge the most evident distinctions that stem from gender and thus budgets have different outcomes for different groups. As such, budgets offer a year-to-year basis on which to work, in order to translate national commitments regarding gender equality and the advancement of women into concrete action. Gender-oriented budget analysis can thus be considered a tool for accountability.

The lack of recognition of underlying gender differences has adverse impact on women especially poorest and marginalized sections of the society. Again, their access to the needed basic services in order to improve their conditions relies on the government's expenditures. However, the power of women to influence budgetary decisions is small in comparison to that of other interest groups who are either closer to the budget decision-makers or have more political leverage. As a result, the needs of women are usually addressed in a limited way. While mitigating immediate economic and social problems, these isolated efforts leave the gender inequalities untouched at all levels of social, economic and political relations. Furthermore, the budget allocations oriented towards specific groups might even widen the inequalities.

Initiatives in the direction of GoBs have to be designed to facilitate a gender analysis in the formulation of government budgets and the allocation of resources. Gender budgets are not separate budgets for women or for men. It is a dissection of the government budget to establish its gender-differential impacts and to translate gender commitments into budgetary commitments. The main objective of a gender-oriented budget is to improve the analysis of incidence of budgets, attain more effective targeting of public expenditure and offset any undesirable gender-specific consequences of previous budgetary measures. They are attempts to break down or disaggregate the government's mainstream budget according to its impacts on women and men. These budgets are emphasized because national budgets formulated usually ignore social and economic roles, responsibilities and capacities of women. These differences are generally structured in a way that leaves women at a disadvantage position in the society by creating inequality gaps. Therefore GoB is an important tool for analyzing the gap between commitments by governments and the decision involved in how governments raise and spend money. Gender oriented budgets can contribute to narrowing such gaps. Since progress towards gender equality is slow, there is need to attach money to policy commitments. Overall research reveals that not enough attention is given to allocate resources and this serves to perpetuate gender biases even though budgets is considered as potential instrument to bring gender balance. A good gender policy requires understanding both the impact of policy and how it might be better designed to achieve outcomes, which meet the needs of women and men as well as different groups of people.

IMPORTANCE OF GENDER-ORIENTED BUDGETS

Evidence suggests that the economic gains of gender equality lead to increased output and better development of people's capacities. Women's economic empowerment could provide possibilities to increase productivity, less stress and better overall health. The need for gender-oriented budget arises after looking into the direct and indirect impacts of current government budgets and economic policies, which are generally, gender neutral. The ultimate aim is to mainstream gender budget initiatives into public policy. This in turn is linked to the millennium development goal of eliminating gender disparity in primary and secondary schools. Equal access for girls and boys to education is identified as a key measure of progress towards gender parity. Research has demonstrated that education for girls is one of the most effective ways of reducing poverty and the failure to invest in female education lowers the gross national product (Cagatay 1998).

Gender-oriented budget analysis was pioneered in Australia during the eighties, when the government conducted assessments of the impact of expenditure on women. South Africa and the Philippines followed by implementing gender-sensitive budget analysis during the mid-nineties. After the 1995 Beijing conference, interest on gender budgeting spread among governments and women's organizations, and initiatives were launched in several Commonwealth countries. To date, more than 40 countries worldwide have conducted some kind of gender budget initiative (Budlender 2002). Efforts have been made to assess the way in which past and current budgets acknowledge and respond to differentiate needs of men and women.

Most sustained and evolving initiatives in South Africa, Tanzania, Philippines, and Mexico aimed at incorporating gender awareness into all aspects of the budget and promoting a more effective allocation of resources (Hewitt and Mukhopadhyay 2002). The analysis of the budget through gender lens has carried different names worldwide. Both the Australian and the South African initiatives in formulating gender budgets are mainly to uplift women who are left in a position of subordination (Budlender, Hicks and Vetten 2002). More recent initiatives use names ranging from 'gender budgets' to 'gender-responsive budgets' or 'gender-sensitive budgets'. It is argued that this shift relates to the transformation of the Women in Development (WID) paradigm (1970s and 1980s) into Gender and Development (GAD) in the 1990s. Whereas the first approach focused on women as a disadvantaged or oppressed group, the latter uses gender as a way of referring to the power relations between women and men. This approach emphasizes the need for assessing the impact of the budget on women and men (Cagatay *et al.* 2000).

Gender budgeting is gaining increasing acceptance as a tool for engendering macro economic policy-making. The Fourth World Conference of Women (UNO 1995) called for a gender perspective in all macroeconomic policies and their budgetary dimensions. The UN General Assembly Special Session on Women also called upon all the Nations to mainstream a gender perspective into key macroeconomic and social development policies and national development programmes.

Australia was the first country to develop a gender-sensitive budget, with the Federal government publishing in 1984 the first comprehensive audit of a government budget for its impact on women and girls. Women's budget exercises were also undertaken by each of the Australian State and Territory governments at various times during the 1980s and 1990s. South Africa followed and initiated formation of gender sensitive budget in 1995, through a participatory process of involving parliamentarians and NGOs. The Commonwealth initiative to integrate gender into national budgetary processes was started in 1997 in four countries other than South Africa such as Fiji, St Kitts and Nevis, Barbados and Sri Lanka (Hewitt and Raju 1999). Several other nations have also taken steps to engender their national budget (Canada, UK, Mozambique, Namibia, Tanzania and Uganda). Gender budget initiatives are currently being attempted in more than 40 worldwide countries after thorough discussions in terms of the process and partners involved in undertaking the activity in the context of macro economic development (Budlender and Hewitt 2002).

In general, budgets in developing countries face certain problems especially those which have particular relevance to gender issues. The single most widespread problem in developing countries is lack of adequate and relevant information, which is essential in assessing underlying structures of inequality and responding accordingly. Identifying the kind of information needed and gender-relevant data is just a first step that might lead to a long process of formulating and implementing gender budgets (Shapiro 2001).

Further, the absence of useful budget information restricts the opportunities to engage with the government in a constructive way. Detailed information regarding the allocation of resources to different programmes is only available months after the budget has been approved. Evaluating the measures taken by the government to achieve gender equity is extremely difficult under such conditions. In order to realize the potential of women's participation, it is necessary to initiate gender budgets (Shapiro 2001). This is again meant to introduce gender as criteria into planning activities and the consequent allocation of resources. Clearly, gender-sensitive budget analysis is needed to identify what has to be done in order to reach a gender-sensitive formulation of the budget. Although most of the initiatives worldwide are still at the analysis stage, important steps have been taken towards gender-sensitive budgets in diverse countries.

CONTRIBUTION OF GENDER-ORIENTED BUDGETS

GoBs can contribute in a variety of ways to reshaping the policy goals and associated resource allocations of governments since different groups of women and men are being affected by budgetary decisions, allocations and expenditures.

Equitable Distribution of Resources: The main objective of budgets is to ensure the redistribution of wealth and resources within a country. If this objective is taken seriously into account, an equitable distribution of resources between men and women has to be a central policy goal as gender inequality continues to be one of the most persistent issues. However, achieving gender equity requires more than equality of opportunity and resources. It requires equality of outcomes for women and men. This implies recognizing different needs, preferences and interests, which affect the way women and men benefit from the same policy (Reeves and Baden 2000). Adequate resource allocations for programmes meant for women is an important step in this direction. Gender-oriented budget analysis can provide factual information that reaches beyond legal entitlements into governmental action regarding specific rights of women. It can do this by attempting to measure the gaps between policy commitments, adequacy of resource allocations and the outcomes of policies.

Economic Productivity: It is argued that gender inequality has an economic cost since it is adversely affecting sustained and prosperous growth, lowering output and limiting the development of people's capacities, and diminishing overall well-being (Hewitt and Mukhopadhyay 2002). The economic empowerment of women would result in higher levels of productivity, improved human resources, and better health (Elson 2002). Gender-sensitive budget analysis can also contribute to the effectiveness of public spending, by identifying the needs of particular groups and analyzing ways in which neutrally defined programmes fail or succeed to address them. If particular needs of women are disregarded and the gender-specific impact of a policy is not taken into account, the policy might fail to reach half of its potential beneficiaries (Himmelweit 2001). This would amount to ineffective or wasteful use of resources.

Good Governance: Good governance becomes an integral part of the budget process in order to improve the delivery of goods and services to women and men, in a fair and responsible way (Hewitt and Mukhopadhyay 2002). In addition, good governance requires a participatory approach to the policy-making process with representation of different groups of citizens, including women. Budgets, which are gender-sensitive and that, incorporate the participation of citizens, including women, help to ensure that policy design and the allocation of resources respond to the coexisting but differentiated needs of people.

Gender-oriented budget analysis can establish the link between the government's commitments regarding gender equity and the way in which public resources are spent. If an impact evaluation is carried out on policy and associated expenditures, and is made publicly available, the potential for citizens to hold government to account is significantly increased. In this sense, it is also a powerful tool for holding governments accountable in terms of commitments to gender equality and targets. In a country where women and the poor are usually marginalized, GoBs contribute to good governance by opening channels for women's participation and influence in decision-making processes. GoBs can make a significant contribution to the achievement of overall political, social and economic development objectives.

STRATEGIES NEEDED

Suitable strategies for gender-oriented budgets should be formulated by recognizing the wide array of interests and objectives behind GoBs. These can include the recognition of women's contribution to the economy, their integration into the productive sector, participation in decision-making processes, access to political structures, equity and the reduction of poverty.

- GoB requires specific breakdown of each agency's expenditure into a) Women-specific targeted expenditures by allocating resources for programmes that specifically target women; b) equal employment opportunity expenditures i.e., resources allocated to affirmative action in order to promote employment of women and men in equal numbers; and c) mainstream expenditures, the bulk of the remaining expenditures not covered by the first two categories.
- GoBs should start off with the approach like that Australia or using some sort of country-specific adaptation. Countries have to identify and introduce programmes of

expenditures explicitly oriented towards women. The main reason behind this is that tracking targeted expenditures is much easier than analyzing the overall gender-awareness of mainstream expenditures. Tackling these can make impact on the extent of gender inequality.

- GoBs have to integrate crucial advocacy-oriented activities by women's organizations. However, advocacy can also be an essential element in government initiatives. Both resistance and support to gender sensitivity in the budget process can be found within the government. Women's machineries, gender-sensitive officials and female members of the legislature can play decisive advocacy roles in many initiatives.
- For outside government initiatives, GoBs must combine research with advocacy in order to be effective. The importance of this combination has to be considered since the obligation to women is emphasized in the formulation of the budget. This is even more so when dealing with the issues relating to the allocation of public resources. Here the availability of technical facts and figures is important for making government officials to consider the arguments about gender more seriously (Budlender *et al.* 2001). By showing that they develop a sound perspective on the budget process as well as the technicalities involved in budgets. Furthermore, the knowledge of these technical facts will support the arguments in favour of these budgets (Budlender *et al.* 1998). Facts are needed in order to counter some technical explanations on the gender-neutrality of budgets put forward by opponents in government.
- The gender advocates have to make the technical discussions more accessible to the people. By transmitting simple but powerful messages about the differentiated impact the budget has on different groups, gender-oriented budget analysis can become relevant to the work of women's groups who are not familiar with the technical issues of the budgets. For example, the research findings on gender budget initiatives of South Africa are well

documented (Budlender *et al.* 2002). The idea is mainstreaming of gender concerns into the budgetary processes, so that both men and women can benefit from public expenditure.

- Workshops, training and short presentations on gender-sensitive issues important means for transmitting the idea of gender-oriented budgets and sharpening its profile within the political agenda. In the case of workshops run for government officials acquainted with planning and budgetary issues, they might represent a much-needed initial step in terms of raising gender-awareness. Discussions in the workshops can also be used as a means for pushing the topic into the public agenda by running them for parliamentarians with simultaneous release of information to the media. When run for actors outside the government, workshops and training might be the necessary step for demystifying the budget and building up initial awareness on gender budget. In most of the cases, workshops consist of a combination of budget literacy and raising gender-awareness, with different levels of sophistication, technicalities, discussions and exercises. Workshops will also be used to get feedback from actors such as sectoral specialists on the results of gender budget analysis.
- A more generalized strategy of GoBs is to work with the legislature. The budget, though formulated and executed by the executive, it has to be approved by the legislature, which has the responsibility of control and oversight. The legislature should play a crucial role within the political arrangement of checks and balances. Interacting members with the members of the legislature and providing them with solid information about the differentiated impact expenditures have on women and men is crucial in order to build up their capacities for holding the executive accountable. This is especially relevant since legislatures have played a crucial advocacy role in South Africa, Uganda, and Scotland (Budlender and Hewitt 2002).

- The natural objective of GoBs should become to engender the budget, which implies mainstreaming gender into the whole budget, with substantial implications for planning activities. If the legislature has sufficient amendment powers, it can hold the executive accountable, and offers steps towards engendering the budget. Gender-disaggregated information from the executive has to be included in the budget documents, in the form of assessments of the problems being addressed, the design of specific actions, as well as the evaluation of their outcomes.
- GoBs have to focus strategically on success criteria. This may mean working initially on selected sectors on expenditure only. GoB initiatives have to achieve a broad-range of successes by making gender-sensitive budgets a part of the government's agenda. This implies acknowledging and challenging long-standing practices regarding the budget, planning activities and policy design.
- It is necessary to shed light on the importance of generating sex-disaggregated data so that it is collected systematized and fed into the planning and budget process. This also implies the recognition of already existing information, whether generated inside or outside government. The South African initiative has generated a significant amount of information and analysis since 1995. However, the lack of gender-disaggregated data at the local level in South Africa highlights that many obstacles remain unresolved (Pearl 2002).
- Changes have to be made in policy design of specific programmes by integrating gender awareness issues with specific allocations. (St Hill 2002). It is also essential to maintaining the level of spending in programmes relevant to women. Under particularly harsh conditions of fiscal austerity and lack of budgetary flexibility and income insufficiency, maintaining levels of spending in programmes relevant to women definitely constitutes significant aspect of gender budgets.

MEASURES TOWARDS ACHIEVING A GENDER-ORIENTED BUDGET

Gender budgeting is now considered as a process to achieve gender equality with its own characteristics. There are no readily applicable procedures that guarantee success. This stems from the fact that GoBs are part of political processes, which are connected to and influenced by larger political contexts. It is possible, however, to isolate some features that can make a significant difference in the overall strength of GoBs:

- People's involvement based on the lines of the Australian women's budget, as well as on the success of the South African and the Tanzanian initiatives is important. Governments' efforts can add considerable value to the success. Initiative should come from gender experts besides public pressure, to make the government accountable for concrete actions. People's involvement is a prerequisite if transparency, accountability, and good governance are among the objectives of the initiatives.
- Budget analysis and advocacy cannot become sporadic activities, since they must build on solid knowledge. Gender-sensitive budget analysis is no exception. Initiatives located in civil society necessarily have to consolidate in-house capacities if they aim at seriously advocating for gender-sensitive budgets. Each initiative has valuable lessons to share, both positive and negative aspects.
- Evaluation of different initiatives towards GoBs and their relevance and impact on overall objective of women empowerment and equity is important. The generation of new initiatives will help to illustrate in a politically meaningful way the positive effects of incorporating gender into the formulation of the budget.
- The identification and documentation of methodologies that break out of the analytical framework in order to build towards integrating gender as a criterion in the formulation of budgets is necessary. Most of the time, however, the

concrete steps towards a gender-sensitive formulation of the budget have not been documented and sufficiently analyzed. It would therefore be relevant to develop a handbook that explains and analyses these approaches developed by different initiatives in order to work towards gender-sensitive budgets.

- Capacity building for those working on GoBs continues to be a much-needed activity for most of the initiatives. Those that are starting could benefit from the many relevant experiences and formats used for workshops and training in different initiatives. Those who are already engaged have to develop new capacities in order to respond to the practical questions that arise when gender-oriented budget analysis gives way to gender-sensitive formulation of the budget. This is particularly the case for outside government initiatives. Though it might not be the role of civil society to formulate the budget itself, civil society needs to understand the formulation of the budget in order to push forward the process of making it gender-sensitive. For both cases, knowing what other GoBs are doing and learning about the many ways in which similar difficulties are being handled could make a significant contribution.
- Extensive sensitization within government must be a continuous and sustained activity even when governments are willing to incorporate gender among the criteria for budgeting. Expressing commitment at high levels is crucial in order to set the governmental machinery into motion. Further, increased participation of women in budgetary debates and decision-making is important.
- People with strategic vision, strong initiatives and commitment for gender equality are key to the success of GoBs. The long-term process necessary to arrive at gender-sensitive budgets will be guaranteed if the government's priorities are not subject to change.

For many initiatives already on their way, both inside and outside government, the real challenge is in breaking out of analysis, into the arena of implementation. If GoBs fail to develop more concrete tools and recommendations, they could fail to deliver tangible results. What is needed is consistent follow up action based on the evaluation of the results from GoBs. This is currently lacking and hinders cross learning and comparison among different initiatives. This is particularly needed since the initiatives are carried out by the governments of countries. Officials responsible for implementing GoBs should not operate under traditional schemes that ignore the socially determined position of men and women. It is necessary to train officials involved in assessing existing problems, designing policies and programmes, allocating resources, developing indicators, collecting data and running actual programmes. Otherwise, the purpose of mainstreaming gender into the budget can be lost at lower levels of the government, despite being supported at the top. Hence it is important to evaluate GoBs for concrete follow-up action.

The processes of people's involvement in the formulation of budgets have to be explored in order to advance gender issues as a relevant concern. Gender-sensitive participatory research techniques have to be further explored, developed and documented. There are many issues that affect specific groups of women on a day-to-day basis. If GoBs should find ways of responding to these issues, and allow their research to be driven by and respond to the needs of particular groups of women. Development of ways to integrate a rights-based approach into GoBs could be a relevant contribution to the evolution of these initiatives. The budget can be a tool for evaluating a government's compliance with international norms of gender equality and holding it accountable.

The above are some of the activities that could be relevant and contribute to the development of new gender budget initiatives. It is also important to avoid creating unrealistic expectations.

CONCLUDING REMARKS

Budget is one of the important instruments in the hands of any government of a country. Managing resources, in addition to performing its traditional functions, government can use budget

as a strong instrument that provides a unique opportunity for addressing gender issues. The prevailing gender inequalities can be corrected by changing the allocation of resources in the budget to various programmes and also formulating gender specific programmes. Gender-oriented budgets are just one tool, aimed at changing the gender-blind nature of the budget.
However, the progress made in the direction of GoB is not adequate although some countries took initiatives and chalked out the programmes to empower women. But it is too early to evaluate the impacts that this analysis is having on redressing the gender imbalance. Much of the work is still at the early stages of developing tools, which help to analyze national budgets. They are, therefore, one step along the lengthy way implicit in breaking the existing gender disparities and building towards equitable societies. If their potential is to be realized, there needs to be a clear vision of what they can achieve, in order to take the further steps required.

REFERENCES

Budlender, D. (2002), A Profile of Country Activities. In: D. Budlender, D. Elson, G. Hewitt and T. Mukhopadhyay (eds.). *Gender Budgets Make Cents: Understanding Gender Responsive Budgets.* Commonwealth Secretariat, London.

Budlender, D., Buenaobra, M., Rood, S., and Sadorra, M. S. (Eds.) (2001), *Gender Budget Trail: The Philippine Experience.* Asia Foundation, Makaty City.

Budlender, D. and Hewitt, G. (2002), *Gender Budgets Make More Cents: Country Studies and Good Practice.* Commonwealth Secretariat, London.

Budlender, D., Hicks, J. and Vetten, L. (2002), South Africa: Expanding into Diverse Initiatives. In: D. Budlender and G. Hewitt (eds.). *Gender Budgets Make More Cents: Country Studies and Good Practice.* Commonwealth Secretariat, London.

Budlender, D., Sharp, R. and Allen, K. (1998), *How to do a Gender-sensitive Budget Analysis: Contemporary Research and Practice.* Commonwealth Secretariat, London.

Cagatay, N. (1998), *Engendering Macroeconomics and Macroeconomic Policies.* Working Paper 6, UNDP, New York.

Cagatay, N., Keklik, M., Lal, R. and Lang, J. (2000), *Budgets as if People Mattered: Democratizing Macroeconomic Policies.* UNDP Conference Paper Series, UNDP, New York.

Commonwealth Secretariat (2002), *Committing to the Global Vision that all Governments Should Engage in Gender Responsive Budgeting by 2015.* Commonwealth Secretariat, London.

Elson, D. (2002), Integrating Gender into Government Budgets in the Context of Economic Reform. In: D. Budlender, D. Elson, G. Hewitt and T. Mukhopadhyay (eds.). *Gender Budgets Make Cents: Understanding Gender Responsive Budgets.* Commonwealth Secretariat, London.

Hewitt, G. and Mukhopadhyay, T. (2002), Promoting Gender Equality through Public Expenditure. In: D. Budlender, D. Elson, G. Hewitt and T. Mukhopadhyay (eds.). *Gender Budgets Make Cents: Understanding Gender Responsive Budgets.* Commonwealth Secretariat, London.

Hewitt, G. and Raju, S. (1999), *Gender Budget Initiative.* A Commonwealth Initiative to Integrate Gender into National Budgetary Processes, Commonwealth Secretariat, London.

Himmelweit, S. (2001), *Tools for Budget Impact Analysis: Taxes and Benefits.* UNIFEM-OECD-Nordic Council Conference on Gender Responsive Budgeting, Brussels.

Klein, N. (2000), *Can Civil Society Adds Value to Budget Decision-making? A Description of Civil Society Budget Work.* International Budget Project, Washington DC, Available at www. internationalbudget. org

Pearl, R. (2002), Gender-responsive Budgets in the Andean Region. In: D. Budlender and G. Hewitt (eds.). *Gender Budgets Make More Cents: Country Studies and Good Practice,* Commonwealth Secretariat, London.

Reeves, H. and Baden, S. (2000), *Gender and Development: Concepts and Definitions,* BRIDGE Report 55, Institute of Development Studies, Brighton.

Shapiro, I (Ed.) (2001), *A Guide to Budget Work for NGOs.* International Budget Project, Washington DC.

St Hill, D. (2002), The UK Women's Budget Group. In: D. Budlender and G. Hewitt (eds.). *Gender Budgets Make More Cents: Country Studies and Good Practice.* Commonwealth Secretariat, London.

UNDP (2002), *Human Development Report*. Oxford University Press, New York.

UNO (1995), *Beijing Declaration and Platform of Action of the Fourth World Conference on Women*. New York.

World Bank (2001), *Attacking Poverty*. World Development Report 2000/2001,Oxford University Press, New York.

Index